ARCHAEOLOGIES OF LANDSCAPE

Social Archaeology

General Editor: Ian Hodder, University of Cambridge

Advisory Editors

Margaret W. Conkey, University of California at Berkeley
Mark Leone, University of Maryland
Alain Schnapp, U.E.R. d'Art et d'Archéologie, Paris
Stephen Shennan, University of Southampton
Bruce Trigger, McGill University, Montreal

ARCHAEOLOGIES OF LANDSCAPE

Contemporary Perspectives

Edited by

Wendy Ashmore

and

A. Bernard Knapp

BLACKWELL
Publishers

First published 1999

Reprinted 2000

Transferred to Digital print 2003

Blackwell Publishers Inc.
350 Main Street
Malden, Massachusetts 02148
USA

Blackwell Publishers Ltd
108 Cowley Road
Oxford OX4 1JF
UK

Library of Congress Cataloging-in-Publication Data

Archaeologies of landscape : contemporary perspectives / edited by
Wendy Ashmore and A. Bernard Knapp.
p.   cm. — (Social archaeology)
Includes bibliographical references and index.
ISBN 0–631–21105–5 (acid-free paper). — ISBN 0–631–21106–3 (pbk.: acid-free paper)
1. Landscape archaeology.   2. Antiquities.   3. Land settlement–History
I. Ashmore, Wendy, 1948.   II. Knapp. Arthur Bernard.   III. Series.
CC75.A655   1999   99–10434
930.1—dc21   CIP

British Library Cataloguing in Publication Data
A CIP catalogue record for this book is available from the British Library.

Typeset in 11 on 12.6 pt Garamond
by Newgen Imaging Systems (P) Ltd, India

This book is printed on acid-free paper

For Tom, Rebecca, and Laurie
W.A.

To my stepdaughter Joanna Sumner, who has a very special relationship with a very different kind of landscape in F.N.Q.

A.B.K.

Contents

Preface

The roots of this volume lie in spirited e-mail correspondence between the two editors, beginning in 1993. Sharing interests in landscape and settlement, we of course noted parallels and contrasts in how ancient people occupied the world in the areas we each knew best, and commented as often on the different – often strikingly different – ways archaeologists approached such inquiry in our own and other regions. We saw our own differences as broadly emblematic of larger intellectual traditions and schools of thought, especially Americanist processual approaches and postprocessual perspectives associated more with British, Australian, and other Old World archaeologies. Although studies of ancient landscapes had begun proliferating rapidly by the time we were corresponding, we felt we were learning a great deal specifically from our interaction, each pointing the other to ideas and works we might not otherwise have encountered as readily. By extension, we thought everyone might profit if we could bring together a group of scholars who might not ordinarily share the same forum. And we saw the burgeoning study of meaning in landscapes as a possible meeting ground for discussion.

As a result, we organized a symposium on "Sacred Landscapes: Constructed and Conceptualized" for the 1996 meeting of the American Anthropological Association, in San Francisco. The symposium title reflected our dual concerns with meaningfully constituted, often sacred landscapes, and with the interface between formally constructed and "simply" recognized or conceptualized landscapes. As we indicate in the first chapter, we sought participants with diverse theoretical and geographic backgrounds, who could span collectively the range of approaches pursued in the archaeological study of landscape. And we asked them to consider, from their own intellectual perspective, the make-up of meaningfully constituted landscapes within the cultural traditions they knew best. To what elements of landscape was

meaning attached? What significances did these elements or arrays of
them have? How formally was landscape marked?

When we decided to work towards publication of the very successful
session, all symposium participants signed on, and we are grateful for
their continued efforts and spirit of collaboration. We were and are
pleased to include authors with quite distinct backgrounds and viewpoints, and have not tried to force consensus on a group selected for its
diversity of perspective. They surely would not all agree with us or
with one another on every point raised in this book, but we see that as
a strength, a reflection of the vitality of landscape archaeologies at the
present time. To round out the volume, we invited several additional
authors to join us, representing further views or areas we had not been
able to include in the original set of oral presentations: Gina Barnes,
James Snead, and Robert Preucel provided important area contributions, and toward the end, Peter van Dommelen agreed to contribute
one of the critical commentaries. Regrettably, Clark Erickson had to
withdraw from the volume before its completion, but we are grateful
for his participation as discussant in the 1996 symposium, and for his
encouragement and substantive input as the volume progressed.

Our proposal for publication was accepted quickly and enthusiasti-
cally by Blackwell. It is important to note the manner in which the
volume grew. The substantive case studies were written in response to
the kind of general charge described earlier, and most for a symposium
explicitly highlighting "sacred" landscapes. In the interests of promot-
ing the diversity we had sought to stress in selecting contributors, we
imposed neither uniform theoretical perspective nor vocabulary on
them. The result, in our view, is a creatively eclectic collection representing much of the range of current archaeologies of landscape. We
leave more focused comments on this to our two discussants, Carole
Crumley and Peter van Dommelen. Their perspectives are quite distinct, as their chapters clearly show. Our own initial chapter was developed as the volume took shape, informed by our contributors'
writings, *not* as part of the charge to which they were asked to
respond. As a consequence, the chapter has allowed us both to provide
some historical context and to explore issues we encountered as we
considered the nature of meaningfully constituted landscapes and the
often subtle distinctions between conceptualized meaning and its formal expression in construction.

In addition to our authors, a number of other friends and colleagues
gave timely support and inspiration during creation of the volume.
At Blackwell, we have enjoyed working with Tessa Harvey, Louise
Spencely, and Lorna Berrett, and thank them for their advice,

assistance, and encouragement, and we also thank Valery Rose for her help with the copy-editing. In Philadelphia, Jerry Sabloff provided early and sustained intellectual encouragement, and Greg Possehl shaped a work setting conducive to the project's completion. Wendy Ashmore would also like particularly to thank Bob Preucel, Clark Erickson, Jane Buikstra, Rebecca Huss-Ashmore, Ginny Ebert, and Tom Patterson for generous support, in tasks and morale. In Glasgow, Bernard Knapp would like to thank Peter van Dommelen for his judicious reading of the introduction, and both Peter van Dommelen and Steve Driscoll for input on various issues related to this volume. Thank you all; this book would not exist without your contributions.

Wendy Ashmore, *Philadelphia*
A. Bernard Knapp, *Glasgow*

Archaeological Landscapes: Constructed, Conceptualized, Ideational

A. Bernard Knapp and Wendy Ashmore

landscape everywhere in the world is a construct of human beings —
whether through human ascription to it of mythological creation, or
through physical actions by the humans themselves. ... Whatever the
difficulties of recognizing such special sites from the archaeological
record — all societies in the past would have recognized, as do all societies in the present, some features of their landscapes (if not all the
earth) as special.

(Ucko 1994: xviii–xix)

Introduction and Background

As long as archaeologists have studied the human past, they have been
interested in space, and consequently in landscapes. What has changed
significantly, however, is archaeological thinking about the nature of
landscape, and thereby the perceived nature of its role in archaeological inquiry. In minimalist terms, a landscape is the backdrop against
which archaeological remains are plotted. From economic and political
perspectives, landscapes provide resources, refuge and risks that both
impel and impact on human actions and situations. Today, however,
the most prominent notions of landscape emphasize its socio-symbolic
dimensions: landscape is an entity that exists by virtue of its being perceived, experienced, and contextualized by people.

Long interest notwithstanding, only recently have archaeologists
begun to pay close attention to a domain frequently called "sacred landscapes." This is only one of several terms used to highlight non-
economic perspectives on human–land relations. Whatever the labels
used, study of these landscapes is hampered by ambiguity in material
clues to social meaning: we know from modern peoples that meaning in

a landscape is not directly related to how obtrusively it has been marked in material, archaeologically detectable ways. Such interpretive challenges have in part inspired the present volume, which offers diverse perspectives on what we distinguish as a continuum of conceptual and constructed landscapes. To consider this continuum, we discuss potential distinctions among conceptual, constructed, and ideational qualities of past landscapes. First, however, we note that several theoretical sources encourage studies of meaning in landscape, in particular historical changes in how archaeologists think about space, and growing applications of social theory in archaeological interpretation.

As already noted, archaeology has traditionally incorporated attention to space and landscape, particularly in what is called settlement archaeology. The difference is that what was once theorized as a passive backdrop or forcible determinant of culture is now seen as an active and far more complex entity in relation to human lives. In part, the change stems from archaeologists' expanding their interpretive gaze beyond the isolable "hot spots" termed sites, to consider a more comprehensive distribution of human traces in and between loci, now often termed "places of special interest" (Cherry et al. 1991; Given et al. n.d.). The resulting perspectives are variably termed siteless archaeology (e.g., Dunnell 1992), off-site archaeology (e.g., Foley 1981), distributional archaeology (e.g., Ebert 1992), and several approaches that fall under the rubric of landscape archaeology (e.g., Gosden and Head 1994; Knapp 1997; Rossignol and Wandsnider 1992; Yamin and Metheny 1996). In practice, these diverse approaches facilitate the study of diffuse human remains – such as field systems, farms, industrial sites, roads, and the generally more ephemeral traces of non-sedentary peoples – that never fit comfortably within traditional operational definitions of "sites." In so doing, they also remind archaeologists of how complicated and often subtle people's interaction with the land can be. At the same time, growing recognition of social meaning of space as *place* mandates examination of what Western scholars often classify as "natural" places of significance, such as caves, mountain peaks, woods, rivers and springs, or even physically "empty" spaces (Carmichael et al. 1994: 1; Hirsch 1995: 4). Ascribing significance to a specific configuration of natural or geographic features is never self-evident but rather culturally determined (e.g., Hirsch 1995; Saunders 1994: 172). More important, taking a holistic landscape perspective compels us to stress the *interrelationships* among people and such traces, places and features, in space and through time.

Architectural mimicry often calls attention to important landscape features, as identified within many societies in the equation of pyramids or other buildings with mountains (e.g., Townsend 1982; Vogt 1969; see also Scully 1989). Sometimes these involve elaborate detailing, such as the artificial watercourses built into the Akapana of Tiwanaku (Kolata and Ponce Sanginés 1992). At other times, architectural assemblages emulate the embracing sweep of local topography, as in the artificial, valley-like depressions within which Chacoan pueblos were set (Stein and Lekson 1992), the landscape mimicry Colin Richards identifies in Orcadian henge monuments (1996; compare Hall 1977), or Arthur Miller's analysis of Monte Albán (1995: 24–7; compare Broda 1991: 101–2). Perhaps more often than we have yet recognized, the sky provides the cues to spatial order on the terrestrial plane, as argued eloquently by Gary Urton (1981) for the Andes, and by numerous authors with respect to the Maya (e.g., Aveni 1980; 1991; Freidel et al. 1993; Tedlock 1992).

Several fields besides archaeology have grappled with landscape issues, informed increasingly by concerns rooted in social theory. Geographers, historians, anthropologists, urban planners, folklorists, and others have engaged concepts of memory, continuity, discontinuity, and transformation (e.g., Rowlands 1993; Schama 1995), often reflecting on the consequences of accelerated change in the late twentieth century (e.g., Bender 1998; Morphy 1995). Their writings have secured such concepts within the intellectual mainstream. Not surprisingly, geographers became involved quite early with studying the meaningful constitution of landscapes (e.g., Cosgrove 1984; Harvey 1980; Tuan 1977). The American geographer Carl Sauer (1925) first formulated the concept of a "cultural" landscape as fashioned from the "natural" landscape. Human geographers now seek meaning in the landscape as a "repository of human striving" (Tuan 1971: 184), and postmodernist perspectives visualize the landscape as a "cultural image" whose verbal or written representations provide images, or "texts" of its meaning, or "reading" (Daniels and Cosgrove 1988: 1; Head 1993: 489–90). Emerging inquiries by social and cultural anthropologists have yielded rich insights (e.g., Feld and Basso 1996; Hirsch and O'Hanlon 1995; Rappaport 1989). Prominent among these studies are phenomenological approaches and linguistic perspectives, emphasizing "landscape" as constituted by humans' dwelling in it, a set of potentials instantiated by human choice and action. In Hirsch's (1995) oft-cited view, landscape is a "process" yielding a foregrounded, everyday social life from a background range of potential social existence.

Archaeological study of landscapes is particularly lively at this time (e.g., Barrett et al. 1991; Bender 1993; 1998; Carmichael et al. 1994;

Knapp 1996a; Parcero Oubiña et al. 1998; Tilley 1994; Townsend 1992), and we may expect such studies to continue expanding in interpretative potential. Within the burgeoning literature, Barbara Bender's (1993) volume offered the first critical study of landscapes to include archaeologists as well as geographers and anthropologists; the contributors examined landscapes from a subjective, locally situated perspective, as something that not only shapes but is shaped by human experience. Tilley's (1994) influential study is concerned explicitly with phenomenology, of landscape as experience, but focuses on monuments rather than on more ephemeral traces of human activity. In that respect it is similar to the case studies in Bender's volume, which deal more with structures and modern-day urban centers than with archaeological space and place. Monuments – like "sites" more generally – make up a real but very limited part of the landscape. However significant a role they played in a community's ceremonial or public life, a more nuanced analysis requires more comprehensive understanding of the total landscape (Derks 1997: 129). The present volume seeks to expand upon these earlier studies and exemplifies some of the innovative directions in archaeological landscape studies today.

It is important to recall explicitly at this juncture the pronounced differences in archaeological theory and interpretation that pertain among intellectual traditions, highlighted especially between "American" and "British" spheres of scholarship, and particularly between processualist and postprocessualist approaches (e.g., Knapp 1996b; Patterson 1990; Preucel 1991; Shanks and Hodder 1995). Debates among practitioners of these various "schools" of thought can be richly productive, but too often become heated confrontation rather than constructive engagement. Archaeologists of diverse backgrounds pursue studies of socially constituted, meaningful landscapes. In so doing, they have tended, not surprisingly, to address the audiences of their closest theoretical peers, and consequently to frame their inquiries in particular epistemic contexts and with reference to interpretive issues most salient in their own traditions. Within the archaeologies of landscape, we see considerable diversity but also many underlying commonalties of concern and approach. We join those who see landscape study as a domain for fruitful interaction, "cross-cultural" communication in multiple senses. In this volume, therefore, we have sought to include authors who have distinct intellectual approaches, and who also work in varied ancient cultures. We have not sought to resolve artificially the real distinctions among their approaches, but highlight them all as contributions to a larger whole.

Following this introduction, then, are ten chapters, divided loosely into sections that move progressively further from ethnographic and historical grounding into deep prehistory. Each is a substantive consideration of landscapes in a particular part of the world, with specific temporal and cultural referents, and with a perspective conditioned by local as well as global traditions. Chronologically, the chapters range from the present day in Australia back into the Neolithic of the Old World and the Archaic of North America. The geographic scope includes all continents except Antarctica. The third and final section of this volume offers two discussion papers by scholars with established commitments to landscape studies; whereas those discussions assess the relevance and coherence of the individual chapters, we focus instead on introducing key concepts and themes.

Because archaeological writing on ideational, conceptualized or constructed landscapes is relatively new (but see, among others, Drennan 1976; Flannery and Marcus 1976; Hall 1977; Piggott 1937), our introduction outlines what we regard as the theoretical wellsprings and underpinnings to this domain of inquiry. We acknowledge from the outset the concerns of those who feel that any attempt to engage the mindset of prehistoric or of any other past culture – analogically or otherwise – is fraught with problems, in particular the overdetermination of archaeological data or the use of circular reasoning. We feel, however, that the issues are not intractable (e.g., Hodder et al. 1995; Renfrew et al. 1993; Renfrew and Zubrow 1994; Schmidt 1997; Wylie 1991), and that the volume's case studies speak strongly for themselves. We have given the contributors free reign to express, even celebrate their diversity. We have purposely *not* imposed our terminology on their work; rather we invited them to present their case studies from the perspective (and with the terminology) out of which their research grew. The volume's discussants consider critically the resultant diversity as exemplified by the specific contributions. Here we do not review the chapters in such specific fashion. Instead, we present themes that we see as pervading the chapters collectively: landscape as memory, landscape as identity, landscape as social order, and landscape as transformation. We use this thematic discussion to place the volume as a whole in the larger context of landscape studies, archaeological and otherwise. Before turning to the thematic review, however, we look briefly but more closely at the concept of landscape.

Landscapes Considered

All too often the prehistoric landscape is studied for evidence of settlement and subsistence. This is the task of "landscape archaeology".

Monuments associated with ritual and ceremonial are usually studied separately, and these are the province of "social archaeology". Such a division of labour is faint-hearted, and ultimately it is impossible to maintain.

(Bradley 1997: 216)

Although we agree that the schism Bradley describes often holds, we believe the contributors to this volume are among those who seek to remove such a divide, to achieve a more integrated and holistic view. In so doing, they – and we – draw on a rich body of thought concerning landscapes and their roles and meanings. "Landscape" is variously defined by archaeologists, anthropologists, geographers, historians, social theorists, poets, and philosophers (Knapp 1997: 14–18). Several scholars have traced the etymology and relative recency of the term, and examined the historical and philosophical contexts of Western Europe and America in which it gained currency (e.g., Derks 1997: 127–31; Hirsch 1995; Jackson 1984; Lemaire 1997; Schama 1995; Thomas 1993). We acknowledge that landscape is an "unstable" concept, moving to and fro along a natural–cultural continuum (Tilley 1994: 37), and that the meaning and understanding of the "countryside" are relative, the result of specific human preconceptions or the expression of particular artistic and scientific viewpoints (Fowler 1995: 100–1). We accept, furthermore, that concepts of space and place or other binary equivalencies (e.g., visual and hidden, inside and outside) cannot define, alone or collectively, an abstract "absolute landscape," because the relevance and relationships of such pairs derive from specific historical or cultural contexts (Hirsch 1995: 23). We even concede that landscape is a "cultural construct of modern European society" and that, in many ways, employing the concept of landscape as widely as archaeologists now do may reveal as much about scholarship today as about society in the past (Lemaire 1997: 6–9). But we would argue that, as a positive consequence, such instability and relativity actually serve to explain the appeal of exploring landscapes, as a catalyst to draw upon diverse approaches and to examine differing domains of human action and experience. There are multiple different ways of "knowing" the earth and the socially recognized places upon it.

Three examples illustrate archaeological definitions for this common-sense term. Drawing on her long involvement with historical ecology, Carole Crumley defines landscape succinctly as "the material manifestation of the relation between humans and the environment" (Crumley 1994: 6). John Barrett (1991: 8, emphasis in original) is more expansive:

Landscape is thus the entire surface over which people moved and within which they congregated. That surface was given meaning as people acted upon the world within the context of the various demands and obligations which acted upon them. Such actions took place within a certain *tempo* and at certain *locales*. Thus landscape, its form constructed from natural and artificial features, became a culturally meaningful resource through its routine occupancy.

Going even further, Robert Johnston's "inherent" approach refuses to distinguish between "real" and "perceived" landscapes, and maintains that "there is still no answer to what landscape is [;] it is still very much a case of 'what it can be.' Landscape is, in the broadest sense, contextual" (Johnston 1998: 56). Although even this trio of definitions offer clearly divergent perspectives, all recognize or imply the human, social nature of landscape.

Previously archaeologists tended to view the human landscape mainly in terms of demography, social interaction, economic resources and risks (e.g., Carneiro 1970; Sanders 1977; Steward 1955; Willey 1953). That is, they focused on topography, technology, resources and land use – on what people did to the land and how it aided or constrained them, rather than what they thought or felt about it (Bender et al. 1997: 148). Models of landscape partitioning, which considered the correlation of mounds and monuments with the spread of farming and village life (e.g., Renfrew 1973), were derived from inferences about territorial claims. The social aspects of these inferred claims, in their reifying of group identities through material connections to the land, began to turn archaeological thinking more pointedly toward social relations, with the land as the medium of social expression (e.g., McAnany 1995). The coincident rise of archaeoastronomy turned archaeological thoughts toward another interpretively promising trajectory, namely to the potential for assessing ancient cognition through the landscape (e.g., Aveni 1980; Hawkins 1965; compare Martlew and Ruggles 1996; Renfrew 1982). In these studies, however, landscape was still viewed primarily as a relatively passive index of technology and belief, a background vellum on which stories of the active sky were written.

Ancient peoples were conceived largely as undifferentiated societies and cultural systems, the analytical units of mainstream (processual) archaeology in the 1970s and 1980s (e.g., Fritz 1978; Schmidt 1983). Postprocessual critiques have significantly restructured discussion outside the Americas (with growing impact in the latter as well), focusing attention on the active role of individuals in constructing and interpreting the world around them, and in continually reshaping culture and society. Symbolic expression is central to maintaining communication and social integration, but these shared symbols become reworked in individual use. Structuration (Giddens 1984), practice (e.g., Bourdieu 1977), and feminist theory (e.g., Conkey and Gero 1997; Wylie 1992), as well as phenomenology (e.g., Gosden 1994; Thomas 1996) have proven useful to many analysts in deciphering the form and meaning of symbolic expressions in the past. As important with respect to landscape, local physiographic features are recognized increasingly as the source and subjects of the symbols, often linked to ancestral beings (Morphy 1995: 186–8). In the archaeologies of landscape, the effect has often been to regard such features and their meanings as mediating the selection, use, modification or avoidance of particular locales. Indeed, archaeologists seem to be moving toward actively recognizing what Keith Basso (1996: 55) calls "interanimation:" implicitly recalling Sir Winston Churchill's famous dictum ("we shape our buildings and they shape us" – Hall 1966: 106), Basso offers this term to describe the constant mutual molding of landscapes and the people who dwell in them. While we may never know the precise content of stories told from ancient landscapes, we can increasingly infer some of the contours of their telling and the social impact that they had.

Landscape as actively inhabited space, and particularly landscape as the arena for ritual or ceremonial activity, are already prominent themes in archaeology (e.g., Alcock 1993; Bradley 1993; Derks 1997; Stein and Lekson 1992; Thomas 1991; 1993). And whereas an ideational or conceptual landscape might also be a "sacred" landscape, it is also a stage constructed in the mind to convey meaning to those who inhabit it (e.g., Ashmore 1998). This is one illustration of how the specific label "sacred landscapes" captures only part of the domain we target in this volume. A landscape embodies more than a neutral, binary relationship between people and nature, along any single dimension. Space is both a medium for and the outcome of human activity: it is recognized by means of specific places, and in this sense, does not exist apart from that activity (Tilley 1994: 10, 23; compare Casey 1996). Individuals and communities conditioned by different social, politico-economic and ideological forces project differing configurations of meaning onto the landscape, thus implying that measurable economic impacts notwithstanding, no *landscape* – aesthetic, poetic, moral, material, or surreal – has an objective appearance or significance independent of the beholder (Fitter 1995: 8–9).

Terms and Themes

Within the foregoing sense of landscape, we highlight three non-exclusive, even overlapping aspects important to specifying the range of landscape described in this volume. These are terms we have found useful as we worked on the volume, not ones we asked volume contributors either to adopt or to critique. In defining the terms, we draw both on the preceding theoretical discussion and on practical terminology developed in UNESCO World Heritage work (Cleere 1995). That is, whereas the study of landscapes in archaeology attracts diverse theoretical and methodological viewpoints, both Sherratt (1996: 14) and Derks (1997: 127) attribute much of the current fascination with landscape to the rapid pace and dramatic scale of development or encroachment on traditional landscapes. The emerging focus of "cultural heritage" adopts concepts related to tradition, memory and the cultural landscape in evaluating potentially significant sites. In the urgently pragmatic effort to identify, preserve and unify the study of unique "cultural" or "natural" landscapes, UNESCO has specified criteria (Cleere 1995: 65–6) for recognizing three categories of cultural landscape:

- "Clearly defined" landscapes were "designed and created intentionally." These include gardens and parklands, often associated with religious or other monumental structures, and Cleere (1995: 65) cites Versailles in France or the Garden Tomb of Humayun (India) as examples.
- "Organically evolved" landscapes began as a particular socio-economic, administrative or religious initiative which evolved subsequently in association with and response to the natural environment. Sub-categories include *relict* (or *fossil*) archaeological landscapes such as mines or quarries (e.g., the "Gold Rush" lands of the USA or Australia), or ancient agricultural complexes (e.g., Erickson 1993), and *continuing* landscapes such as cultivation terraces in Southeast Asia.
- Finally, "associative cultural" landscapes are identified by such features as sacred promontories, or "religious settlements in outstanding landscapes." Examples include Uluru/Ayers Rock, or Meteora and Mount Athos (see further discussion under "Conceptualized Landscapes," below).

The UNESCO definitions stem from a need to capture a wide and internally varied set of meaningful landscapes in a single protective net. Although these categories are essential for that context and useful as clarifying referents here, they differ somewhat from the distinctions we offer. What we propose here are three interpretive descriptors – constructed, conceptualized, ideational – for thinking about meaning-laden landscapes. We acknowledge (see further below) that it is often difficult to differentiate among these aspects of landscape, and emphasize anew that it is we – the editors – who sought to distill these aspects from the contributions to this volume; that is, we did not assign them as structuring principles to the contributors. Furthermore, we would suggest that landscape is essentially all of these things at all times: it is the arena in which and through which memory, identity, social order and transformation are constructed, played out, re-invented, and changed.

Constructed landscapes

While the erection of monuments alters the visual character of a landscape to varying degrees, even subtle construction may transform its meaning without radically changing the topography (Bradley 1993: 23–4). In general, mobile human groups create their landscapes by projecting ideas and emotions onto the world as they find it – on trails, views, campsites or other special places. Sedentary people, on the other hand, structure their landscapes more obtrusively, physically constructing gardens, houses and villages on the land, often in the near vicinity of notable natural landmarks (Ingold 1986: 153; Wilson 1988: 50). Several contributions in this volume treat such predominantly *constructed landscapes*.

Under our rubric of constructed landscape, we would place UNESCO's "clearly defined" and in part, their "organically evolved" landscapes. In this volume, we would include under constructed landscapes the burial mounds of prehistoric Britain (Barrett), prehistoric cultures in the North American midcontinent (Buikstra and Charles), and the Egyptian state temples as microcosms of the sun or the horizons (Richards). An example of an industrial landscape (sub-category of the organically evolved landscape) would be the towering (modern) spoil heaps and (ancient) slag heaps that dominate the northern Troodos foothills on the island of Cyprus and represent a striking human construction which emulates the foothills that comprise and encompass this very landscape (Knapp, this volume).

Contemporary beliefs, visions and myths can and often do lead to metaphorical and physical (re)construction of the archaeological record, and constructed landscapes are particularly susceptible to such "freezing" of meaning (Ucko 1994: xv–xvi). That is, modernization of landscapes often leads to truncation and impoverishment of their living embodiment of memory, to a rupture in their "cultural biography" – the long interaction between people and their environment

(Lemaire 1997: 16; compare Denevan 1992; Spirn 1996). In considering the relationship between archaeology as past discourse and archaeology as contemporary practice, Bender, Hamilton, and Tilley (1997)
maintain that excavation inspires alternative interpretive constructions
that may be perpetuated, transformed or abandoned. Archaeologists
and heritage managers alike need to be aware that physical and verbal
(re)constructions invoke assumptions about a particular site or region
which may bear little or no relationship to the "traditional" value
placed on the land by the various native or aboriginal peoples who
inhabit and utilize it. The pragmatics and realities that archaeologists
must confront in this ongoing conflict between science and the arts,
among humanism, cultural heritage and legislated regulation, is
poignantly presented by Lekson (1996) in his review of several studies
cited repeatedly in this volume.

Conceptualized landscapes

As earlier discussion should make clear, landscapes offer a variety of
images, which are interpreted and given meaning through localized
social practices and experience (Richards 1996: 314). These *conceptualized landscapes* are mediated through and to some extent constitutive of
social processes, which in turn are integral to their reproduction as
concepts (Morphy 1995: 197).

Our notion of conceptualized landscapes comes closest to
UNESCO's "associative cultural" landscapes. Such landscapes are characterized by powerful religious, artistic or other cultural meanings
invested in natural features rather than in material culture or monuments, which are insignificant or absent (Cleere 1995: 66–7). In fact,
the first property inscribed on the World Heritage list as a cultural
landscape was in the associative category, the site of Tongariro in New
Zealand, a mountain sacred for the Maoris but one where they are for-
bidden to venture. Although many chapters in this volume describe
what we would call conceptual landscapes, the most obvious examples
are Buddhist cave temples and mountains (Barnes), Australian
Aboriginal Dreaming Tracks (Taçon), and the known but often physically unmarked features of the Inka world (van de Guchte). The other
three Native American case studies combine constructed and conceptualized landscapes (Brady and Ashmore; Buikstra and Charles;
Snead and Preucel). The principal aim in recognizing these distinctions, however, is less to categorize, *per se*, than to highlight *variation
along a continuum* of ancient human material intervention in landscapes.

Ideational landscapes

"Ideational" is a term necessarily both comprehensive and vague. The *Oxford English Dictionary* gives two basic definitions: (1) the formation of ideas or mental images of things not present to the senses; and (2) culture based on spiritual values or ideas. By extension, "ideational" could also mean the formation of a concept or external object correlative with an idea, or more simply something concerned with an idea. Within archaeology, *prima facie*, "ideational" has been taken to be the simple equivalent of sacred and symbolic, or else – in a happy convergence of metaphor – has been equated with "landscapes of the mind" (Bintliff 1996: 250). Is this "mental landscape" imaginative and emotional, or simply empirical? Is it an insider (emic) or outsider (etic) point of view?

Our answer is that an ideational landscape is both "imaginative" (in the sense of being a mental image of something) and emotional (in the sense of cultivating or eliciting some spiritual value or ideal). The term is also meant to elicit an insider's perspective, but archaeologists clearly impose ideational notions from the outside. "Ideational" should be regarded as distinct from "ideological" and is intended to be broader than "sacred" or "symbolic." Ideational landscapes may provide moral messages, recount mythic histories, and record genealogies, but we cannot assume that they always or necessarily comprise the kind of unified, fully articulated doctrine commonly implied by the term "ideology." And concerning the "sacred" nature of landscapes, Bender, Hamilton, and Tilley (1997: 148; compare Sherratt 1996: 146) suggest that all societies centralize ritual in the reproduction of power and authority. Like many other contributors to this volume, we certainly have found reference to the "sacred" useful for distinguishing these aspects of landscapes in our own work (e.g., our chapters herein). We suggest it may prove helpful, however, to recognize *as well* an alternative, more encompassing domain, one with fewer specific implications for how particular meanings might have been generated or perpetuated in antiquity. Just as "ideational" is far less linked to an articulated system than are the terms "ideology" or "ideological," so is it also intended to embrace sacred as well as other kinds of meanings attached to and embodied in landscapes.

Every part of a prehistoric landscape would have been mediated by peoples' ideas about their world, by their social identities, and by their cognitive understandings (Bender et al. 1997: 150). A fundamental value in the concept of an ideational landscape, in our view, is that it can encompass both the range of meaning archaeologists recognize in landscapes, and the pair of analytic "realms" – conceptualized, and constructed. Indeed, although it is useful to distinguish the latter two analytically, in actuality they often lack a perceptible boundary. If so, then we have in "ideational landscape" a construct approaching Johnston's (1998) "inherent" notion, where landscape is not separately perceived but embedded within ways of living and being.

Themes

Taking into account these theoretical and terminological considerations, we review four closely interrelated themes in the current archaeological study of ideational, conceptual and constructed landscapes. Expression of these themes varies greatly among particular landscapes and in the writings of individual landscape analysts, including the contributors to this volume. These themes are (1) landscape as memory, (2) landscape as identity, (3) landscape as social order, and (4) landscape as transformation.

Landscape as memory   Landscape is often regarded as the materialization of memory, fixing social and individual histories in space. Research in cognitive science suggests that human memory constructs rather than retrieves, and that the past thus originates from the elaboration of cultural memory, which is itself socially constituted (Holtorf 1997: 48–50). The outcome of such a process maps mythic and moral principles for a society, reminders of triumphs and catastrophes in the social past. Schama (1995) points to the many "mythical" elements of the landscape that could be and have been appropriated from our rich, pre-modern heritage. Perhaps the most frequently cited embodiment of memory in land is the intricately conceptualized landscape array of Aboriginal Australians (e.g., Taçon, this volume). In a more recently recognized example, Dietler (1998) examines three "Celtic" (Iron Age) hilltop settlements which in recent history have been symbolically converted into part of the collective memory and national identity of modern France. Without the enduring capacity and institutionalized power of landscape myths and memories, national identity would lose much of its "ferocious enchantment" with contemporary territorial mystiques (Schama 1995: 15; compare Hirsch 1995).

Nora's (1989) "sites of memory" – which range from cathedrals and cemeteries to concepts, commemorations and symbols – represent media that together help to formulate a nation's political and ethnic identity. Landscapes are also commonly thought to embody the cosmos in miniature, wherein one's own town, home and body occupy the symbolic center of the universe. The concept of an *axis mundi* is effectively a cultural universal, and "sites of memory" form an integral part of all cultural traditions (e.g., Eliade 1959; Vogt 1969; Brady and Ashmore, this volume; Richards, this volume). But how do we know which elements were significant in the memory of a particular society or at a specific time? Chinese geomancy, or *feng shui*, is a particularly well-known set of beliefs for situating oneself in harmony with the landscape; although similar beliefs likely pertain elsewhere, *feng shui*, as such, is not a universal belief system (e.g., Carlson 1980). Nor are archaeological notions about "natural" or "cultural" landscapes universal categories: each society tends to characterize and conceptualize the landscape in its own way (Oosten 1997: 152). Embedded in the collective memory of a community and in the individual memories of its members are mythical or cosmological concepts, as well as folk memories of burial grounds, meeting places, valleys, mountains, and more, all situated in a specific temporal and historical context. Such concepts or memories are not simply reflections of landscape, but also often the means of organizing, using, and living in the landscape (e.g., Brady and Ashmore, this volume; van de Guchte, this volume; compare Basso 1984; 1996; Jackson 1980).

Memory stresses continuity in the landscape, often through re-use, reinterpretation or restoration, and reconstruction. From Stonehenge to Persepolis, from Ayodhya to Ayers Rock (Uluru), from Teotihuacan to Machu Picchu, there is a genre of research and heritage management that seeks to reinscribe past meaning onto a present landscape by demonstrating its social, sacred, or ceremonial *longue durée* (e.g., Bender 1998; Bradley 1998a; Holtorf 1997; Barrett, this volume). Together with this comes the notion that the people who previously lived in such a landscape may well have thought of it in similar terms (Sherratt 1996: 146). But meaning is mutable, with or without tangible change in the physical reminders by which such meaning is remembered (e.g., Kubler 1962; Rowlands 1993: 146; Tilley 1996). Schama (1995: 14) argues passionately and at length that the myths and memories inscribed in contemporary landscapes can contribute dramatically to a better understanding of the complexity and antiquity of local traditions of landscape (compare, for example, Jackson 1980; 1984; Kniffen 1965). Landscape as memory is linked in this sense to the identity of its inhabitants.

Landscape as identity   People recognize, inscribe, and collectively maintain certain places or regions in ritual, symbolic, or ceremonial terms;

conversely, these places create and express sociocultural identity. Landscape provides a focus by which people engage with the world, and create and sustain a sense of their social identity. The genesis of contemporary cultural or political identity is reflected at least indirectly in the etymology of "landscape," and in the development of interest in landscape as a "piece of land" or a "picture representing such a piece of land" (Lemaire 1997: 5–7). Bradley (1993: 26) suggests that "special attention" markers single out socially significant features in the landscape. Often the locations so identified are visually prominent landmarks; others designate important transitions between what we consider ecological zones. Still others may signal loci of important past events and notable people, political or mythic. The famed Nazca lines, for example, have been interpreted in part as pointing to sources of water in a quintessentially arid land (e.g., Aveni 1986). Prominent features of the Aboriginal Australian landscape mark events in the Dreamtime and embody supernatural ancestors (Ingold 1996: 137; Morphy 1995: 195).

The forms of "special attention" range from rock markings (e.g., Bradley 1991), to deposits of offerings (e.g., McEwan and van de Guchte 1992), to shrine construction (e.g., Aldenderfer 1990; Barnes, this volume) – or they may be as intangible as oral linkage with important events and transitions (e.g., Basso 1984; Bauer 1991; Gell 1995; Snead and Preucel, this volume; van de Guchte, this volume). The most obtrusive and formal markings, of course, are architectural and depictive. Mount Rushmore dominates its landscape with portraits of four US presidents (e.g., Olwig 1993); the ancient Egyptian temple at Abu Simbel is one of many imposing portrait monuments commissioned by Ramses II to identify his domain. These exemplify ready avenues for probing spatial cognition and social identity. But even in societies reliant on strong oral traditions, landscape marking is often evident. The global distribution and deep antiquity of rock marking or "rock art" is ample testimony (e.g., Bradley 1997; Conkey 1980; Flood 1996; Fullager et al. 1996; Marshack 1972). Studies of rock art, in fact, have helped to break down the distinction between an economic archaeology based on settlements and land use, and a social archaeology based on monuments and material culture; Bradley (1997: 215) maintains, accordingly, that "some of the images associated with ceremonial centres also extended to natural places in the landscape."

No matter the form, all these means of identifying the landscape refer to the diachronic constructed or conceptual landscape. At any particular moment in time, certain places become vested with identity, be it supernatural, social, or self-identity (Ucko 1994: xviii). Whereas landscapes generally become intensely marked and socialized as time passes, those sites with remarkable "natural signifiers" are the ones considered most powerful by various contemporary groups (Taçon 1994: 126; this volume). Where landscape is identity and memory, a tangibly marked landscape is memory-enhanced. Labels such as "built environment" are useful in this regard, but by reifying bounded cate-gories like built and unbuilt, we have collectively obscured what increasingly appears as an unbroken continuum in how people inhabit and identify with their surroundings. This growing recognition is part of the reason we proposed the three terms outlined earlier.

Landscape as social order   Just as landscape maps memory and declares identity, so too it offers a key to interpreting society. This is a question not simply of the spatial ordering of residential, civic and other activi-ties but rather of the broader, conceptual landscape. More than being a metaphor for human actions taking place at some independent level, the land itself, as socially constituted, plays a fundamental role in the ordering of cultural relations (Ashmore 1991; Layton 1995: 229; Schmidt 1997). And, as a community merges with its *habitus* through the actions and activities of its members, the landscape may become a key reference point for expressions of individual as well as group iden-tity (similarly, Derks 1997: 126; Barnes, this volume; van de Guchte, this volume). This theme is much explored in American historical archaeology, especially with respect to the creation of garden land-scapes by assertively affluent Colonial landholders (e.g., Leone 1984; Yamin and Metheny 1996; Kealhofer, this volume).

Basso (1984, 1996) describes the moral landscape of the Western Apache, wherein ethical lessons are affixed to natural features, and offer constant ambient cues to right living (compare Kahn 1996). To be absent from the natal landscape is to lose one's moral bearings. Social roles, relations and identities, too, are mapped on the land, as frequently implied in referential conflations of foreignness, chaos, and barbarism. Fear and fascination go hand in hand with concepts of dis-tance and the exotic (e.g., Helms 1988; 1992; Knapp 1998); Janet Richards' chapter here alludes to the role of ordered Egyptian space in keeping chaos at bay. Social order in the landscape is also implied by Buikstra and Charles's analysis (this volume), wherein the dead and the ancestors are firmly situated in specific locales marking their roles in the social and natural worlds of the North American Middle Archaic.

In reconstructing past landscapes, archaeologists must avoid imposing their own, often hierarchical notions of social order. The more heter-archical concept of "nested landscapes," where family, kin, community, gender, and age/experience would have linked land, dwellings and ceremonial spaces (Bender 1998: 60; Bender et al. 1997: 174; compare Chang 1972; Crumley 1979; 1986), offers one possible way out of this dilemma and a means of interpreting prehistoric landscapes. With regard to contemporary landscapes, Morphy (1995) argues that the landscape is central to reproducing the Dreaming as a component of the cultural structure of contemporary Australian Aboriginal society and thus of generating information about the ancestral past of Aborigines (see also Taçon, this volume). As members of social groups, individuals negotiated their interests and manipulated their sociospatial world: it is the closest link we can make between mind, meaning and social order in the prehistoric context. We believe, however, that the interpretive potentials here are far from realized.

Recognizing nested landscapes implies acknowledging diversity in social identity, a challenge embraced by postprocessual, Marxist, and feminist archaeologists. By the latter, we mean not simply those who seek to identify gender-specific individuals in the archaeological record, but rather those who seek to explore more broadly what the existence of such distinctions as gender, sex, age, kin group, class, and ethnicity might imply for understanding and interpreting the archaeological record (e.g., Conkey and Gero 1997). Certainly, ancient women and men have been recognized in the past, and increasingly in terms of space (e.g., Crown and Fish 1996; Gilchrist 1994; Hastorf 1990; Tringham 1994) but seldom yet at the scale of landscape studies. Hodder's (1984, 1990) structuralist models are perhaps the most widely known, but focus more precisely on communally held gender symbolism. Peter Schmidt (e.g., 1983, 1997) links landscape features with sexual imagery and gender symbolism in East Africa. Thomas Jackson (1990) offers an ethnographically derived model for gendered landscape marking and resource control among the Mono of California. Watson and Kennedy's (1990) model for development of Native North American horticulture is one that implicitly genders landscape use and experience. We recognize increasingly, however, that gender – and other social – distinctions do not always translate to spatial or landscape maps (e.g., Bodenhorn 1993; Kent 1997); in fact, Bodenhorn (1993: 199) notes provocatively that whereas a modern Iñupiat woman's place is physically at the hearth, she – particularly the whaling-captain's wife – is considered metaphorically to accompany her husband to sea, and it is she who attracts the whales to the hunters. The quest to identify gendered landscapes may prove quixotic as often as not. Approaches informed by feminist theory will, nonetheless, fruitfully advance pursuit of "nested landscapes," by acknowledging the diversity of experience and meanings held by the socially varied people who co-inhabit the land (compare Meskell 1998a; 1998b).

Landscape as transformation In any society, individuals will, for their own reasons, locate themselves in different places, hold differing conceptions of the world and their place within it, and make differing demands on that world: the result can be tension, contestation or transformation (Bender 1998: 63). The transformation of landscapes is most often linked interpretively with cyclical time, and with the perpetuation or change of the social order (e.g., Schmidt 1997). Indeed, rituals re-create the universe on a frequent basis and at nested social and spatial scales, of which landscape is only one (e.g., Bradley 1998a; Derks 1997; Hanks 1990; Vogt 1969; several chapters in this volume). It is the repetitive use and structured modification of an ideational landscape that yields the palimpsest archaeologists study, often sorted analytically into chronological slices, excising from the accumulated whole, arrays of sites pertaining to particular archaeological periods. Virtually all landscape analysts have recognized the intimate and complex relationship between space and time: one of Marx's central tenets on capitalist logic was that space may be annihilated by time (e.g., Hirsch 1995: 15). Perhaps more to the point here is that landscapes embody time at different scales as well. Philosopher Edward Casey (1996: 36, emphasis in original) notes that, phenomenologically, "*space and time come together in place*;" since landscapes embody multiple times as well as multiple places, they thereby materialize not only continuity and sequence, but potentially change and transformation as well.

Ingold (1993) draws particular attention to the annual round of human activities linked to different places and conditions in the landscape. On a short time scale, the daily transit of the sun and other celestial bodies is a potent orienting device for human activity and for using the landscape to chart, celebrate and perpetuate this fundamental cycle (e.g., Aveni 1980; 1991; Carrasco 1991; Richards, this volume). On a long time scale, landscapes embody social continuity, the most frequently cited traces of which are monuments to mortuary ritual and ancestor veneration (e.g., McAnany 1995; Renfrew 1973; Buikstra and Charles, this volume). As Barrett, Bradley, Buikstra, Charles and others have argued, however, changes in the designated use of the landscape may indicate disruptions to cyclical time, or within the society invoking time cycles.

Archaeologists tend to focus on monuments when they were built and while they remained in active use, but the "afterlife of monuments" (Bradley 1993) remains under-appreciated. We forget that a seemingly abandoned monument is still part of an active landscape. Ancient sites, monuments and even entire landscapes may be transformed and re-used as people encounter and interact with particular places, as they re-create the past (Bender et al. 1997: 149). Teotihuacan, for example, remained a powerful place of pilgrimage and ritual in Aztec times, nearly a millennium after the core of the city was burned; today, of course, it continues to draw thousands of visitors annually as an emblem of Mexico's pre-Columbian past. Monument afterlife can have different sources and take different forms (Bradley 1998a); even geological formations may have been understood as ancestral monuments, maintained and embellished by later generations living in the same space (Bradley 1998b: 20–1; Morphy 1995; Brady and Ashmore, this volume). Here, the constructed and conceptualized landscapes become inextricably merged.

Landscape transformation takes many forms, with many instigating causes. Conquest frequently involves the destruction of history or destiny for the vanquished, through obliteration of their monuments (e.g., Chapman 1994; Crumley and Marquardt 1987; Low 1995): the landscape is remade, its symbolic markings no longer visible, and society becomes disoriented. Resistance can likewise be expressed in landscape destruction, as in the toppling of the Berlin Wall, or rebellious settlers' trampling of a governor's estate in seventeenth-century South Africa (Markell 1995; Yentsch 1996). Less catastrophic fates for monuments and landscapes may be no less socially profound, as John Barrett argues in this volume, inasmuch as what we might call benign neglect may signal a fundamental change in the social perception of the landscape, its past, and the society it represents (consider Buikstra and Charles, this volume; Kealhofer, this volume). Like all human realities, the landscape has a plurality of coda by which it may be interpreted; inventing a tradition or re-writing a tradition is also re-writing the landscape (Parcero Oubiña et al. 1998: 174).

Archaeological Landscapes in Contemporary Perspective

Like any other human product, landscape objectifies an intention, meaning and rationality. These result in specific formal elements which should reflect in some way the contours of that rationality.

(Parcero Oubiña et al. 1998: 159)

We may assume, for the sake of discussion, that contemporary, etic, archaeological perceptions of the landscape were not those used by prehistoric or early historic societies to conceptualize their environments. If current concepts of landscape have any validity, then, they do so only if archaeologists remain fully aware of their own cultural or historical configuration and mediation. The problem, according to Lemaire (1997: 11–12), is that we have to think of the past using concepts associated with the rise of modernity, without falling victim to their distortions. However, as Cosgrove (1997: 25) points out, the relationship between modernity and landscape is complex, ambiguous, and negotiated, especially when one accepts that landscape is "a nexus of community, justice, nature and environment, a contested territory that is as pertinent today as it was when the term entered the modern English language at the end of the sixteenth century" (Olwig 1996, cited by Cosgrove 1997: 25).

In pre-modern, non-Western societies, landscape may have been regarded as largely mythic space, but one in which humans actively participated. Contemporary interpretations or reconstructions of past landscapes often implicate a rupture in history – the invention of landscape – that not by chance, coincided with or derived from catastrophic disruption to this mythical ordering of space (e.g., Denevan 1992; Olwig 1993: 334). This is most obvious in areas of colonial expansion. Archaeology, after all, became popular only when the modern world emerged, when nation-states became the political norm, and when people attempted to validate their presence in the world by excavating and exposing the ancient substrates of modern dwellings (Lemaire 1997: 19). There are significant, ongoing differences in both the meanings and uses of landscape, the result of diverse social and environmental histories within different regions of the world (Cosgrove 1997: 25).

In their recent field work at Leskernick in Cornwall, Bender, Hamilton, and Tilley (1997: 165) confronted a landscape that was "somehow the equivalent of a tropical jungle, with stones substituting for trees, in which the huts looked like stone and the stones like huts, a seamless web of the cultural and natural." To polarize nature and culture, perception and interpretation, is commonplace, but in fact hinders conceptualizing past landscapes (Tilley 1994: 23). Whatever our own traditional views, it is now clear that landscape is neither exclusively natural nor totally cultural: it is a mediation between the two and an integral part of Bourdieu's *habitus*, the routine social practices within which people experience the world around them. Beyond *habitus*, however, people actively order, transform, identify with and memorialize landscape by dwelling within it. The environment manifests itself as landscape only when people create and experience space as a complex of places. People's sense of place, and their engagement with the world around them, are invariably dependent on their own social, cultural, and historical situations.

As archaeologists, we have chosen to explore the meaning and legacies of individual ideational landscapes. We have argued in this introduction that the study of archaeological landscapes is at a critical point in the development of both theory and practice. Heightened global awareness of landscapes and their mutability, changes in theorizing space within archaeology, and recent archaeological applications of social theory, all have converged in the past few years to ignite several dynamic and creative efforts in understanding ancient landscapes; the already large literature continues to grow steadily. We have outlined here what we see as the formative developments in forging the current state of interpretation, and have proposed that by recognizing constructed, conceptual and, more abstractly, ideational landscapes, archaeologists may find it possible to sharpen reference to landscape phenomena. Others, including some volume contributors, would not always agree with what we have asserted or proposed. But we believe they would join us in optimism about the prospects of further critical growth in studying social meaning in ancient landscapes.

ACKNOWLEDGMENTS

We thank Virginia Ebert, Tom Patterson, Jeremy Sabloff, and Peter van Dommelen for helpful comments on earlier drafts.

REFERENCES

Alcock, S. E. 1993: *Graecia Capta: The Landscapes of Roman Greece*. Cambridge: Cambridge University Press.

Aldenderfer, M. 1990: Late Preceramic ceremonial architecture at Asana, Southern Peru. *Antiquity*, 64, 479–93.

Ashmore, W. 1991: Site-planning principles and concepts of directionality among the ancient Maya. *Latin American Antiquity*, 2, 199–226.

Ashmore, W. 1998: Monumentos políticos: sitios, asentamiento, y paisaje por Xunantunich, Belice. In A. Ciudad Ruiz, Y. Fernández Marquínez, J. M. García Campillo, Ma. J. Iglesias Ponce de León, A. L. García-Gallo, and L. T. Sanz Castro (eds), *Anatomía de una Civilización: Aproximaciones Interdisciplinarias a la Cultura Maya*, Madrid: Sociedad Española de Estudios Mayas, 161–83.

Aveni, A. F. 1980: *Skywatchers of Ancient Mexico*. Austin: University of Texas Press.

Aveni, A. F. 1986: The Nazca lines: patterns in the desert. *Archaeology*, 39 (4), 32–9.

Aveni, A. F. 1991: Mapping the ritual landscape: debt payment to Tlaloc during the month of Atlcahualo. In D. Carrasco (ed.), *To Change Place: Aztec Ceremonial Landscapes*, Niwot: University Press of Colorado, 58–73.

Barrett, J. 1991: The archaeology of social reproduction. In J. Barrett, R. Bradley, and M. Green, *Landscape, Monuments and Society: The Prehistory of Cranborne Chase*, Cambridge: Cambridge University Press, 6–8.

Barrett, J., Bradley, R., and Green, M. 1991: *Landscape, Monuments and Society: The Prehistory of Cranborne Chase*. Cambridge: Cambridge University Press.

Basso, K. H. 1984: "Stalking with stories": names, places, and moral narratives among the Western Apache. In S. Plattner and E. M. Bruner (eds), *Text, Play, and Story: The Construction and Reconstruction of Self and Society*, Washington, DC: 1983 Proceedings of the American Ethnological Society, 19–55.

Basso, K. H. 1996: Wisdom sites in places: notes on a Western Apache landscape. In S. Feld and K. H. Basso (eds), *Senses of Place*, Santa Fe: SAR Press, 53–90.

Bauer, B. 1991: Pacariqtambo and the mythical origins of the Inca. *Latin American Antiquity*, 2, 7–26.

Bender, B. (ed.) 1993: *Landscape: Politics and Perspectives*. Oxford: Berg.

Bender, B. 1998: *Stonehenge: Making Space*. Oxford: Berg.

Bender, B., Hamilton, S., and Tilley, C. 1997: Leskernick: stone worlds; alternative narrative; nested landscapes. *Proceedings of the Prehistoric Society*, 63, 147–78.

Bintliff, J. 1996: Interactions of theory, methodology and practice. *Archaeological Dialogues*, 3, 246–55.

Bodenhorn, B. 1993: Gendered spaces, public places: public and private revisited on the North Slope of Alaska. In B. Bender (ed.), *Landscape: Politics and Perspectives*, Oxford: Berg, 169–203.

Bourdieu, P. 1977: *Outline of a Theory of Practice*. Cambridge: Cambridge University Press.

Bradley, R. 1991: Rock art and the perception of landscape. *Cambridge Archaeological Journal*, 1, 77–101.

Bradley, R. 1993: *Altering the Earth: The Origins of Monuments in Britain and Continental Europe*, Monograph Series, 8. Edinburgh: Society of Antiquaries of Scotland.

Bradley, R. 1997: *Rock Art and the Prehistory of Atlantic Europe*. London: Routledge.

Bradley, R. 1998a: *The Significance of Monuments: On the Shaping of Human Experience in Neolithic and Bronze Age Europe*. London: Routledge.

Bradley, R. 1998b: Ruined buildings, ruined stones: enclosures, tombs and natural places in the Neolithic of south-west England. *World Archaeology*, 30, 13–22.

Broda, J. 1991: The sacred landscape of Aztec calendar festivals: myth, nature, and society. In D. Carrasco (ed.), *To Change Place: Aztec Ceremonial Landscapes*, Niwot: University Press of Colorado, 74–120.

Carlson, J. 1980: A geomantic model for the interpretation of Mesoamerican sites: an essay in cross-cultural comparison. In E. P. Benson (ed.), *Mesoamerican Sites and World-Views*, Washington, DC: Dumbarton Oaks, 143–215.

Carmichael, D. L., Hubert, J., and Reeves, B. 1994: Introduction. In D. L. Carmichael, J. Hubert, B. Reeves, and A. Schanche (eds), *Sacred Sites, Sacred Places*, One World Archaeology, 23, London: Routledge, 1–8.

Carmichael, D. L., Hubert, J., Reeves, B., and Schanche, A. (eds) 1994: *Sacred Sites, Sacred Places*. One World Archaeology, 23. London: Routledge.

Carneiro, R. 1970: A theory of the origin of the state. *Science*, 169, 733–8.

Carrasco, D. (ed.) 1991: *To Change Place: Aztec Ceremonial Landscapes*. Niwot: University Press of Colorado.

Casey, E. S. 1996: How to get from space to place in a fairly short stretch of time: phenomenological prolegomena. In S. Feld and K. H. Basso (eds), *Senses of Place*, Santa Fe: SAR Press, 13–52.

Chang, K. C. 1972: *Settlement Patterns in Archaeology*, Modules in Anthropology, 24. Menlo Park, CA: Addison-Wesley.

Chapman, J. 1994: Destruction of a common heritage: the archaeology of war in Croatia, Bosnia and Hercegovina. *Antiquity*, 68, 120–6.

Cherry, J. F., Davis, J. L., and Mantzourani, E. 1991: *Landscape Archaeology as Long-Term History: Northern Keos in the Cycladic Islands*, Monumenta Archeologica, 16. Los Angeles: UCLA Institute of Archaeology.

Cleere, H. 1995: Cultural landscapes as world heritage. *Conservation and Management of Archaeological Sites*, 1, 63–8.

Conkey, M. W. 1980: The identification of prehistoric hunter-gatherer aggregation sites: the case of Altamira. *Current Anthropology*, 21, 609–30.

Conkey, M. W., and Gero, J. M. 1997: Programme to practice: gender and feminism in archaeology. *Annual Review of Anthropology*, 26, Palo Alto: Annual Reviews Inc., 411–37.

Cosgrove, D. E. 1984: *Social Formation and Symbolic Landscape*. London: Croom Helm.

Cosgrove, D. E. 1997: Inhabiting modern landscape. *Archaeological Dialogues*, 4, 23–8.

Crown, P. L., and Fish, S. K. 1996: Gender and status in the Hohokam Pre-Classic to Classic transition. *American Anthropologist*, 98, 803–17.

Crumley, C. L. 1979: Three locational models: an epistemological assessment for anthropology and archaeology. In M. B. Schiffer (ed.), *Advances in Archaeological Method and Theory*, 2, New York: Academic Press, 141–73.

Crumley, C. L. 1986: A dialectical critique of hierarchy. In T. C. Patterson and C. M. Gailey (eds), *Power Relations and State Formation*, Washington, DC: Archeology Section, American Anthropological Association, 155–69.

Crumley, C. L. 1994: Cultural ecology: a multidimensional ecological orientation. In C. L. Crumley (ed.), *Historical Ecology: Cultural Knowledge and Changing Landscapes*, Santa Fe: SAR Press, 1–16.

Crumley, C. L., and Marquardt, W. H. 1987: Regional dynamics in Burgundy. In C. L. Crumley and W. H. Marquardt (eds), *Regional Dynamics: Burgundian Landscapes in Historical Perspective*, San Diego: Academic Press, 609–23.

Daniels, S., and Cosgrove, D. E. 1988: Introduction: iconography and landscape. In D. E. Cosgrove and S. Daniels (eds), *The Iconography of Landscape: Essays on the Symbolic Representation, Design and Use of Past Environments*, Cambridge: Cambridge University Press, 1–10.

Denevan, W. M. 1992: The pristine myth: the landscape of the Americas in 1492. *Annals of the Association of American Geographers*, 82, 369–85.

Derks, T. 1997: The transformation of landscape and religious representation in Roman Gaul. *Archaeological Dialogues*, 4, 126–47.

Dietler, M. 1998: A tale of three cities: the monumentalization of Celtic oppida and the politics of collective memory and identity. *World Archaeology*, 30, 72–89.

Drennan, R. D. 1976: Religion and social evolution in Formative Mesoamerica. In K. V. Flannery (ed.), *The Early Mesoamerican Village*, New York: Academic Press, 345–68.

Dunnell, R. C. 1992: The notion site. In J. Rossignol and L. Wandsnider (eds), *Space, Time, and Archaeological Landscapes*, New York: Plenum Press, 21–41.

Ebert, J. I. 1992: *Distributional Archaeology*. Albuquerque: University of New Mexico Press.

Eliade, M. 1959: *The Sacred and the Profane*. New York: Harcourt Brace.

Erickson, C. L. 1993: The social organization of prehispanic raised field agriculture in the Lake Titicaca basin. In V. L. Scarborough and B. L. Isaac (eds), *Economic Aspects of Water Management in the Prehispanic New World*, Research in Economic Anthropology, Supplement 7, Greenwich, CT: JAI Press, 369–426.

Feld, S., and Basso, K. (eds) 1996: *Senses of Place*, Santa Fe: SAR Press.

Fitter, C. 1995: *Poetry, Space, Landscape: Toward a New Theory*. Cambridge: Cambridge University Press.

Flannery, K. V., and Marcus, J. 1976: Formative Oaxaca and the Zapotec cosmos. *American Scientist*, 64, 374–83.

Flood, J. 1996: Culture in early Aboriginal Australia. *Cambridge Archaeological Journal*, 6, 3–36.

Foley, R. 1981: Off-site archaeology: an alternative approach for the short-sited. In I. Hodder, G. Isaac, and N. Hammond (eds), *Pattern of the Past: Studies in Honour of David Clarke*, Cambridge: Cambridge University Press, 157–83.

Fowler, P. J. 1995: Writing on the countryside. In I. Hodder, M. Shanks, A. Alexandri, V. Buchli, J. Carman, J. Last, and G. Lucas (eds), *Interpretive Archaeology: Finding Meaning in the Past*, London: Routledge, 100–9.

Freidel, D. A., Schele, L., and Parker, J. 1993: *Maya Cosmos: Three Thousand Years on the Shaman's Trail.* New York: William Morrow.

Fritz, J. M. 1978: Paleopsychology today: ideational systems and adaptation in prehistory. In C. L. Redman, M. J. Berman, E. V. Curtin, W. T. Langhorne, Jr, N. M. Versaggi, and J. C. Wanser (eds), *Social Archeology: Beyond Subsistence and Dating,* New York: Academic Press, 37–59.

Fullager, R. L. K., Price, D. M., and Head, L. M. 1996: Early human occupation of northern Australia: archaeology and thermoluminescence dating of Jinmium rock-shelter, Northern Territory. *Antiquity,* 70, 751–73.

Gell, A. 1995: The language of the forest: landscape and phonological iconism in Umede. In E. Hirsch and M. O'Hanlon (eds), *The Anthropology of Landscape: Perspectives on Place and Space,* Oxford: Clarendon Press, 232–54.

Giddens, A. 1984: *The Constitution of Society: An Outline of the Theory of Structuration.* Berkeley: University of California Press.

Gilchrist, R. 1994: *Gender and Material Culture: The Archaeology of Religious Women.* London: Routledge.

Given, M., Knapp, A. B., and Meyer, N. n.d.: The Sydney Cyprus Survey Project: an interdisciplinary investigation of long-term change in the north central Troodos, Cyprus. Submitted to *Journal of Field Archaeology.*

Gosden, C. 1994: *Social Being and Time.* Oxford: Blackwell.

Gosden, C., and Head, L. 1994: Landscape – a usefully ambiguous concept. *Archaeology in Oceania,* 29, 113–16.

Hall, E. T. 1966: *The Hidden Dimension.* Garden City, NY: Doubleday.

Hall, R. 1977: Ghosts, water barriers, corn, and sacred enclosures in the Eastern Woodlands. *American Antiquity,* 41, 360–4.

Hanks, W. F. 1990: *Referential Practice: Language and Lived Space among the Maya.* Chicago: University of Chicago Press.

Harvey, D. 1980: *The History of Topographical Maps: Symbols, Pictures and Surveys.* London: Thames and Hudson.

Hastorf, C. L. 1990: Gender, space and food in prehistory. In J. M. Gero and M. W. Conkey (eds), *Engendering Archaeology: Women and Prehistory,* Oxford: Blackwell, 132–59.

Hawkins, G. S. 1965: *Stonehenge Decoded.* Garden City, NY: Doubleday.

Head, L. 1993: Unearthing prehistoric cultural landscapes: a view from Australia. *Transactions of the Institute of British Geographers,* n.s. 18, 481–99.

Helms, M. 1988: *Ulysses' Sail: An Ethnographic Odyssey of Power, Knowledge, and Geographical Distance.* Princeton: Princeton University Press.

Helms, M. 1992: Thoughts on public symbols and distant domains relevant to the chiefdoms of lower Central America. In F. W. Lange (ed.), *Wealth and Hierarchy in the Intermediate Area,* Washington, DC: Dumbarton Oaks, 317–29.

Hirsch, E. 1995: Landscape: between place and space. In E. Hirsch and M. O'Hanlon (eds), *The Anthropology of Landscape: Perspectives on Place and Space,* Oxford: Clarendon Press, 1–30.

Hirsch, E., and O'Hanlon, M. (eds) 1995: *The Anthropology of Landscape: Perspectives on Place and Space.* Oxford: Clarendon Press.

Hodder, I. 1984: Burials, houses, women and men in the European Neolithic. In D. Miller and C. Tilley (eds), *Ideology, Power and Prehistory*, Cambridge: Cambridge University Press, 51–68.

Hodder, I. 1990: *The Domestication of Europe*. Oxford: Blackwell.

Hodder, I., Shanks, M., Alexandri, A., Buchli, V., Carman, J., Last, J., and Lucas, G. (eds) 1995: *Interpreting Archaeology: Finding Meaning in the Past*. London: Routledge.

Holtorf, C. J. 1997: Megaliths, monumentality and memory. *Archaeological Review from Cambridge*, 14 (2), 45–66.

Ingold, T. 1986: Territoriality and tenure: the appropriation of space in hunting and gathering societies. In T. Ingold (ed.), *The Appropriation of Nature: Essays on Human Ecology and Social Relations*, Manchester: Manchester University Press, 130–64.

Ingold, T. 1993: The temporality of the landscape. *World Archaeology*, 25, 152–74.

Ingold, T. 1996: Hunting and gathering as ways of perceiving the environment. In R. Ellen and K. Fukui (eds), *Redefining Nature: Ecology, Culture and Domestication*, Oxford: Berg, 117–55.

Jackson, J. B. 1980: *The Necessity for Ruins, and Other Topics*. Amherst: University of Massachusetts Press.

Jackson, J. B. 1984: *Discovering the Vernacular Landscape*. New Haven: Yale University Press.

Jackson, T. L. 1990: Pounding acorns: women's production as social and economic focus. In J. M. Gero and M. W. Conkey (eds), *Engendering Archaeology: Women and Prehistory*, Oxford: Blackwell, 301–25.

Johnston, R. 1998: Approaches to the perception of landscape: philosophy, theory, methodology. *Archaeological Dialogues*, 5, 54–68.

Kahn, M. 1996: Your place and mine: sharing emotional landscapes in Wamira, Papua New Guinea. In S. Feld and K. H. Basso (eds), *Senses of Place*, Santa Fe: SAR Press, 167–96.

Kent, S. M. 1997: Invisible gender – invisible foragers: Southern African hunter-gatherer spatial patterning and the archaeological record. In S. Kent (ed.), *Gender in African Prehistory*, Walnut Creek, CA: AltaMira Press, 39–67.

Knapp, A. B. 1996a: The Bronze Age economy of Cyprus: ritual, ideology, and the sacred landscape. In V. Karageorghis and D. Michaelides (eds), *The Development of the Cypriot Economy: From the Prehistoric Period to the Present Day*, Nicosia: University of Cyprus and Bank of Cyprus, 71–106.

Knapp, A. B. 1996b: Archaeology without gravity: postmodernism and the past. *Journal of Archaeological Method and Theory*, 3, 127–58.

Knapp, A. B. 1997: *The Archaeology of Late Bronze Age Cypriot Society: The Study of Settlement, Survey and Landscape*, Occasional Paper, 4. Glasgow: University of Glasgow, Department of Archaeology.

Knapp, A. B. 1998: Mediterranean Bronze Age trade: distance, power and place. In E. H. Cline and D. Harris-Cline (eds), *The Aegean and the Orient in the Second Millennium: Proceedings of the 50th Anniversary Symposium, Cincinnati, 18–20 April 1997*, Aegaeum, 18, Liège: Université de Liège, 260–80.

Kniffen, F. B. 1965: Folk housing: key to diffusion. *Annals of the Association of American Geographers*, 55, 549–77.

Kolata, A., and Ponce Sanginés, C. 1992: Tiwanaku: the city at the center. In R. F. Townsend (ed.), *The Ancient Americas: Art from Sacred Landscapes*, Chicago, Munich: Art Institute of Chicago, Prestel Verlag, 317–33.

Kubler, G. 1962: *The Shape of Time: Remarks on the History of Things*. New Haven: Yale University Press.

Layton, R. 1995: Relating to the country in the western desert. In E. Hirsch and M. O'Hanlon (eds), *The Anthropology of Landscape: Perspectives on Place and Space*, Oxford: Clarendon Press, 210–31.

Lekson, S. H. 1996: Landscape with ruins: archaeological approaches to built and unbuilt environments. *Current Anthropology*, 37, 886–92.

Lemaire, T. 1997: Archaeology between the invention and destruction of the landscape. *Archaeological Dialogues*, 4, 5–21.

Leone, M. P. 1984: Interpreting ideology in historical archaeology: the William Paca garden in Annapolis, Maryland. In D. Miller and C. Tilley (eds), *Ideology, Power and Prehistory*, Cambridge: Cambridge University Press, 25–35.

Low, S. M. 1995: Indigenous architecture and the Spanish-American plaza in Mesoamerica and the Caribbean. *American Anthropologist*, 97, 748–62.

Markell, A. 1995: The historical archaeology of Vergelegen, an early farmstead at the Cape of Good Hope. *Historical Archaeology*, 29 (2), 10–34.

Marshack, A. 1972: *The Roots of Civilization*. New York: McGraw-Hill.

Martlew, R. D., and Ruggles, C. L. N. 1996: Ritual and landscape on the west coast of Scotland: an investigation of the stone rows of northern Mull. *Proceedings of the Prehistoric Society*, 62, 117–31.

McAnany, P. A. 1995: *Living with the Ancestors: Kinship and Kingship in Ancient Maya Society*. Austin: University of Texas Press.

McEwan, C., and van de Guchte, M. 1992: Ancestral time and sacred space in Inca state ritual. In R. F. Townsend (ed.), *The Ancient Americas: Art from Sacred Landscapes*, Chicago, Munich: Art Institute of Chicago, Prestel Verlag, 359–71.

Meskell, L. 1998a: Intimate archaeologies: the case of Kha and Merit. *World Archaeology*, 29, 363–79.

Meskell, L. 1998b: An archaeology of social relations in an Egyptian village. *Journal of Archaeological Method and Theory*, 5, 209–43.

Miller, A. G. 1995: *The Painted Tombs of Oaxaca: Living with the Ancestors*. Cambridge: Cambridge University Press.

Morphy, H. 1995: Landscape and the reproduction of the ancestral past. In E. Hirsch and M. O'Hanlon (eds), *The Anthropology of Landscape: Perspectives on Place and Space*, Oxford: Clarendon Press, 184–209.

Nora, P. 1989: Between memory and history: *les lieux de mémoire*. *Representations*, 26, 7–25.

Olwig, K. 1993: Sexual cosmology: nation and landscape at the conceptual interstices of nature and cultures; or what does landscape really mean? In B. Bender (ed.), *Landscape: Politics and Perspectives*, Oxford: Berg, 307–43.

Olwig, K. 1996: The substantive nature of landscape. *Annals of the Association of American Geographers*, 86, 630–53.

Oosten, J. 1997: Landscape and cosmology. *Archaeological Dialogues*, 4, 152–4.

Parcero Oubiña, C., Criado Boado, G., and Santos Estévez, M. 1998: Rewriting landscape: incorporating sacred landscapes into cultural traditions. *World Archaeology*, 30, 159–78.

Patterson, T. C. 1990: Some theoretical tensions within and between the processual and postprocessual archaeologies. *Journal of Anthropological Archaeology*, 9, 189–200.

Piggott, S. 1937: Prehistory and the Romantic movement. *Antiquity*, 11, 31–8.

Preucel, R. W. (ed.) 1991: *Processual and Postprocessual Archaeologies: Multiple Ways of Knowing the Past*, Occasional Paper, 10. Carbondale, IL: Center for Archaeological Investigations, Southern Illinois University.

Rappaport, J. 1989: Geography and historical understanding in indigenous Colombia. In R. Layton (ed.), *Who Needs the Past?*, London: Routledge, 84–94.

Renfrew, C. 1973: *Before Civilization: The Radiocarbon Revolution and Prehistoric Europe*. New York: Knopf.

Renfrew, C. 1982: *Towards an Archaeology of Mind*. Cambridge: Cambridge University Press.

Renfrew, C., Peebles, C., Hodder, I., Bender, B., Flannery, K. V., and Marcus, J. 1993: What is cognitive archaeology? *Cambridge Archaeological Journal*, 3, 247–70.

Renfrew, C., and Zubrow, E. B. W. (eds) 1994: *The Ancient Mind: Elements of Cognitive Archaeology*. Cambridge: Cambridge University Press.

Richards, C. 1996: Henges and water: toward an elemental understanding of monumentality and landscape in late Neolithic Britain. *Journal of Material Culture*, 1, 313–36.

Rossignol, J., and Wandsnider, L. (eds) 1992: *Space, Time, and Archaeological Landscapes*. New York: Plenum Press.

Rowlands, M. 1993: The role of memory in the transmission of culture. *World Archaeology*, 25, 141–51.

Sanders, W. T. 1977: Environmental heterogeneity and the evolution of Lowland Maya civilization. In R. E. W. Adams (ed.), *The Origins of Maya Civilization*, Albuquerque: University of New Mexico Press, 287–97.

Saunders, N. J. 1994: At the mouth of the obsidian cave: deity and place in Aztec religion. In D. L. Carmichael, J. Hubert, B. Reeves, and A. Schanche (eds), *Sacred Sites, Sacred Places*, One World Archaeology, 23, London: Routledge, 172–83.

Sauer, C. O. 1925: The morphology of landscapes. *University of California Publications in Geography*, 2, 19–54.

Schama, S. 1995: *Landscape and Memory*. New York: Knopf.

Schmidt, P. R. 1983: An alternative to a strictly materialist perspective: a review of historical archaeology, ethnoarchaeology, and symbolic approaches in African archaeology. *American Antiquity*, 48, 62–79.

Schmidt, P. R. 1997: *Iron Technology in East Africa: Symbolism, Science, and Archaeology*. Bloomington and Oxford: Indiana University Press and James Curry.

Scully, V. 1989: *Pueblo, Mountain, Village, Dance*, 2nd edn. Chicago: University of Chicago Press.

Shanks, M., and Hodder, I. 1995: Processual, postprocessual and interpretive archaeologies. In I. Hodder, M. Shanks, A. Alexandri, V. Buchli, J. Carman, J. Last, and G. Lucas (eds), *Interpreting Archaeology: Finding Meaning in the Past*, London and New York: Routledge, 3–28.

Sherratt, A. 1996: "Settlement patterns" or "landscape studies"? Reconciling reason and romance. *Archaeological Dialogues*, 3, 140–59.

Spirn, A. W. 1996: Constructing nature: the legacy of Frederick Law Olmsted. In W. Cronon (ed.), *Uncommon Ground: Rethinking the Human Place in Nature*, New York: W. W. Norton, 91–113.

Stein, J. R., and Lekson, S. L. 1992: Anasazi ritual landscapes. In D. E. Doyel (ed.), *Anasazi Regional Organization and the Chaco System*, Anthropological Papers, no. 5, Albuquerque: Maxwell Museum of Anthropology, 87–100.

Steward, J. M. 1955: *Theory of Culture Change*. Urbana: University of Illinois Press.

Taçon, P. S. C. 1994: Socialising landscapes: the long-term implications of signs, symbols and marks on the land. *Archaeology in Oceania*, 29, 117–29.

Tedlock, B. 1992: The road of light: theory and practice of Mayan skywatching. In A. F. Aveni (ed.), *The Sky in Mayan Literature*, Oxford: Oxford University Press, 18–42.

Thomas, J. 1991: *Rethinking the Neolithic*. Cambridge: Cambridge University Press.

Thomas, J. 1993: The politics of vision and the archaeologies of landscape. In B. Bender (ed.), *Landscape: Politics and Perspectives*, Oxford: Berg, 19–48.

Thomas, J. 1996: *Time, Culture and Identity*. London: Routledge.

Tilley, C. 1994: *A Phenomenology of Landscape: Places, Paths and Monuments*. Oxford: Berg.

Tilley, C. 1996: The power of rocks: topography and monument construction on Bodmin Moor. *World Archaeology*, 28, 161–76.

Townsend, R. F. 1982: Pyramid and sacred mountain. In A. F. Aveni and G. Urton (eds), *Ethnoastronomy and Archaeoastronomy in the American Tropics*, *Annals of the New York Academy of Sciences*, 385, 37–62.

Townsend, R. F. (ed.) 1992: *The Ancient Americas: Art from Sacred Landscapes*. Chicago, Munich: Art Institute of Chicago, Prestel Verlag.

Tringham, R. 1994: Engendered spaces in prehistory. *Gender, Place and Culture*, 1, 169–203.

Tuan, Y. 1971: Geography, phenomenology, and the study of human nature. *Canadian Geographer*, 15, 181–92.

Tuan, Y. 1977: *Space and Place: The Perspective of Experience*. Minneapolis: University of Minnesota Press.

Ucko, P. J. 1994: Foreword. In D. L. Carmichael, J. Hubert, B. Reeves, and A. Schanche (eds), *Sacred Sites, Sacred Places*, One World Archaeology, 23, London: Routledge, xiii–xxiii.

Urton, G. 1981: *At the Crossroads of the Earth and the Sky*. Austin: University of Texas Press.

Vogt, E. Z. 1969: *Zinacantan: A Maya Community in the Highlands of Chiapas*. Cambridge, MA: Belknap Press.

Watson, P. J., and Kennedy, M. C. 1990: The development of horticulture in the Eastern Woodlands of North America: women's role. In J. M. Gero and M. W. Conkey (eds), *Engendering Archaeology: Women and Prehistory*, Oxford: Blackwell, 255–75.

Willey, G. R. 1953: *Prehistoric Settlement Patterns in the Viru Valley, Peru*, Bulletin 155. Washington, DC: Bureau of American Ethnology.

Wilson, P. 1988: *The Domestication of the Human Species*. New Haven: Yale University Press.

Wylie, A. 1991: The interplay of evidential constraints and political interests: recent archaeological research on gender. *American Antiquity*, 57, 15–35.

Wylie, A. 1992: Feminist theories of social power: some implications for a processual archaeology. *Norwegian Archaeological Review*, 25, 51–68.

Yamin, R., and Metheny, K. B. (eds) 1996: *Landscape Archaeology: Reading and Interpreting the American Historical Landscape*. Knoxville: University of Tennessee Press.

Yentsch, A. E. 1996: Introduction: close attention to place – landscape studies by historical archaeologists. In R. Yamin and K. B. Metheny (eds), *Landscape Archaeology: Reading and Interpreting the American Historical Landscape*, Knoxville: University of Tennessee Press, xxiii–xlii.

Part I

Ethnographic and Historical Cases

2

Identifying Ancient Sacred Landscapes in Australia: From Physical to Social

Paul S. C. Taçon

Introduction

Debates about what makes us human have focused on our tool-making abilities, language, the production of "art," the use of symbols, and our genetic heritage. In most cases, similarities rather than differences from other species are highlighted and it seems that, in terms of behaviors such as tool use, language and art, humans are the creatures that practice these things to the extreme. Our physical selves are aided by our material culture and symbolic communication but it is the concept of "landscape" that is integral to this process. Other species have home-ranges, preferred travel routes, or dwellings used by many generations of individuals, but with humans landscape use, modification and manipulation have become obsessions. Our oldest ancestors initiated the process of transforming natural wilderness into cultural places and spaces many thousands of years ago, by the mythologizing, marking and mapping of landscapes (Cosgrove 1989; 1993; Taçon 1994). Today there are few areas of the world that have not been built upon, mapped, marked, or otherwise modified for human use. Indeed, a driving urge for many people is to be the first to conquer the last few remaining areas of what they perceive to be "wilderness" – supposed but perhaps now mythical places untouched by humankind. Yet what we perceive to be wilderness is also landscape, with some people going to great lengths to preserve these "places." However, "wilderness" too is sectioned off, marked, mapped, and mythologized into networks of national parks or reserves, becoming another type of humanly defined landscape in the process.

There are many definitions of landscape and even more perceptions and conceptions (e.g., Bender 1993; Cosgrove and Daniels 1988;

Gosden and Head 1994; Ingold 1993). "Landscape is a term which both invites and defies definition" (Gosden and Head 1994: 113) – consequently, there is a vast body of landscape literature that attempts to dissect the very essence of landscape use and understanding but ultimately we are forced to conclude that landscape as a concept is infinitely variable. Landscape, like "beauty," is in the mind of the beholder and, as such, varies widely from one personal or cultural perspective to the next. Experience, history, value systems, relationships, circumstance, and individual choices all play a part in how landscapes are seen or described. The important point is that they are seen and described from a human perspective – often personified, deified and/or defined in terms of human history and exploitation. Landscapes are socialized; landscapes are conceived. But are there certain physical landscapes that share common features which make them recognizably special, sacred or sublime, no matter what one's cultural background? For example, Nash (1997) makes a case for archetypal landscapes founded in nature. How have humans responded to these places, converting them from physical to social landscapes? And what of the world's earliest surviving human landscapes? Is there good evidence that humans have always been obsessed with socializing large-scale landscapes?

In order to answer these questions we must turn to rock art, that great body of enduring human-made marks produced with both symbolic and aesthetic intent. For it is this form of ancient human activity that is most directly linked to early perceptions of landscape – the very location and organizational structure of rock art speaks of human relationships to places and spaces (see Hodder 1993 and Tilley 1994 for definitions and other relationships between material culture and landscapes). We will never be able to decipher the full meaning of ancient rock art but we can define its structure and organizing principles (Chippindale and Taçon 1998). These, in turn, can be related to the larger landscapes of which they are a part. As Richard Bradley (1995: 107) notes for the "Atlantic" style of rock art found on natural surfaces from Scotland to Spain: "It is a scheme based largely on geography." Many other forms of rock art are similarly structured, with striking examples found in some parts of Australia, the Americas, and southern Africa. In all these regions one of the earliest surviving forms of rock art consists of cup-shaped marks known as "cupules" (Parkman 1995; Taçon et al. 1997). It is these that may give us insight into very early landscape use at the symbolic level (figure 2.1).

However, in Australia (figure 2.2) there is also a large body of ethnographic evidence to consult about landscape perceptions and

Figure 2.1 Large panels of cupules, such as this one at Jinmium, Northern Territory, are found scattered across the northern portions of Western Australia and the Northern Territory (photo: Paul Taçon).

conceptions. Furthermore, visual art and landscape feature prominently in modern politics, from urban "multi-cultural" to remote "traditional" settings. For instance, Luke Taylor (1988: 381) has shown that some "X-ray" paintings from the remote region of Arnhem Land:

> encode "inside" meanings relating to the spatial relationship between topographic features of clan lands. At an "outside" level these paintings are also interpreted to show the body parts and internal organs and bones of ancestral beings. The metaphors of these paintings express the way Kunwinjku conceive of the spatial organization of sites in their lands in terms of an abstract model of the divided yet organically related body parts of the ancestral being that created those lands. Such sites are described as transformations of the actual body parts of the ancestral being, and all the sites thus created are considered to be intrinsically connected. The association between body parts and landscape is developed principally within the Mardayin ceremony and in X-ray paintings used in the Mardayin. Paintings interpreted to show X-ray features occur in a number of contexts in this ceremony.

According to Djon Mundine (1992: 11) similar layered levels of relationship between people and places underpin Indigenous urban art, even though the specific ways in which they are expressed and the

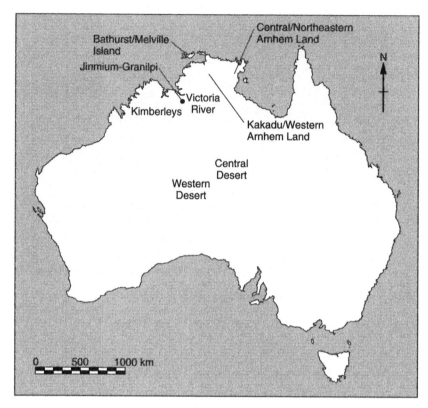

Figure 2.2 Map of Australia showing places mentioned in the text.

particular meanings are quite different:

> As in ancient times, Aboriginal people are returning to a multi-layered artistic culture: to interactive forms of song, dance, literature, and newer forms in film and video. Through their expansion of subject matter and range of work, employing new media alongside ones long-used, Aboriginal people are again finding ways to access their inner, vital, dynamic spirit. They are giving voice to a wounded history but also reaching beyond anger, speaking again with pride about the land called Australia and their long, strong, enduring and once again confident relationship to it.

Sacred Landscapes, Sacred Sites

In areas of the world where ethnographic or historic information is available we know that certain landscape features invoke common responses in human beings — feelings of awe, power, majestic beauty, respect, enrichment among them. Most commonly these subjective feelings occur in response to perceiving four types of places: (a) where the results of great acts of natural transformation can be best seen, such as mountain ranges, volcanoes, steep valleys or gorges (figure 2.3); (b) at junctions or points of change between geology, hydrology, and vegetation, or some combination of all three, such as sudden changes in elevation, waterfalls, the places where rainforest meets other vegetation (figure 2.4); (c) where there is an unusual landscape feature, such as a prominent peak, cave, or hole in the ground that one comes upon suddenly (figure 2.5); and (d) places providing panoramic views or large vistas of interesting and varied landscape features (figure 2.6). Often these are places where concepts of an upper world, a lower world and the earth plain come together visually in a striking manner. These are places where the center of the world may be experienced, where an *axis mundi* is located (Eliade 1964; 1978; Ouzman 1998; Paper 1990), for it is at these places that it is claimed a powerful connection between different levels and states of

Figure 2.3 Outstanding and unusual geological features, such as those that define Rainbow Valley in central Australia, are important landscapes associated with the activities of Ancestral Beings who created, shaped, and formed the land in the ancient eras of the Dreamtime (photo: Paul Taçon).

Figure 2.4 Waterfalls, permanent pools and other liminal places where there is visual evidence of transformation between water, geology, and vegetation are usually considered to be sacred places. They may have either open or restricted stories and access depending on their context within larger Dreaming Tracks. This example is of an open site within Kakadu National Park but there are other closed, dangerous places nearby (photo: Paul Taçon).

existence can be encountered. For Indigenous people of northern Australia:

> Most often, these nodes or focal points are unusual or outstanding aspects of the natural landscape, such as the tops of hills or raised areas, the centres of plains, areas marking the interfaces of water, rock, earth and sky (i.e., the underworld, middle world and skyworld), waterfalls, darkened deep pools of permanent water surrounded by rock, unusually sculptured and eroded geological forms or shaped boulders and rocky outcrops and areas in general. At some of these locations, the power is believed to be so concentrated that it is dangerous for all but those initiated into the highest levels of religious knowledge to approach them.

Figure 2.5 Near the Mann River this unusual geological feature is said to mark the spot where a Rainbow Serpent turned to stone (photo: Paul Taçon).

Figure 2.6 Meredith Wilson records rock paintings at a site that has magnificent panoramic views. These places were often marked with rock art imagery from a number of different periods (photo: Paul Taçon).

At others, correctly conducted rituals or observances, such as rock
painting, song, ceremonies, and blowing water in Australia...allow
individuals to tap into the power of places or to be protected from it.

(Taçon 1990: 13)

The ancient Greeks, Romans, Maya, Chinese, Vikings, and peoples
of Southeast Asia, among others, responded similarly to these powerful
landscape nodes, as is evidenced by their stories, literature, visual art,
and architecture. Indeed, places of worship are invariably modeled on
the more striking features of geology, with temples, cathedrals,
churches and monasteries placed in relation to mountains or pillars of
stone or shaped to resemble them. Often their insides re-create a cave
or cavern-like environment and water invariably features in some of
the rituals performed inside. Physical manifestations of upper, lower,
and middle worlds can be found in the architecture, highlighting
aspects of belief systems founded on landscape qualities. These human-
made sacred places are also richly adorned with elaborate imagery –
with symbols and senses of aesthetics that reflect the unique identities
and experiences of their makers. Ouzman (1998) argues that southern African rock art sites represented physical and conceptual places
where upper, lower, and middle worlds believed to exist by San
communities intersect. Vastokas and Vastokas (1973) have argued similarly for many North American rock art sites. Thus we see a common
pattern – human-made sacred places modeled on a core set of natural
places but embellished with unique artistry to reflect the cultural distinctiveness of given groups of people.

Similar patterns may be observed with many Australian rock art
sites. First of all, rock art sites may be situated near naturally defined
"sacred" locations but usually they do not occur right at them. Instead,
they more often overlook, indicate the approach to or mark the limits
of the more sacred and restricted landscape zones. Secondly, rock art
sites are invariably located not far from water, whether the sites were
once places of habitation or not. Thirdly, the rock shelters or platforms
that were most extensively used for painting and/or engraving are
those with prominent, often magnificent, panoramic views. In other
words, significant stretches of what may be perceived to be powerfully
charged or "beautiful" landscapes can be seen from the sites or vantage
points nearby. It is almost as if people were situating themselves to
take advantage of the visual results of nature's creativity in order to
produce or enhance their own.

And this connection did not end with death for an important feature
of secondary mortuary ceremonies in northern Australia is the reinte-
gration of the deceased with the special, more sacred parts of the land.

Figure 2.7 Tiwi burial grounds on Melville and Bathurst Islands were traditionally liminal spaces where rainforest meets eucalypt (photo: Paul Taçon).

Many of the significant locations chosen for rock art were also used to house human remains, often painted with ochre. In areas where the geology is such that there are few suitable rocky locations other sorts of significant landscapes were chosen. For instance, among the Tiwi of Bathurst and Melville Islands the transitional spaces between eucalypt and rainforest were used to inter human remains, with elaborately carved and painted Pukumani poles erected to memorialize the dead (figure 2.7; Goodale 1959; Mountford 1958: 60–118; Spencer 1914: 238–9).

In Australia, most other important rituals and ceremonies that emphasize rites of passage or intensification were and, in some areas, continue to be performed in these sorts of powerful, unusual, and visually striking natural places. In the process, "the rituals effectively bonded people with nature, with geography and with the landscape ... people anchored themselves in both space and time and gained insight and direction" (Taçon 1990: 30). Ultimately this is conceived and expressed as a religious experience and cultural practice, with divine knowledge, insight or encounters a primary feature. When practices continue at the same locations over many generations these places and their surrounding landscapes become increasingly symbolically charged, patterned, and contextualized – traditions of landscape experience and enrichment are perpetuated and expressed as "Ancestral Law."

Finally, it should be noted that there are many levels of sacredness used to define and describe landscapes, with some more sacred than others. Often these are related to issues of restriction and access, powerlessness and authority, initiate and initiated. As people move through different levels of knowledge acquisition, access to more varied sacred sites – hence landscapes – becomes culturally possible. It is because of the power perceived to exist and believed to be directly experienced at some locations that restrictions of access are made but it also has to do with the power and authority of those already initiated into the secrets of those unusual places. This is true not only for Indigenous Australians but also for many other, if not most, peoples of the world. It is said to protect both uninitiated individuals and the nature of special places. This process began with natural places but continues with sacred architecture across the globe.

However, as Paper (1990: 44) notes for North America, there is a fundamental difference between Western and Indigenous religions in terms of the understanding of the natural world and landscape: "In western religions, the earth itself is not sacred; it is created by the sacred, by God. In Native American religions, the landscape is sacred; it is deity." Paper further notes that sacred space is "delineated from the standpoint of center and periphery" in Native American religions. This can be said of Indigenous Australian religions as well but there is an important difference in that a large number of centers may be linked together along *Dreaming Tracks*, routes that define the journeys of the *First People* – Ancestral Beings that shaped the land into its present form.

Dreaming Tracks

Dreaming Tracks, popularized as "Songlines" by Bruce Chatwin (1988), are the key to understanding Australian landscapes. For Aboriginal people it is these vast stretches of landscape that link particular individuals and language groups to other people, to the past, to other creatures and to the land itself. Individuals or clans may be responsible for particular sacred sites along Tracks but there is a shared interest in their safeguarding and maintenance by all people associated with the routes. Often individuals of different backgrounds would come together at nodal points along Tracks to engage in a joint ceremony, make contact with the power of Ancestral Beings and the landscapes they created, as well as to reaffirm human relationships. In many cases, the stories associated with Dreaming Tracks are used to describe human origins, codes of conduct, and the nature of landscapes in their present form – they also inspire great works of contemporary art (e.g., Morphy 1991; Ryan 1989). Often the most powerful involve

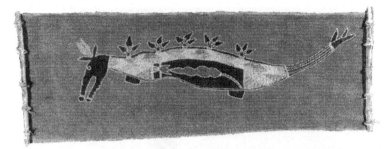

Figure 2.8   The Rainbow Serpent is the most powerful and universal Aboriginal Ancestral Being associated with significant and sacred landscapes. In this painting by Bruce Nabegeyo the Serpent is shown in its composite form, linking various creatures associated with different landscapes, as well as the clans responsible for those lands (photo: Carl Bento, Australian Museum).

Beings collectively referred to as Rainbow Serpents – gigantic, powerful snake-like creatures that combine elements of male and female, lower world, middle world, and upper world, and features of the land's more significant animals, in both its perceived physical form and its behavior (figure 2.8). The key elements of earth, water, rock, and air are also brought together in the Rainbow Serpent stories (Taçon 1989a; 1989b; Taçon et al. 1996; Taylor 1987; 1990).

In the western Arnhem Land region of Australia's Northern Territory, for example, it is believed there once were many Ancestral Beings and Heroes, all originally with human form, but it was a form of Rainbow Serpent, the most powerful of all Ancestral Beings, that was responsible for the birth of human beings and other creatures, as well as much of the land as it exists in its present form. This Being is described as a Rainbow Snake/Woman called *Yingarna* by the Kunwinjku, a Woman named *Imberombera* or *Warramurrungundji* by Gagudju and Iwaidja people, and an Ancestral Woman that turned into the powerful Rainbow Serpent *Almudj* according to the Gundjeibmi (Taçon 1989b: 239). Today she is depicted in either Rainbow Serpent or human female form, often carrying dilly bags full of babies or shown with a womb full of developing children (figure 2.9). This Ancestral Woman/Rainbow Serpent came from the sea northeast of the Cobourg Peninsula and the various tribes and clans of western Arnhem Land trace her travels through their territories (Spencer 1928: 742). She created *Bininj*, people, and told the different tribes which language they should speak. She also prepared the land, told people what foods they could eat, and began the process of human reproduction by depositing spirit children at ten different localities in the landscape. Most of these

Figure 2.9 Thompson Yulidjirri painting *Yingarna*, the most powerful Rainbow Serpent, in her human female form. Dilly bags hanging from her shoulders carried babies that became the first people and ancestors of Aboriginal clans (photo: Paul Taçon).

are permanent clan wells, significant and sacred water holes surrounded by unusual rocky outcrops and other powerfully charged features of the land. At these locations spirit children are said to resemble small fish, or bundles of rainbow color (Taçon 1989a; 1989b). All subsequent Ancestral Beings who passed through the region, forming, shaping and modifying landscapes in the process, are said to have derived their powers from the great Woman/Rainbow Snake "and were supposed to be acting under her instructions in everything they did" (Chaloupka et al. 1985: 75).

Spencer (1928: 753) credits *Imberombera* with making "creeks, hills, animals and plants," but contemporary Aborigines explain many features of landscapes as having been shaped by other Beings. Ultimately, however, they derived their power from her and the changes they made can be considered an indirect result of her activities. As well, many animals arose more as a result of some of her activities rather than as a matter of accident. Indeed, *Yingarna* or her son *Ngalyod* are said to have later killed or transformed other Ancestral Beings and humans by sending great storms and floods or through swallowing them whole. Regurgitated Beings, or their bony remains, are believed to form many of the region's escarpments and rock outliers. At other locations Ancestral Beings were turned to stone on the spot for igniting the Rainbow Serpent's fury. In some cases, they were transformed from their human-like forms into the animal species that now populate the region by the Serpent flooding or otherwise transforming vast stretches of land. In its most general sense the Rainbow Serpent is a symbol of the creative and destructive forces of the universe, what Western peoples refer to as *nature* or *Mother Nature*.

Rainbow Serpent Dreaming Tracks dissect much of Australia but other powerful Beings, such as the *Wandjina* of the Kimberley, *Bula* from southern Arnhem Land, or *Biaime* and others from the greater Sydney region of New South Wales also transformed and linked together great and vast landscapes. A variety of lesser Beings and Cultural Heroes formed other tracks, such as those associated with the native cat that runs north–south through central Australia (Gunn 1997; Taçon 1994). Taken together they map the more significant parts of the entire Australian continent, highlighting both places integral to human survival and those best avoided.

The Oldest Surviving Rock Art

At many sites Ancestral Beings are said to have left images of themselves behind when they entered rock walls, and some old, sizable, and more elaborate rock art is attributed to them. Other old painted art is said to have been made by tall, thin human-like spirit beings, such as the Mimi of Arnhem Land, who taught the first humans about physical and spiritual survival in newly settled landscapes. Rock art sites are common along major Dreaming Tracks and many motifs, whether believed to be human or divinely inspired, are said to relate to the oral histories that surround the Beings of the Tracks, as well as that of the creatures and peoples that followed. In this sense rock art is intimately related to both landscape and history for contemporary knowledgeable elders; rock art sites are described as Aboriginal history books that highlight continuing environmental, social, and landscape change (Taçon in press).

Of course, these contemporary readings of rock art sites, and the landscapes of which they are an integral part, may differ widely from those of the past. However, not only do they provide analogies based on oral history worth testing as explanatory devices but they also suggest landscape organizing principles or structures that may have both great antiquity and an archaeological signature (e.g., Taçon et al. 1997).

As noted earlier, the oldest surviving form of Australian rock art consists of cup-shaped engraved marks known as "cupules" (see figure 2.1). They are purposely made circular depressions constituting one of the world's most widespread and universal forms of rock art, second perhaps only to hand stencils and prints in both distribution and antiquity (see Taçon et al. 1997). In northern Australia, these round, cup-like marks, arranged in clusters of up to several thousand, are unanimously recognized to be the region's oldest surviving form of rock art (Chaloupka 1993; Flood 1996; 1997; Taçon and Chippindale 1994; Walsh 1994; Welch 1992), in some instances dating to many tens of thousands of years ago (Fullagar et al. 1996; Taçon et al. 1997). They are found on vertical and sloping shelter walls, horizontal ledges, boulders and large slabs of sloping or horizontal pavements (figure 2.10). They were made by pecking and pounding and are not to be confused with grinding hollows that resulted from food processing – thousands of cupules were often arranged to cover vertical surfaces in orderly, tightly packed rows and could not be the by-products of non-symbolic, purely practical activities. On wall panels, the average diameter of cupules ranges between 26 and 34 mm, while on boulders they average 58 to 66 mm.

Cupules were not used to define figures, such as animals or humans. Rather, they tend to be more related to the nature of the surface they were pecked and/or abraded into, their extent often conforming to or accentuating the surface's natural cracks, crevices, and boundaries. Occasionally, a symmetrical geometric shape was defined with an orderly arrangement of a dozen or more cupules but this is rare. For the most part, the cupule designs are abstract in appearance and enigmatic in meaning.

Landscapes, Art, and Meaning

We may never know exactly why cupules were made on an individual or widespread basis or much of the specific meaning these marks had for their makers. Many plausible reasons for their existence can be

Figure 2.10 The main Jinmium, N.T., cupule panels are located on the inner walls of two shelters that face in opposite directions. The marks not only signify that the location is important but also relate to the Dreaming story of the site and the Track on which it lies (photo: Paul Taçon).

suggested, some of which are not mutually exclusive, such as use in ritual, in communicating ideas about places, as decoration and so forth; it is probable that cupules were made, used, or interpreted in many ways at particular times and over time. Indeed, it is likely that a number of levels of meaning could be derived from cupule arrangements when they were in common use, just as has been found with more recent Aboriginal art (e.g., Morphy 1984; 1991; Munn 1966; 1973; Taçon 1989a; 1989b; Taylor 1987; 1990).

Because the detailed study of patterning at cupule sites is preliminary, only general observations can be made. What is clear, however, is that cupule-covered wall panels lie close to the major river systems, from central Arnhem Land to the western Kimberley; are found mainly on plains rather than plateaus; are among a given region's more prominent geological features; and that today many lie on important Dreaming Tracks. For instance, the Jinmium–Granilpi complexes – the best studied to date – lie on a major Rainbow Serpent Dreaming Track that runs from the coast near the Northern Territory– Western Australia border, through and across Keep and Victoria Rivers, and on to the Gulf of Carpentaria. The track links many diverse language groups together, just as does the *Yingarna/Imberombera* Rainbow Serpent Track of western Arnhem Land. Many cupule sites can be found along the track but they are not exclusive to it (Fullagar et al. 1996; Taçon et al. 1997).

The most important result of an analysis of cupule distribution at sites is that they are found to be organized very particularly in relation to natural signs and features of rock surfaces. Whether the cup-shaped marks resulted from ritual activities, record keeping, art making, decoration, communication, or some unknown pastime or activity they were placed in accordance with natural marks and boundaries. At Jinmium and Granilpi, for instance, cupules most commonly were used to infill sizable portions of rock shelter wall panels, with natural cracks, crevices, and contours defining the limits of their execution (4 localities); to mark high points on the tops of geological features (up versus down; 4 localities); to mark the edges of shelter floors and shelter limits (inside versus outside; 5 localities); and to mark/accentuate the outside edges of natural holes/tunnels/passageways through the rock but not the insides (outside versus inside versus other side; 12 localities). Sometimes rows of cupule-covered boulders link different locations within sites or across landscapes, and massive, shaped boulders with hundreds of cupules oriented in all directions dominate some shelters (Taçon et al. 1997). Although not fully investigated, similar patterns of cupule placement can be found in Kakadu National Park and Arnhem Land to the west and the Kimberley region to the east, at sites thought to be of comparable antiquity. Perhaps then the oldest enduring human-made symbolic marks in Australia are structured by natural landscape features rather than by random or an organizing principle that overrides or ignores the nature of place and space, such as the placement of marks on surfaces in a disfiguring manner rather than one that enhances surfaces. There is evidence to suggest this occurred on both macro (landscape) and micro (panel/site) scales.

Many of the forms of rock art that followed cupules in Australia were arranged differently but retain a landscape focus in terms of marking and signifying important spaces, places, and landscapes and in regard to subject matter. For example, in the engraved, painted or beeswax rock art of Australia, the most common subjects are tracks of animals, humans or Ancestral Beings, as would be seen on the land; the key animals, such as macropods, large birds or fish, from and of the land and its waterways (figure 2.11); Ancestral Beings that created the land; and human beings – the people who were born on, lived in, fought over, and died on the land (e.g., Flood 1997; Layton 1992; Taçon and Chippindale 1994). Even some more abstract motifs, such as circles and concentric circles, are said to represent camp sites, sacred sites, caves, trees, water holes, or other significant places – sometimes

Figure 2.11 Recent panels of polychrome rock paintings in the "Top End" of the Northern Territory are dominated by depictions of Ancestral Beings that created the land, animals seen on the land, and humans that manage the land. This site in Kakadu National Park has paintings over earlier cupules, showing two very distinct and separated periods of landscape marking (photo: Paul Taçon).

more than one or all of these at once (Dussart 1988; Munn 1966; 1973; Taçon 1994). Contemporary Aboriginal art continues the process with most bark painting, central Australian acrylic painting on canvas (figure 2.12), and urban art of a variety of media (e.g., prints – see McGuigan 1992) directly or indirectly relating to land or dispossession from it:

> Aboriginal art is strong in country and law: that is both its politics and blood. In its present form, this art is born of white colonisation and dispossession of Ancestral land. The weight and chains of *kardiya* (white) control and oppression have left their mark. Although some may see it as the colonisers' plaything, art is a means of empowerment for its makers, a political tool in the fight to regain sovereignty over the land. Beneath most Aboriginal paintings lie the principles of Land Rights. (Ryan 1993: 60)

Coming to terms with landscapes

The whole history of Australian Aboriginal art includes an emphasis on coming to terms with changing landscapes. This is true of both rock

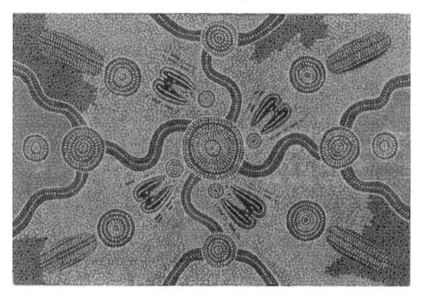

Figure 2.12 Contemporary acrylic paintings, such as this depiction of
the creation of the Alice Springs region (*Yeperenye* Dreaming) by
Wenten Rubuntja Tjabanati, tend to take an aerial view of landscapes and
are intimately concerned with the creation of land, its special attributes
and stories that revolve around its history (photo: Carl Bento, Australian
Museum).

art and recent music, performance and visual art. Furthermore, I contend that when people first arrived on the continent, whether 40,000
(Allen and Holdaway 1995), 60,000 (Roberts et al. 1993) or 120,000
(Fullagar et al. 1996) years ago, there was a need not only to colonize
but also to humanize and socialize what may have been perceived as a
hostile landscape. On a grand scale, vegetation was transformed
through burning practices (Haynes 1985; Head 1994; Jones 1969;
1975; 1980), animal populations were changed through hunting practices (Flannery 1994), and geological places were socialized through
rock art and ritual, including cupule marking. Places were also socialized through stories – the Dreamtime sagas of landscape creation and
adventure. In many ways the journeys recount or relate to some of the
initial colonization of the continent but they also describe subsequent
changes to land experienced during the many millennia of human
occupation – from volcanic eruptions to the great flooding that
occurred at the end of the last glaciation.

   Much contemporary art tells about further changes to landscapes
and people, brought about by visits of Macassans in the north and
invasions of Europeans initially through the country's south. And

across the continent, contemporary Indigenous peoples reaffirm their connections to landscapes through art and ritual as a vital part of both their physical and spiritual survival. But this is done differently in various parts of the country, partly as a reflection of the particular landscapes and terrain people grew up in and partly as a reflection of the nature of their social networks. For instance, it is believed the geographic, hydrological, vegetation and food resource differences between central Australia and the Top End of the Northern Territory led to differences in each region's social networks, and that these differences are mirrored in the art systems of each area. This is argued for both ancient rock art, that is non-figurative "Panaramittee" versus figurative (Smith 1992a; 1992c), and contemporary painting, such as acrylic on canvas versus ochres on bark (Ryan 1993; Smith 1989; 1992b; 1992c). As Smith (1992c: 44) explains:

> Art in fertile regions, characterised by high population densities and relatively high levels of territoriality, is more heterogeneous than art in infertile regions characterised by low population densities and low levels of territoriality. Style in ethnographic Aboriginal art can serve to both delineate territory and to create cohesion between groups ...
>
> In relatively fertile regions such as that of northern Australia, it is likely that the increased regionalisation of rock art sequences through time reflects a change from open to closed social networks. Open social networks were essential to the colonisation of the continent, but after a threshold in population numbers had been reached at some stage in the mid-Holocene (and this would vary according to the region), social networks in infertile regions, such as the Western Desert, would have remained open as such networks are essential to the effective exploitation of resources in such regions.

In more precisely defining some of these differences, Ryan (1993: 62) adds: "If bark paintings generally are site-specific, narrow verticals, then large desert canvas[es] enclose the viewer in the vastness of the continent, leading him or her through a succession of named sites – on journeys of wandering." This is the key difference in the art of each region: the northern art features focused, clan-specific landscapes while that to the south addresses expansive tracts that have significance for many clans and linguistic groups. But in each art body, connections to landscapes are emphasized and elaborately expressed, as are specific Ancestral Beings that created the varied landscapes and the particular creatures that dwell in them. In turn, individual and corporate identity is reaffirmed. In some cases the connection is so strong "they learn to see their own body as a metaphor of the topographic organization of their clan lands, features such as birthmarks on their body being seen as equivalent to sacred sites within their clan lands" (Taylor 1988: 384). Valuable lessons about land management are also often emphasized. Importantly, urban art, although more heterogeneous in style, form and media and often made by people of mixed descent, features the same themes, but with the added political element of loss of land and invasion by foreigners (Kleinert 1997; Mundine 1992; Ryan 1993; Taçon 1996).

This sense of roots, belonging to land and taking responsibility for it, has developed over a lengthy period of time in Australia and it is because of this that many non-Aboriginal people, recent arrivals, have difficulty grasping the full significance or consequence of this form of bonding. Having severed their own roots and transformed their own landscapes into thoroughly artificial places, cities and cityscapes being the most poignant (Cosgrove 1993 argues that "Wilderness," "Garden" and "City" are distinct archetypal landscapes with differing concerns and mythologies), they have long been bent on doing the same to Indigenous lands. A driving concern is to not "waste" land, to see its full potential through "development," something seen to be of value in Western eyes. This is at odds with the Indigenous perspective, which instead focuses on managing and caring for land by way of burning practices, hunting restrictions, food-sharing responsibilities, art and ritual. But above all else the Indigenous perspective is expressed through knowledge of and relations to land – and thus to other people, plants, and animals. Knowledge about a landscape's past – its creation, transformations and particular history – is fundamental. Thus it is not only the human past that is of interest or importance but also the landscape past. For it is the web and chains of past landscape relationships, as expressed by Dreaming Tracks and so forth, that define present human relationships alongside those of kinship and language.

In Aboriginal English, "my mother's country," "my father's country" are two common descriptions that express this strong link between human kinship and landscape but it is reaffirmed at much deeper levels as well – with connections to animals through totem systems or restricted ceremonies that honor specific creatures or Ancestral Beings responsible for the creation and sustenance of both people and places. Indeed, as Indigenous Australian Kumantjayi Ross (1994: vii) has emphasized at the beginning of his forward to a book about the Central Land Council: "Aboriginal spirituality, culture and society can be defined in one word: land." However, although land has always been important to Indigenous Australians, the specific ways and meanings in which this has been expressed vary over time and across space – resulting in a heritage consisting of a mosaic of metaphoric landscape meaning and relationship, in need of continual visual display and reaffirmation. Obviously, the power of place can never be understated for Indigenous Australians, for without it the world would not exist.

ACKNOWLEDGMENTS

I would especially like to thank the dozens of Aboriginal elders who have patiently taught me about art, life, and landscape since 1981, when my own journey into and across Australian landscapes began. In particular: David Canari, Paddy Carlton, Peter Jatbula, Nipper Kapirigi, Mick Kubarkku, Bardayal Nadjamerrek, Bobby Nganjmirra, Bill Neidjie, Biddy Simon, and Peter Sullivan.

Bernard Knapp and Wendy Ashmore are thanked for the invitation to participate in their 1996 symposium, "Sacred landscapes: constructed and conceptualized" (American Anthropological Association, San Francisco), and for comments on this paper that made it stronger. Thanks, too, to Robin Torrence (Australian Museum) for comments.

Richard Fullagar, Lesley Head, Sven Ouzman, and Ken Mulvaney are thanked for opening my eyes to cupule rock markings and assistance in related field work. Christopher Chippindale is acknowledged for contributing to my greater comprehension of Australian and world rock art through the joint studies we have engaged in since 1990. The Australian Museum is thanked for supporting landscape research through the People and Place Research Centre.

REFERENCES

Allen, J., and Holdaway, S. 1995: The contamination of Pleistocene radiocarbon determinations in Australia. *Antiquity*, 69, 101–12.

Bender, B. (ed.) 1993: *Landscape: Politics and Perspectives*. Oxford: Berg.

Bradley, R. 1995: Rock carvings and decorated monuments in the British Isles. In K. Helskog and B. Olsen (eds), *Perceiving Rock Art: Social and Political Perspectives*, Oslo: Instituttet for Sammenlignende Kulturforskning, 107–29.

Chaloupka, G. 1993: *Journey in Time*. Sydney: Reed Books.

Chaloupka, G., Kapirigi, N., Nayidji, D., and Namingum, G. 1985: *Cultural Survey of Balawurru, Deaf Adder Creek, Amarrkananga, Cannon Hill and the Northern Corridor: A Report to the Australian National Parks and Wildlife*

Service. Darwin: Australian National Parks and Wildlife Service and the Museum and Art Galleries Board of the Northern Territory.

Chatwin, B. 1988: *The Songlines*. London: Picador.

Chippindale, C., and Taçon, P. S. C. (eds) 1998: *The Archaeology of Rock-Art*. Cambridge: Cambridge University Press.

Cosgrove, D. 1989: Geography is everywhere: culture and symbolism in human landscapes. In D. Gregory and R. Walford (eds), *Horizons in Human Geography*, London: Macmillan, 118–35.

Cosgrove, D. 1993: Landscapes and myths, gods and humans. In B. Bender (ed.), *Landscape: Politics and Perspectives*, Oxford: Berg, 281–305.

Cosgrove, D., and Daniels, S. (eds) 1988: *The Iconography of Landscape: Essays on the Symbolic Representation, Design and Use of Past Environments*. Cambridge: Cambridge University Press.

Dussart, F. 1988: Women's acrylic paintings from Yuendumu. In M. West (ed.), *The Inspired Dream: Life as Art in Aboriginal Australia*, South Brisbane: Queensland Art Gallery, 35–8.

Eliade, M. 1964: *Shamanism: Archaic Techniques of Ecstasy*. New York: Pantheon.

Eliade, M. 1978: *A History of Religious Ideas*, Volume 1: *From the Stone Age to the Eleusinian Mysteries*, transl. W. R. Trask. Chicago: University of Chicago Press.

Flannery, T. 1994: *The Future Eaters: An Ecological History of the Australasian Lands and People*. Chatswood (Sydney): Reed Books.

Flood, J. 1996: Culture in early Australia. *Cambridge Archaeological Journal*, 6, 3–36.

Flood, J. 1997: *Rock Art of the Dreamtime*. Sydney: Angus and Robertson.

Fullagar, R., Price, D., and Head, L. 1996: Early human occupation of northern Australia: archaeology and thermoluminescence dating of Jinmium rock-shelter, Northern Territory. *Antiquity*, 70, 751–73.

Goodale, J. 1959: The Tiwi dance for the dead. *Expedition*, 2 (1), 3–13.

Gosden, C., and Head, L. 1994: Landscape – a usefully ambiguous concept. *Archaeology in Oceania*, 29, 113–16.

Gunn, R. G. 1997: Rock art, occupation and myth: the correspondence of symbolic and archaeological sites within Arrernte rock art complexes of central Australia. *Rock Art Research*, 14 (2), 124–36.

Haynes, C. D. 1985: The pattern and ecology of munwag: traditional Aboriginal fire regimes in north-central Arnhem-land. *Proceedings, Ecological Society of Australia*, 13, 203–14.

Head, L. 1994: Landscapes socialised by fire: post-contact changes in Aboriginal fire use in northern Australia, and implications for prehistory. *Archaeology in Oceania*, 29, 172–81.

Hodder, I. 1993: The narrative and rhetoric of material culture sequences. *World Archaeology*, 25, 268–82.

Ingold, T. 1993: The temporality of the landscape. *World Archaeology*, 25, 152–74.

Jones, R. 1969: Fire-stick farming. *Australian Natural History*, 16, 224–8.

Jones, R. 1975: The Neolithic, Palaeolithic and the hunting gardeners: man and land in the antipodes. In R. P. Suggate and M. M. Creswell (eds), *Quaternary Studies*, Wellington: Royal Society of New Zealand, 21–34.

Jones, R. 1980: Hunters in the Australian coastal savanna. In D. R. Harris (ed.), *Human Ecology in Savanna Environments*, New York: Academic Press, 107–46.

Kleinert, S. 1997: Aboriginal landscapes. In G. Levitus (ed.), *Lying about the Landscape*, North Ryde, Sydney: Craftsman House, 82–99.

Layton, R. 1992: *Australian Rock Art: A New Synthesis*. Cambridge: Cambridge University Press.

McGuigan, C. 1992: *New Tracks Old Land: Contemporary Prints from Aboriginal Australia*. Surry Hills (Sydney): Aboriginal Arts Management Association.

Morphy, H. 1984: *Journey to the Crocodile's Nest*. Canberra: Australian Institute of Aboriginal Studies.

Morphy, H. 1991: *Ancestral Connections: Art and an Aboriginal System of Knowledge*. Chicago: University of Chicago Press.

Mountford, C. P. 1958: *The Tiwi – Their Art, Myth and Ceremony*. London: Phoenix House.

Mundine, D. 1992: "If my ancestors could see me now." In B. Murphy (ed.), *Tyerabarrbowaryaou: I Shall Never Become a White Man*, Sydney: Museum of Contemporary Art, 4–11.

Munn, N. 1966: Visual categories: an approach to the study of representational systems. *American Anthropologist*, 68, 936–50.

Munn, N. 1973: *Walbiri Iconography*. Ithaca: Cornell University Press.

Nash, R. 1997: Archetypal landscapes and the interpretation of meaning. *Cambridge Archaeological Journal*, 7, 57–69.

Ouzman, S. 1998: Toward a mindscape of landscape: rock-art as expression of world-understanding. In C. Chippindale and P. S. C. Taçon (eds), *The Archaeology of Rock-Art*, Cambridge: Cambridge University Press, 30–41.

Paper, J. 1990: Landscape and sacred space in Native North American religion. In J. Vastokas (ed.), *Perspectives of Canadian Landscape: Native Traditions*, North York: York University, 44–54.

Parkman, E. B. 1995: "California Dreaming": cupule petroglyph occurrences in the American West. In J. Steinbring (ed.), *Rock Art Studies in the Americas*, Monograph 45, Oxford: Oxbow, 1–12.

Roberts, R., Jones, R., and Smith, M. A. 1993: Optical dating at Deaf Adder Gorge, Northern Territory, indicates human occupation between 53,000 and 60,000 years ago. *Australian Archaeology*, 37, 58.

Ross, K. 1994: Foreword. In *The Land is Always Alive: The Story of the Central Land Council*, Alice Springs: Central Land Council, vii–ix.

Ryan, J. 1989: *Mythscapes: Aboriginal Art of the Desert*. Victoria: National Gallery of Victoria.

Ryan, J. 1993: Australian Aboriginal art: otherness or affinity. In B. Luthi and G. Lee (eds), *ARATJARA – Art of the First Australians*, Dusseldorf: Kunstsammlung Nordrhein-Westfalen, 49–63.

Smith, C. 1989: Designed Dreaming: assessing the relationship between style, social structure and environment in Aboriginal Australia. BA (Honors) thesis, University of New England, Armidale.

Smith, C. 1992a: Colonising with style: reviewing the nexus between rock art, territoriality and the colonisation and occupation of Sahul. *Australian Archaeology*, 34, 34–42.

Smith, C. 1992b: The articulation of style and social structure through Australian Aboriginal art. *Aboriginal Studies*, 1, 28–34.

Smith, C. 1992c: The use of ethnography in interpreting rock art: a comparative study of art from the Arnhem Land and Western Desert regions of Australia. In M. J. Morwood and D. Hobbs (eds), *Rock Art and Ethnography*, Melbourne: Occasional AURA Publication, No. 5, 39–45.

Spencer, W. B. 1914: *Native Tribes of the Northern Territory of Australia*. London: Macmillan.

Spencer, W. B. 1928: *Wanderings in Wild Australia*. London: Macmillan.

Taçon, P. S. C. 1989a: Art and the essence of being: symbolic and economic aspects of fish among the peoples of western Arnhem Land, Australia. In H. Morphy (ed.), *Animals into Art*, London: Unwin Hyman, 236–50.

Taçon, P. S. C. 1989b: From Rainbow Serpents to "x-ray" fish: the nature of the recent rock painting tradition of western Arnhem Land, Australia. PhD dissertation, Australian National University.

Taçon, P. S. C. 1990: The power of place: cross-cultural responses to natural and cultural landscapes of stone and earth. In J. Vastokas (ed.), *Perspectives of Canadian Landscape: Native Traditions*, North York: York University, 11–43.

Taçon, P. S. C. 1994: Socialising landscapes: the long-term implications of signs, symbols and marks on the land. *Archaeology in Oceania*, 29, 117–29.

Taçon, P. S. C. 1996: Indigenous modernism: betwixt and between or at the cutting edge of contemporary art? *Bulletin of the Conference of Museum Anthropologists*, 27, 33–55.

Taçon, P. S. C. in press: Australian indigenous rock art – the human story. In D. Whitley (ed.), *The Handbook of Rock Art Research*, San Francisco: Altamira Press.

Taçon, P. S. C., and Chippindale, C. 1994: Australia's ancient warriors: changing depictions of fighting in the rock art of Arnhem Land, N.T. *Cambridge Archaeological Journal*, 4, 211–48.

Taçon, P. S. C., Fullagar, R., Ouzman, S., and Mulvaney, K. 1997: Cupule engravings from Jinmium-Granilpi (Northern Australia) and beyond: exploration of a widespread and enigmatic class of rock markings. *Antiquity*, 71, 942–65.

Taçon, P. S. C., Wilson, M., and Chippindale, C. 1996: Birth of the Rainbow Serpent in Arnhem Land rock art and oral history. *Archaeology in Oceania*, 31, 103–24.

Taylor, L. 1987: "The same but different": social reproduction and innovation in the art of the Kunwinjku of western Arnhem Land. PhD dissertation, Australian National University.

Taylor, L. 1988: Seeing the "inside": Kunwinjku paintings and the symbol of the divided body. In H. Morphy (ed.), *Animals into Art*, London: Unwin Hyman, 371–89.

Taylor, L. 1990: The Rainbow Serpent as visual metaphor in western Arnhem Land. *Oceania*, 60, 329–44.

Tilley, C. 1994: *A Phenomenology of Landscape: Places, Paths and Monuments*. Oxford: Berg.

Vastokas, J. M., and Vastokas, R. 1973: *Sacred Art of the Algonkians: A Study of the Peterborough Petroglyphs*. Peterborough: Mansard Press.

Walsh, G. 1994: *Bradshaws: Ancient Rock Paintings of Australia*. Geneva: Édition Limitée.

Welch, D. 1992: The Early Rock Art of the Kimberley, Australia. Paper presented in Symposium F, Second AURA Congress, Cairns.

3

Creating Social Identity in the Landscape: Tidewater, Virginia, 1600–1750

Lisa Kealhofer

Men and their gardens have forever been interdependent and insepar-
able, each other's true revelation. ... Gardening offers a chance for man
to regulate at least one aspect of his life, to control his environment and
show himself as he wishes to be.

(Leighton 1970: 3, 6)

Introduction

The men who sailed to Virginia in the early seventeenth century were
fortune seekers eager to create new identities. Many died before they
succeeded. Establishing a new identity was not merely a matter of
changing places or names, but entailed transforming the New World
to authenticate a new identity. Landscapes, both as smaller gardens
and as larger regions, not only record how these new identities were
created, but they also played an active role in how individuals and
communities defined themselves.

During the Colonial period the definition of individual social identity
was re-formulated in Virginia. Reference-group size increased in the seventeenth century, and identity became increasingly individualized (Deetz
1977; Yentsch 1990). Arguably, people define themselves relative to
other people, their family and/or other social groups. Previously, familial
or corporate relationships defined who an individual was (e.g., Braudel
1984; Deetz 1993). While familial relationships continued to be important, other factors also became influential in defining individual identity.
Material goods and social, economic, and political networks became
more accessible, more malleable, and were used increasingly to define
one's position in the world (Douglas and Isherwood 1979; Foucault
1972). Philosophically, as well as economically, these ideas can be traced

to a convergence of Renaissance ideas, the development of capitalism, the frontier, and the emerging world system (Braudel 1984; Deetz 1993; Johnson 1996; Leone 1988; Lewis 1984; Shackel 1993; 1994; Wallerstein 1974; 1980). However, rather than tracing these links anew here, discussion will focus on how landscapes reveal the development of the different components of social identity in colonial Virginia.

The Chesapeake region provides an unusually long and rich record of English colonial life. Research on historical, archaeological, and architectural creation and transformation of colonial identities has proliferated of late (e.g., Isaac 1982; 1988; Leone 1988; 1994; Upton 1982). Much of this work has defined landscapes as settings for action, rather than as active components in the construction of meaning and social relationships (e.g., Isaac 1982; Upton 1988). Traditionally, seventeenth-century colonial society has also been seen as laying the groundwork ideologically, politically, and economically for the formation of a new nation (Shackel and Little 1994: 5). This evolutionary view of colonial social change is at odds with evidence from seventeenth-century Tidewater landscapes, however, where new groups were forming, shifting, and positioning themselves.

Identity is a complex of different scales of statuses and roles, including personal, social, and cultural attributes (Goodenough 1965). These scales and attributes can be linked to material patterning at different scales in the landscape, garden, town, and region. In addition, the creation of identity at these different scales required variable periods of time and changed at different rates. Creating landscapes of social hierarchy, government control, or economic "rationality" took longer than individuals' shaping of personal gardens and plots. This discrepant scheduling influenced the shape and meaning of gardens relative to landscapes over time.

This discrepancy also affected the ideational landscape. Knapp and Ashmore (this volume) note that the distinction between constructed and conceived landscapes is often blurred. In the Chesapeake case, where another "world" was colonized, constructed and conceived landscapes seemed quite distinct. Colonists "conceived" of the their new landscape – often described by English explorers as Eden – but they did not configure it with any complexity or depth of meaning. For example, sacred points of reference did not exist. It takes time to embed meaning, even in a little modified "conceived" landscape.

Initially, colonists' constructed landscapes tended to be small. Homestead and garden stood in stark contrast to their surroundings, carved out of a forested "wilderness" and often temporary. These smaller spaces were more dichotomous, emphasizing the discrepancies between sacred, controlled, and safe space and those that were beyond the "pale." As the landscape was domesticated, through warfare, trade, pastoralism, agriculture, industry, and settlement, the distinction between conceived and constructed landscapes blurred. The landscape increasingly conformed to colonist lifestyles and world views, and the nature of gardens changed. While gardens were always "multivocal," serving a variety of purposes and reflecting various views of the world, by the eighteenth-century elite gardens in Virginia were consciously used to project a revised patriarchal myth and value-system across the landscape (Isaac 1982; Upton 1988). Just as constructed and conceived landscapes overlap, so too did the boundaries between the garden and the landscape (see Jefferson 1787, for example).

Seventeenth-century Virginia represents the end of a transitional period in the development of the capitalist world economy (Braudel 1984; Wallerstein 1980). Several recent studies of landscapes and space have suggested that capitalist and precapitalist views of nature and culture can be seen in dichotomous terms (e.g., Olwig 1993; Tilley 1994). If this is true, then seventeenth-century Virginians' concept of space and place should be on the capitalist side of these dichotomies. However, this polarization misses the contradictions in seventeenth-century, or any contemporary, views of nature and culture, place and space. It is within the contradictions, or variability, that trajectories of social change are defined. This chapter highlights the contradictions apparent in Tidewater gardens and landscapes to suggest that these tensions, as disparate views of nature and culture in the seventeenth century, helped shape the nature of social change in Virginia.

In sum, the creation of identities during the Colonial period occurred at different scales. Two of these scales are discussed here: the region, as political and social community identity, and the family farmstead/plantation, as individual (elite) identity. Landscapes embed aspects of the infrastructures of these groups at both scales. Given the shift to individualized identity during the Colonial period, in the new colony the process of self-definition was enmeshed with the simultaneous creation of the community of colonists. After defining the theoretical approach used here, discussion begins with the creation of community in the seventeenth-century landscape, and then turns to examples of how individuals shaped their identities.

The Active Landscape

Landscape analyses have interested a diverse range of scholars in recent years (e.g., Butzer 1996; Cosgrove 1984; Crumley 1994; Gosden

1994; Rodman 1992). Interest has shifted from the cultural ecological or environmental determinist modes of previous decades to postmodernist perspectives. Individual action, history, politics, and meaning have come to the fore. "Environment," "place," "space," and "landscape" are being deconstructed, redefined, and subjectified (e.g., Bender 1993; Olwig 1993; Rodman 1992; Tilley 1994).

Within archaeology, Tilley (1994) provides a postmodern redefinition of "space" as the medium of action, suggesting it is situationally empowered, with temporally specific and often contradictory meanings. Further, he offers a middle ground between the economic, objectifying view of space used by the New Geography and the New Archaeology (e.g., "locational analyses"), and the idealist view of space as individually subjective. This middle ground can be seen more proactively as a dialectic, where people create places which define space, and people's identities are in turn defined by their place. This rings familiar, as a semantic twist on Giddens' (1979) structure and action, as the dialectic "structuration." Places are both internalized by the meanings they have for individuals, and are places for action — where meaning is created through social interaction.

Giddens (1979), in fact, sees locales as critical for social production and reproduction. Both action and structure are shaped by locales, and locales are part of the action and structure. Because of this, places are value-laden, political, and invested with power. In a similar vein, Upton (1988) argues that architecture is structured experience, used to manipulate time and consciousness, and proposes that this can be extended to landscapes as well. How the landscape is structured shapes individuals' actions, but different individuals and different groups perceive the same landscape differently. In Rodman's (1992) terms, landscapes are "multivocal."

Tilley (1994) goes on to suggest that a major disconformity occurred between understandings of space in capitalist versus precapitalist societies. In capitalist societies, space is desanctified, controlled, economic, a backdrop, and "linear." Capitalism effectively strips meaning from the environment, secularing and desanctifying it. The environment effectively becomes a set of commodities that are exploited and stripped of symbolic meaning.

While seeing landscapes in terms of action and structuration is useful, the capitalist/precapitalist dichotomy oversimplifies the diverse understandings of space and landscapes in "capitalist" colonial Virginia. It masks the significance of variable world views. As Mann (1986) points out, capitalism is not a uniform process; instead, it varies in rate, content, and nature. Nor are precapitalist societies uniform in their interaction with space and place. In many ways, the Powhatan of

the southern Chesapeake had desanctified their landscape by the time
of contact (Rountree 1989), while the English retooled biblical myths
to embed meaning in space and place (Isaac 1982). Similar statements
could be made for the other dichotomies that Tilley (1994) constructs.
For example, the notion of place as backdrop is an analytical one (e.g.,
Isaac 1988), not a difference between capitalist and precapitalist views
of place (e.g., Rodman 1992; Upton 1988). Individuals in modern
societies do create "backdrops," but these are evocative and symbolic,
not two-dimensional and meaningless.

The patterns of settlement in the seventeenth-century Chesapeake
reveal a diverse and often contradictory set of understandings and mis-
understandings about place and landscapes among and between the
colonists and the Powhatan (Potter and Waselkov 1994; Rountree
1989; Smith 1986 [1624]). In addition to the problems with dichotomous historical definitions of space, the actions read out of landscapes
rarely bestow the landscape with the active role that it is often posited
as playing (Rodman 1992; Tilley 1994). It is how the meaning of place
is continuously configured, how the place itself is formed and maintained, and how its contents are involved in interaction that are central
to understanding how landscapes and identities articulate.

The Data: Social Identity, Scale, and Landscape

As discussed above, identity is shaped at a variety of scales. Two of these
scales are examined to identify the landscapes of social identity during
the early Colonial period in the Tidewater region. The goal is to understand how individuals defined not only themselves but also their social
and landscape context. The communities created in Virginia by immigrants were rapidly changing from their English precursors. The first
section below looks at how identity was defined at the community level
as communities were created and consolidated in the seventeenth century, and the second focuses on how individuals within these communities defined themselves as their landscapes and communities changed.

The large scale: establishing a community (1607–50)

Virginia was marketed in England as an earthly paradise, a garden, "a
land of spontaneous fruitfulness holding the promise of easy sustenance, wealth, health and leisure" (Howett 1992: 82). As Seddon
(1997) points out, identifying a place as a veritable Eden was the first

step in English colonization. Maps of the period show coastal outlines and spaces filled with exotic plants and primitive but fecund people (e.g., Smith 1986 [1624]). The "Horn of Plenty" was a symbol often used. This salesmanship brought thousands of people seeking new opportunities to Virginia in the seventeenth century. Several meanings were overlaid in these images: not only the identification of a mythic beautiful place, but also the commodification of the riches found there. As Horn (1979) notes, merchants in the main ports in England most influenced emigrants to come to Virginia through stories of the riches there. However, it was not long before the fall: mortality rates in this reputed Eden were over 50 percent from dysentery, cholera, and other diseases, apparently most virulent near Jamestown (Earle 1979).

The creation of identity relies on a relationship to a defined community or social group. The first colonists were not initially a community: few social ties bound them together. Only in Virginia were relationships forged among those who persevered and survived. Tidewater Virginia was colonized in 1607 by a group of men representing the Virginia Company of London. Jamestown was the first settlement and capital of Virginia (figure 3.1). Within a few decades, however, Jamestown came to serve mainly as an administrative center for the dispersed plantations and homesteads lining the James and York Rivers. The first colonists were in search of a commodity, or commodities, to make them rich. After a decade of experimentation and failure with a variety of industries, Rolfe's introduction of tobacco proved to be the most economically successful commodity. The success of tobacco, in conjunction with the economic depression and population increase in England during the seventeenth century, encouraged emigration to Virginia throughout the era (Horn 1979; 1988).

Producing tobacco was labor-intensive, requiring both people and large areas of cleared land (Kulikoff 1986). Cheap labor was gained in England by buying indentured and bonded servants (Horn 1979). The size of tobacco plantations and the presence of the river network enabled the growth of a dispersed settlement system (Earle 1992). Settlement expansion was tethered to river access for transportation of the export crop and direct importation of English goods. The settlement system shaped the definition of communities in the region. Earle (1992) proposes that the head cities and market centers for the Chesapeake settlements were actually ports back in England, whose primacy effectively limited urban growth in Virginia.

Communities were short-lived in the early years. Several colonizing experiments failed, and the high mortality rate also made communities very unstable (Deetz 1993; Earle 1979; Edwards and Brown 1993).

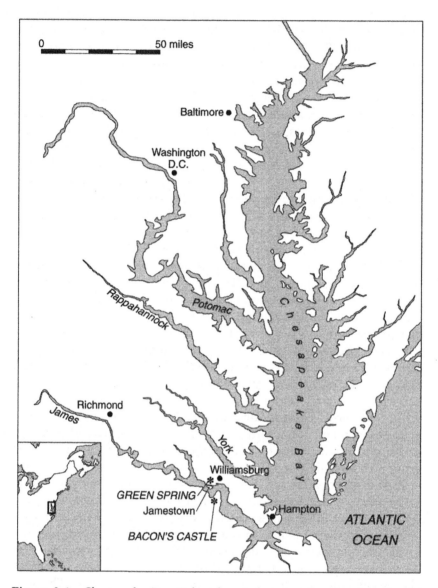

Figure 3.1 Chesapeake Bay Colonial period sites and towns mentioned in the text.

A variety of schemes were used to encourage economic development. Large tracts called "Hundreds" were allotted to small corporations or wealthy individuals who set up communities such as Flowerdew Hundred or Wolstenholme (Deetz 1993; Noël Hume 1983). The Powhatan uprising of 1622 ended settlement in many of these communities along the James River. While these early "Particular Plantations" of the Virginia Company concentrated small populations (e.g., Noël Hume 1983), other plantations comprised only a family and their servants (Kelso 1984; Turner 1993). These communities (Markell 1994) pursued a variety of small-scale industries, as well as pastoral and farming activities.

After the 1622 uprising, colonists often moved into more isolated homesteads of one to two families (e.g., Kelso 1984). These were often fortified or defensively located, until after the middle of the century when the Powhatan were no longer an immediate threat (Hodges 1999). Social and emotional ties, however, developed only over multiple generations. Social and demographic instability was also reflected in political instability (Jordan 1979). The regional community was only slowly interlinked through the exchange of specialized facilities and craftsmen (Earle 1992), a pattern that continued into the nineteenth century.

The settlement pattern that the English forged within Powhatan territory (Potter 1993; Turner 1993), and more generally throughout the Chesapeake (Potter 1993; Potter and Waselkov 1994), usurped indigenous settlements and fields. When Rolfe introduced varieties of West Indian tobacco, plantations developed throughout the region on top of indigenous settlements and fields, as can be seen at Jordan's Journey (Turner 1993). Only limited tracts of land were suitable for tobacco and corn cultivation, particularly with slash-and-burn and hoe technologies. The expansion of English settlements was thus a direct displacement of indigenous groups and their subsistence technologies. English settlements were also often placed in defensive locations: on islands or peninsulas secured by palisades (e.g., Jamestown itself, Eppes Island, Bermuda Hundred; see Gleach 1986; Hodges 1997; Turner 1993). These strategies led to the colonists being dispersed across the regional landscape among their fields, similar to the Powhatan they replaced, despite the major economic shift in settlement, from prehistoric procurement camps to commercial tobacco production (Fausz 1971; Kelly 1979).

Deetz (1987; 1993) and Edwards and Brown (1993) have used archaeological data to show the pattern of settlement expansion and contraction through the seventeenth century, as people responded to the boom and bust of the tobacco economy. During the first half of the seventeenth century tobacco production and sales boomed, and settlement expanded throughout the bottom lands. As tobacco sales collapsed in the last decades of the seventeenth century, and the English market became highly volatile, production declined, populations shrank, and farms were abandoned. Plantation consolidation of farms into larger holdings, with slave-produced tobacco, began in the second decade of the eighteenth century as tobacco sales soared again (Deetz 1987; Morgan 1975). While this pattern glosses over the mechanisms of community change, it reveals at least indirectly the lack of stability in seventeenth-century Virginian communities. This instability also inhibited development of community identity until near the end of the century.

Most of those who came to Virginia did not intend to stay – they wanted to get rich and go home to England. Tobacco cultivation proved to be more than a full-time job. These arguments have been used to explain the lack of investment in houses, infrastructure, landscapes, and material goods in general (Carson et al. 1981). The critical transition to material investment and permanence begins in the second half of the seventeenth century, when second- and, later, third-generation Virginians came of age (Markell 1994). This transition extended more rapidly through the Tidewater during the eighteenth century.

Consolidating the community in the landscape (1650–1720)

After the initial concentration of early plantations along the rivers, freemen moved into often less productive and certainly less accessible tracts further inland where transport was more difficult (Kelly 1979). The southern forest was being transfigured into a mosaic of fields, pasture, and remnant forest patches. Status commonly followed a spatial gradient, with the wealthiest along the river, controlling access to shipping. Threats from the Powhatan recurred until the mid-seventeenth century, when most were displaced from the peninsula after the end of the second Anglo-Powhatan war. After this the regional landscape shifted as individual wealth, security, and infrastructures expanded. Tobacco production continued to thrive and some planters reinvested their earnings in creating more permanent homes and landscapes (e.g., Bacon's Castle, Berkeley/Ludwell, Littletown). At the same time, tobacco farmers began to agitate for control over marketing of their tobacco, and attempts were made to increase economic diversification and manufacturing (Brown 1996).

During this second phase, government involvement in the Colony intensified, although elite factions often manipulated government monies for their own benefit (Brown 1996). Nevertheless, infrastructures were created or expanded through increased taxation, supporting militia, courthouses, markets, churches, and roads (e.g., Morgan 1975; Shea 1983). The process of creating and maintaining these county institutions and facilities served to establish places of interaction for the settlers in the region. Laws multiplied for regulating trade, shipping, town organization and maintenance, land management (e.g., Reps 1972). While the fields and plantations of the region were increasingly bounded, urbanization was not a feature of this transformation (Earle 1992). Meeting places, such as churches, courthouses, racetracks, ordinaries/taverns, and markets were often isolated – places in the midst of spaces – and dispersed across the peninsula (Reps 1972). Nevertheless the number of places with meaning – linked to specific activities or people – increased substantially. Community and social bonds were forged slowly in this non-urban landscape (Walsh 1988). Interaction occurred during court days, market days, at church and home on Sundays and holidays, and in the course of local government administration (often at taverns; Roeber 1988). Hospitality was a social ideal, and guests were eagerly catered to as a measure of status (Brown 1996; Isaac 1982). The lack of central places served to make the creation of discrete places for different types of interaction all the more significant as arenas for group formation.

Toward the end of the seventeenth century, the supply of indentured and bonded labor declined as the tobacco market became increasingly volatile and competition from freeholders increased. Immigrant labor disappeared as economic conditions improved in England (Kulikoff 1986). European wars interrupted trade. This collapse of the tobacco market in the third quarter of the century disrupted and re-oriented settlement expansion (Edwards and Brown 1993). These economic problems played a role in Bacon's Rebellion against Governor Berkeley, laying the ground work for a significant shift in economic and political control, a shift that opened the door for the development of a new patriarchal economic and political configuration in the eighteenth century (Brown 1996; Morgan 1975).

Plantation owners slowly switched to slave labor (Morgan 1975). This served the dual function of reducing competition, as slaves were rarely freed to begin farming themselves, and stabilizing the work force. It also amplified class separation. Slave population increased dramatically during the eighteenth century (Kulikoff 1986). The creation of community, and identity, among slaves thus occurred after the initial definition of Tidewater communities, but was a critical part of their consolidation in the eighteenth century (Isaac 1982; 1988). Slaves understood and used landscapes very differently than did other groups (Upton 1988). Forests and woods served as centers for social and ritual activities not condoned by their owners (Isaac 1988).

At the end of the seventeenth century, the capital of the colony was moved from Jamestown, on the James River, to Williamsburg, a few miles inland in the center of the peninsula. This shift was the culmination of the colonization of the peninsula and the initial transformation of the Tidewater landscape. Governor Nicholson planned Williamsburg, as he had Annapolis, on a baroque model, with long avenues and vistas (Reps 1972). Although Williamsburg was never a major urban center, it did serve as the first central place, linking plantation owners, farmers, and tenants into a strongly intertwined community through the market, the church, and the court for much of the eighteenth century.

At the community scale, colonial landscapes were created in the seventeenth century, defining an increasing number of places that articulated different groups in the colony. The clearance of the forest and the creation of an open, grassy, agricultural landscape was part of the creation of colonial identities. This landscape was also re-shaped through the introduction of European and other exotic species of plants and animals. From another perspective, places created and reconfigured social groups. Churches, courthouses, roads, markets, plantations, and homesteads divided the landscape into separate arenas for action by different groups, and in each arena the social and the political were embedded in the location, content, and structure of the place. The different configurations of these places provide a window into the variation among groups in the Tidewater, and how colonial Virginia was unique in the colonies. If Earle's (1992) argument that the tobacco economy, as it articulated with the English commercial system, limited the growth of urban centers in the Tidewater is taken one step further, the dispersed and fragmented structure and content of the Tidewater landscape in the seventeenth century could also be seen as one cause of the political instability that plagued the colony until the early eighteenth century, and perhaps longer. The structures of place and space allowed divergent and contradictory understandings of power and social relationships, and inevitably led to conflict. This interpretation inverts standard settlement-pattern studies which use settlement organization to interpret political systems, to the view that politics and economics were actively shaped, at least in part, by the structure and content of the landscape.

The small scale: individual houselots and plantations

The creation of individual social identities can be traced through changes in both built and cultivated landscapes. In the built environment the first settlements, from Jamestown to Wolstenholme, were corporate. This follows both from the nature of the commercial organization responsible for colonization and from the organization of traditional communities in England until the sixteenth century (Johnson 1996). In many places medieval economic and social relations continued through the early modern period (e.g., Braudel 1984; Wolf 1982). These relationships were often planted into the colonies, but rarely lasted more than a generation (e.g., Walsh 1988). In Maryland, one example began as a manorial estate, but by the end of the 1600s it was transformed into a series of dispersed freeholds and tenancies whose owners' networks extended well beyond their local "lord." The commercial communities of the Virginia Company period (1607–24) dispersed even more rapidly as few social ties bound them together after the disastrous 1622 uprising.

House Little was invested in shelter, landscape, and identity in these early years. Virginia architecture of this period has been characterized as "impermanent" – earthfast wood structures with a limited life span (Carson et al. 1981). While little evidence exists for the nature of domestic landscapes, the sheet scatters of artifacts around seventeenth-century houses suggest many settlers made little attempt to formalize or ornament their immediate surroundings. Gardens, for economic purposes both herbal and subsistence, are known from both excavations and casual references in documents (Deetz 1993; Kelso 1984; Noël Hume 1983; Yentsch 1995). For example, recent excavations at Rich Neck Plantation reveal an enclosed area between domestic buildings that has typical garden features (Levy 1996). However, ornamental gardens, parks, and landscapes remain unknown, despite their growing popularity in England by the early to mid-seventeenth century (Martin 1991; Martin and MacCubbin 1984).

As the century progressed, individual identity was constructed through domestic spatial separation. Previously communal rooms were divided and distanced from the public by the introduction of halls (Deetz 1977; 1993; Neiman 1993). From multi-unit housing, characteristic of the early corporate communities of the Virginia Company period, houses shifted to fewer and more specialized functions, with activity areas and servants spatially moved into separate structures by the end of the century (e.g., Deetz 1993; Kelso 1984; Neiman 1990).

In addition, more permanent brick features were added to homes and installations, beginning in mid-century (Markell 1994). The transition from "impermanent" to permanent architecture began, paralleling the creation of an increasingly structured community and the enclosure of fields and work areas. More formal entry ways were constructed, increasing social and personal isolation and separation (Neiman 1993), although this trend reversed by the end of the century. Definition of space in the house and by entryways also served to structure space and activities immediately around the house and its dependencies. Neiman (1993) argues that such isolation and separation made labor more efficient and more economical, as less was invested in taking care of laborers. This separation of activities correlates with the imbuing of new places with new meanings, the definition of new relationships, and a proliferation of contexts for individual and group action. These economizing activities parallel increased competition and reduction in tobacco prices during the last decades of the seventeenth century.

In the last quarter of the century, Jamestown underwent a government-instigated revitalization in New Towne – a conscious attempt to create community and urbanity in the Tidewater (Bragdon et al. 1993). New buildings were constructed according to contemporary London styles: rowhouses and apartment blocks. Bricks were used in most of these new constructions. Martin (1991) identified a terraced garden in town. However, government attempts to create towns were frustrated as colonists maintained their plantation residences. The style, technology, and disposition of the buildings in Jamestown did nevertheless make a clear statement about the owner's identity and status in the colony, even if nonresident. When the capital was moved to Williamsburg around 1700, Jamestown was slowly abandoned.

Garden   In addition to this limited urban context, one conscious presentation of self was in the form of landscape gardens (Leslie and Raylor 1992). As Martin (1991) notes, it is one thing to buy English products, such as iron, wool, pewter and porcelain, that provide the trappings of rank, but quite another to invest in moving large amounts of earth, and creating grand artistic landscapes. Two examples of seventeenth-century elite gardens have been excavated to date in the Tidewater, allowing a glimpse of the variability and fluidity of identities in Virginia.

Governor Berkeley's plantation at Green Spring (1641–77), just 4 miles northwest of Jamestown, provides a convincing example of a statement of colonial elite identity (figure 3.2). The house was one of

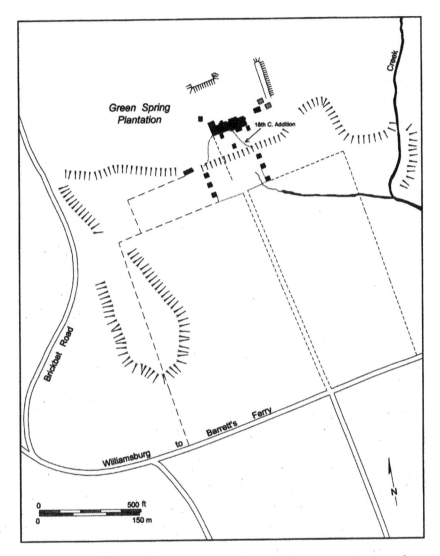

Figure 3.2 Schematic layout of Governor Berkeley's Green Spring plantation (after Martin 1991: 9).

the few buildings in the 1640s to make use of brick and sandstone, and to have a full brick-lined cellar (Caywood 1955). The plantation was near the center of political power and was also within an area of early field clearance. As the forest was cleared for shifting tobacco cultivation a more open pastoral landscape was created. Within this early sector of clearance, this property had the potential for being shaped into an English landscape garden, which capitalized on pastoral views of meadows and trees (Lees 1970).

Extensive gardens were identified during 1920s excavations (Martin 1991; Shurcliff 1929). The plan reveals a landscape garden, falling away from the terrace of the house. Some indications of garden terraces occur, but the content of the garden is unknown. The placement of the house and garden links Green Spring into the increasingly domesticated landscape. The garden becomes part of the natural world as viewed from the house, and the stature of the house was increased when viewed from afar. This style of "naturalized" garden, later popularized by Capability Brown, was very new even in England at this time, and did not become popular in Virginia until the eighteenth century.

Green Spring served as a source of plants, gardeners, and gardening ideas for nearly 150 years. Documents relate a well-stocked nursery (Martin 1991). Berkeley's investment in house, garden, landscape, and plantation created a social and political focus in the colony. The choice of garden styles reflects close knowledge of elite garden styles in England, and thereby Berkeley's desire to situate himself not only in local but in English circles. This elaborate landscape garden clearly revealed his stake in being at the pinnacle of the colonial elite. The garden was part of the cosmopolitan and lavish entertaining that characterized the Berkeley household (Brown 1996).

Berkeley's definition of himself backfired. His conspicuous consumption was seen as excessive to those paying the taxes and suffering the tobacco slump. As the elite factionalized in the 1670s, Berkeley was characterized as one of the "sponges" sucking up the public treasury (Brown 1996: 159). His lifestyle became the target of the opposing faction led by Bacon, and subsequently he lost power.

Seventeenth- and eighteenth-century correspondence reveals a continual exchange of plants among the elite within the colony, and across the Atlantic to England, Africa, and elsewhere (e.g., Martin 1991; Meatyard and Brown 1994; Yentsch 1995). During the seventeenth century horticultural experimentation was globally ubiquitous, if often unsuccessful. Social networks were created and maintained in the idiom of plants, gardening, and landscapes. It is important to emphasize here that, while the landscapes themselves held meaning as structures and places, it was also the ongoing process of creating gardens, maintaining them, and using them as social and political venues – linking action and structure – that Berkeley and others used to define themselves as Virginians and Englishmen.

Another example, excavated in the 1980s by Luccketti (1990), is the garden at Bacon's Castle. One of the oldest houses still standing in Virginia, its Jacobean style is unique in Virginia (figure 3.3). Built in *c*.1665 by Arthur Allen, Bacon's Castle is in Surry County across the James River, south of Jamestown (Kelso 1996; Martin 1991). Very little documentary evidence exists for this more peripheral plantation, but excavations uncovered a stark, geometric 1680s vegetable and herb garden without terracing. This rectangular garden is offset from the house, making clear that it is *not* a landscape garden, attempting to naturalize culture or enculturate nature. The garden is divided into three sets of paired large, raised beds, divided by wide formal paths. Attention is focused internally, on views of the house and the garden itself, as was typical of medieval gardens, rather than as part of a view creating a landscape from the house. Only a few touches offset the basically geometric layout: curvilinear beds against the northern wall and possible exedras at the west end of each of three paths, for viewing the garden and the domestic landscape (Martin 1991). Nor was the garden part of the three-dimensional or volumetric landscape of the house and plantation, serving to link visually or symbolically the house to the land (Lees 1970; Leone 1988). The possible exedras, the raised beds, and the layout were all in the style of a medieval herb or kitchen garden (Lees 1970; cf. Yentsch 1995).

Figure 3.3 Aerial photograph of the garden at Bacon's Castle during excavations by the James River Institute (photo: N. Luccketti).

The two gardens discussed here represent quite different but contemporary elite social statements of the mid-late seventeenth century.
At Bacon's Castle, the imposition of control and order, and the focus
on the domestic landscape suggests Allen was reformulating a more
medieval identity that focused primarily on his extended household,
and himself as a traditional manor lord. His world revolved around the
internal workings of the plantation and his household. At Green Spring,
however, Governor Berkeley created a garden and a landscape for
social and political interaction that extended out into and across the
countryside. Certainly he capitalized on his position to create his
adjoining landscape (Brown 1996), and used the landscape to define
his position. The style, the location, and the position of his garden in
the community and in relation to the house demonstrate Berkeley's
social identity, and the central role he played in the colony.

Field   The organization of house, garden, fields, and worker housing
defines a set of social technologies (cf. Pfaffenberger 1993). The
medieval world views that shaped tenant—lord relationships were very
different from those of the early modern world (Johnson 1996; Walsh
1988). In Virginia, as tobacco plantation owners invested in slaves,
and tobacco farming became the prerogative of the elite in the eighteenth century, patriarchal and biblical myths were re-shaped to justify
the new socio-economic configuration. These myths sought to naturalize and explain the hierarchical social and economic relationships
defined in the landscape (Isaac 1988). Perhaps just as importantly they
defined how both the patriarchal "master" and the slave "children"
should perform according to their duties and rights. These statuses and
roles had long-term impact on the social identities in Virginia's communities.

A strong link is often suggested for the expansion of slavery and the
expansion of landscape/plantation gardening in Virginia (Isaac 1982;
1988). The need to create a social identity is seen as a need to create
social distance (Kryder-Reid 1994; Leone 1988; 1994). Slaves became a
critical part of how elite individuals created and maintained their landscapes. If we examine the timing, however, landscape gardens predate
the expansion of slavery. The presence of gardens such as Berkeley's,
prior to the expansion of slavery, suggests that the creation of social
identity was not a purely capitalist mechanism, but rather, formative in establishing community and international networks within a
dispersed and volatile landscape.

Throughout the seventeenth century, an increasing number of domains
were created, within which individuals could position themselves in

social, ideational, and spatial terms. These domains were given meaning by individuals who belonged to overlapping networks, and identity was expressed by the material manifestation of network participation: goods, gardens, church, education, judicial/political skills. The idiom used to integrate these material identities was literally organic, and relationships were established and maintained in a cultivated landscape (Kryder-Reid 1994). Slavery became part of the social and economic system in Virginia, but it was not a necessary part of the creation of identity. Put another way, the creation of social distance is one outcome of the increasing uniqueness of identities. It goes hand in hand with the creation of new groups in societies, not based on purely familial relationships, but tied to new political economies, new ideals, and new understandings of the world, a process occurring in many parts of the world in the seventeenth century.

Summary

At the household scale, individuals in the seventeenth century began to use garden and landscape style and content to define themselves. These identities are manifest in where and what they chose to grow or produce, where and how they built their houses, and more importantly here, where and how they configured their gardens. The style of garden, its meaning, and its social context, reveals choices made by men to define and legitimate their place in the world (Kryder-Reid 1994; Leone 1994).

Interestingly, however, the ways in which individuals defined themselves in home, garden, and field were structurally different. If the pattern of divide, separate, and isolate associated with the eighteenth-century pattern of Georgianization (see Deetz 1977) is compared with the development of garden structure, a very different pattern is revealed. Where houses are increasingly subdivided, and domestic functions and household members even removed to other structures, gardens increasingly link the house with the larger landscape. Internally gardens may be subdivided, but not any more so than they were previously. Landscape gardens create controlled space to reinforce the hierarchical relationships between the elite, their land, slaves, and freeholders. Urban houselots, such as St George Tucker's in Williamsburg, with ornamental gardens, kitchen gardens, and nurseries, more closely followed the pattern of separation and distancing (Martin 1991). As one moved out into the landscape, into the mosaic of fields and forests, elite control over the meaning of place declined rapidly. More and different meanings were associated with these places, as refuge, religious sanctuary, meeting place, and resource area. Inversions of power, ambiguities in relationships, and competing meanings made elite power irrelevant (cf. Upton 1988).

The transition from the seventeenth to the eighteenth century was one of increasing elite control of the meanings of place, space, and social relationships. As this control increased, so too did the competition among the elite for hegemony. The nature of gardens changed, too, as individuals redefined themselves in a changing landscape of power. Diversity in garden content and structure became a feature in separating classes rather than in defining a class.

More detailed knowledge of the content of these gardens and landscapes would add another dimension to our understanding of who their creators were, just as the study of more vernacular gardens and landscapes would allow better understanding of other groups in colonial society and how they used space and place to create and define themselves.

Discussion

Postmodernists focus on the capitalist era as one in which space is transformed into commodity, breaking old social and communal bonds. However, in this American colonial context, landscapes are not solely created as commodities, but rather are used to establish, negotiate, and maintain community and individual social identity. The shaping of new places in the New World meant the creation of new relationships. Relationships were mediated within these places using plants, structures, and perspectives. By the eighteenth century, Tidewater landscapes were used to naturalize hierarchical social and economic relationships rationalized through patriarchal and biblical myths (Isaac 1982; 1988). The transformation of landscapes by individuals such as Jefferson and Washington reflects an ongoing definition and redefinition of the content of the myth, but reifies the fact that the structure itself – linking and juxtaposing nature and culture – is sacred.

Berkeley and Allen's seventeenth-century landscapes were not mere precursors of eighteenth-century landscapes and relationships. In presenting contradictory values and goals, the gardens actively participated in the continuing formation and reformation of communities and identities, mediating and creating conflict and resolution. The plantation gardens and landscapes structured social action, both as venue and in ongoing acts of creation and maintenance. The identities and relationships defined by the gardens and regional landscapes reflect the factional competition, contradictions, and fragmentation in seventeenth-century Tidewater economies, politics, and social groups.

If we return to Tilley's (1994) suggestion that major disconformities exist between understandings of space in capitalist versus precapitalist societies, with space being desanctified, controlled, economic, a backdrop, and "linear" in capitalist societies, the evidence from seventeenth-century Virginia provides an alternate view. "Capitalist" Tidewater cultivated landscapes were often full of contradictory, mythical, poetic, political, and multi-dimensional meanings, and perhaps most importantly, they were not a backdrop but very much part of an ongoing process of individual social and political negotiation.

The meanings of conceived and constructed landscapes changed over time as community and individual identities re-shaped the land. Jamestown changed from gateway community to agricultural backwater. The Pleistocene terraces of the James River came to be falling terraces in Georgian-styled elite gardens. In the course of these seventeenth-century changes, however, very different meanings became attached to these places. Changes in meaning do not always mean replacement of older ideologies, but often are the embedding of new meanings into older frameworks. As the millennium turns, we are re-inventing the colonial landscapes and once again changing the meaning of the Tidewater.

At each point in time, the configuration of the cultivated landscape has shaped the social and political nature of Tidewater communities. The dispersed and fragmented landscapes of the Tidewater seem to have provoked some of the political instability that plagued the colony. The divergent and contradictory understandings of place and power and social relationships led to conflicts. Perhaps we should consider that cultivated landscapes play an active role in shaping economic and political systems, rather than simply seeing them as passive indicators of political organization.

ACKNOWLEDGMENTS

Discussions with several people over the last few years contributed significantly to this article. I would like to thank J. Bowen, M. R. Brown, K. Meatyard, and F. Neiman. Their interest and scholarship stimulated much of my thinking on landscapes and colonial Virginia. I am grateful also to A. Edwards and G. Brown who assisted with the figures.

REFERENCES

Bender, B. (ed.) 1993: *Landscape: Politics and Perspectives*. Oxford: Berg.

Bragdon, K., Chapell, E., and Graham, W. 1993: A scant urbanity: Jamestown in the 17th century. In T. Reinhart and D. Pogue (eds), *The Archaeology of 17th Century Virginia*, Richmond, VA: Virginia Department of Historic Resources/Dietz Press, 223–49.

Braudel, F. 1984: *Civilization and Capitalism, 15th–18th Century*. New York: Harper and Row.

Brown, K. 1996: *Good Wives, Nasty Wenches and Anxious Patriarchs: Gender, Race and Power in Colonial Virginia*. Chapel Hill: University of North Carolina Press for the Institute of Early American History and Culture, Williamsburg.

Butzer, K. 1996: Settlement histories, agrosystemic strategies, and ecological performance. *Journal of Field Archaeology*, 23, 141–50.

Carson, C., Barka, N., Kelso, W., Stone, G., and Upton, D. 1981: Impermanent architecture in the southern American colonies. *Winterthur Portfolio*, 16, 135–96.

Caywood, L. R. 1955: *Excavations at Greenspring Plantation*. Yorktown, VA: Colonial National Historical Park.

Cosgrove, D. E. 1984: *Social Formation and Symbolic Landscapes*. London: Croom Helm.

Crumley, C. L. (ed.) 1994: *Historical Ecology: Cultural Knowledge and Changing Landscapes*. Santa Fe: SAR Press.

Deetz, J. 1977: *In Small Things Forgotten: An Archaeology of Early American Life*. New York: Doubleday.

Deetz, J. 1987: Harrington histograms versus Binford mean dates as a technique for establishing the occupational sequence of sites at Flowerdew Hundred, Virginia. *American Archaeology*, 6, 62–7.

Deetz, J. 1993: *Flowerdew Hundred: The Archaeology of a Virginia Plantation 1619–1864*. Charlottesville: University of Virginia Press.

Douglas, M., and Isherwood, B. 1979: *The World of Goods: Towards an Anthropology of Consumption*. New York and London: Routledge.

Earle, C. 1979: Environment, disease, and mortality in early Virginia. In T. Tate and D. Ammerman (eds), *The Chesapeake in the Seventeenth Century*, New York: University of North Carolina Press, 96–125.

Earle, C. 1992: Why tobacco stunted the growth of towns and wheat built them into small cities. In C. Earle, *Geographical Inquiry and American Historical Problems*, Stanford: Stanford University Press, 88–152.

Edwards, A., and Brown, M. 1993: Seventeenth century Chesapeake settlement patterns: a current perspective from Tidewater Virginia. In T. Reinhart and D. Pogue (eds), *The Archaeology of 17th Century Virginia*, Richmond, VA: Dietz Press/Council of Virginia Archaeologists, 285–309.

Fausz, J. 1971: Patterns of settlement in the James River basin. MA thesis, College of William and Mary.

Foucault, M. 1972: *An Archaeology of Knowledge*. London: Tavistock.

Giddens, A. 1979: *Central Problems in Social Theory: Action, Structure, and Contradictions in Social Analysis*. Berkeley: University of California Press.

Gleach, F. 1986: "... Where the Pale Ran": Sir Thomas Dale's palisades of seventeenth century Virginia. *Quarterly Bulletin of the Archaeological Society of Virginia*, 41, 160–8.

Goodenough, W. 1965: Rethinking "status" and "role": toward a general model of the cultural organization of relationships. In M. Banton (ed.), *The Relevance of Models for Social Anthropology*, New York: Praeger, 1–22.

Gosden, C. 1994: *Social Being and Time*. Oxford: Blackwell.

Hodges, C. 1999: Seventeenth century fortifications in Colonial Virginia. MA thesis, College of William and Mary.

Horn, J. 1979: Servant immigration to the Chesapeake in the seventeenth century. In T. Tate and D. Ammerman (eds), *The Chesapeake in the Seventeenth Century*, New York: W. W. Norton, 51–95.

Horn, J. 1988: Adapting to a New World: a comparative study of local society in England and Maryland, 1650–1700. In P. Morgan, L. Carr, and J. Russo (eds), *Colonial Chesapeake Society*, Chapel Hill: University of North Carolina Press, 133–75.

Howett, C. 1992: Graces and modest majesties: landscape and garden traditions of the American South. In W. Pun (ed.), *Keeping Eden: A History of Gardening in America*, Boston: Little, Brown, 81–95.

Isaac, R. 1982: *The Transformation of Virginia*. Chapel Hill: University of North Carolina Press.

Isaac, R. 1988: Ethnographic method in history: an action approach. In R. B. St George (ed.), *Material Life in America 1600–1860*, Boston: Northeastern University Press, 39–62.

Jefferson, T. 1787: *The Papers of Thomas Jefferson*. Charlottesville: University of Virginia Press.

Johnson, M. 1996: *An Archaeology of Capitalism*. Oxford: Blackwell.

Jordan, D. 1979: Political stability and the emergence of a native elite in Maryland. In T. Tate and D. Ammerman (eds), *The Chesapeake in the Seventeenth Century*. New York: W. W. Norton, 243–73.

Kelly, K. 1979: "In dispers'd country plantations": settlement patterns in seventeenth century Surry County, Virginia. In T. Tate and D. Ammerman (eds), *The Chesapeake in the Seventeenth Century*, New York: W. W. Norton, 183–205.

Kelso, W. 1984: *Kingsmill Plantations, 1619–1800: Archaeology of Country Life in Colonial Virginia*. Orlando: Academic Press.

Kelso, W. 1996: Big things remembered: Anglo-Virginian houses, armorial devices, and the impact of common sense. In A. Yentsch and M. Beaudry (eds), *The Art and Mystery of Historical Archaeology: Essays in Honor of James Deetz*, Boca Raton, FL: CRC Press, 127–45.

Kryder-Reid, E. 1994: "As is the gardener, so is the garden": the archaeology of landscape as myth. In P. Shackel and B. Little (eds), *Historical Archaeology of the Chesapeake*, Washington, DC: Smithsonian Institution Press, 131–48.

Kulikoff, A. 1986: *Tobacco and Slaves: The Development of Southern Cultures in the Chesapeake 1680–1800*. Chapel Hill: University of North Carolina Press.

Lees, C. B. 1970: *Gardens, Plants, and Man*. Englewood Cliffs, NJ: Prentice-Hall.

Leighton, A. 1970: *Early American Gardens*. Boston: Houghton Mifflin.

Leone, M. 1988: The Georgian order as the order of merchant capitalism in Annapolis, Maryland. In M. Leone and P. Shackel (eds), *The Recovery of Meaning: Historical Archaeology in the Eastern United States*, Washington, DC: Smithsonian Institution Press, 235–62.

Leone, M. 1994: The archaeology of ideology. In P. Shackel and B. Little (eds), *Historical Archaeology of the Chesapeake*, Washington, DC: Smithsonian Institution Press, 219–30.

Leslie, M., and Raylor, T. (eds) 1992: *Culture and Cultivation in Early Modern England: Writing and the Land*. Leicester: Leicester University Press.

Levy, P. 1996: Rich Neck Plantation interim report. Manuscript on file, Department of Archaeological Research, Williamsburg: Colonial Williamsburg Foundation.

Lewis, K. 1984: *The American Frontier: An Archaeological Study of Settlement Pattern and Process*. New York: Academic Press.

Luccketti, N. 1990: Archaeological excavations at Bacon's Castle, Surry County, Virginia. In W. Kelso and R. Most (eds), *Earth Patterns: Essays in Landscape Archaeology*, Charlottesville: University Press of Virginia, 23–42.

Mann, M. 1986: *The Sources of Social Power*. Volume 1: *A History of Power from the Beginning to AD 1760*. Cambridge: Cambridge University Press.

Markell, A. 1994: Solid statements: architecture, manufacturing, and social change in seventeenth-century Virginia. In P. Shackel and B. Little (eds), *Historical Archaeology of the Chesapeake*. Washington DC: Smithsonian Institution Press, 51–64.

Martin, P. 1991: *The Pleasure Gardens of Virginia*. Princeton: Princeton University Press.

Martin, P., and MacCubbin, R. (eds) 1984: *British and American Gardens in the Eighteenth Century*. Williamsburg: Colonial Williamsburg Foundation.

Meatyard, K., and Brown, M. R., III 1994: Paradise found: gardens as discourse in late 18th-century Williamsburg. Paper presented at the 93rd annual meeting, American Anthropological Association, Atlanta.

Morgan, E. 1975: *American Slavery, American Freedom: The Ordeal of Colonial Virginia*. New York: W. W. Norton.

Neiman, F. 1990: An evolutionary approach to archaeological inference: aspects of architectural variation in the 17th century Chesapeake. PhD dissertation, Yale University.

Neiman, F. 1993: Temporal patterning in house plans from the 17th century Chesapeake. In T. Reinhart and D. Pogue (eds), *The Archaeology of 17th Century Virginia*, Richmond, VA: Virginia Department of Historical Resources/Dietz Press, 251–83.

Noël Hume, I. 1983: *Martin's Hundred*. New York: Alfred A. Knopf.

Olwig, K. 1993: Sexual cosmology: nation and landscape at the conceptual interstices of nature and culture; or what does landscape really mean? In B. Bender (ed.), *Landscape: Politics and Perspectives*, Oxford: Berg, 307–43.

Pfaffenberger, B. 1993: The factory as artifact. In P. LeMonnie (ed.), *Technological Choices: Transformations in Material Cultures since the Neolithic*, New York: Routledge, 338–71.

Potter, S. 1993: *Commoners, Tribute, and Chiefs: The Development of Algonquian Culture in the Potomac Valley*. Charlottesville: University Press of Virginia.

Potter, S., and Waselkov, G. 1994: "Whereby we shall enjoy their cultivated places." In P. Shackel and B. Little (eds), *Historical Archaeology of the Chesapeake*, Washington, DC: Smithsonian Institution Press, 23–34.

Reps, J. 1972: *Tidewater Towns: City Planning in Colonial Virginia and Maryland*. Williamsburg and Charlottesville: Colonial Williamsburg Foundation and the University of Virginia.

Rodman, M. C. 1992: Empowering place: multilocality and multivocality. *American Anthropologist*, 94, 640–56.

Roeber, A. G. 1988: Authority, law, and custom: the rituals of Court Day in Tidewater Virginia 1720–1750. In R. B. St George (ed.), *Material Life in America, 1600–1860*, Boston: Northeastern University Press, 419–38.

Rountree, H. 1989: *The Powhatan Indians of Virginia*. Norman: University of Oklahoma Press.

Seddon, G. 1997: Gardens as paradise. *Australian Journal of Garden History*, 8, 8–12.

Shackel, P. 1993: *Personal Discipline and Material Culture: An Archaeology of Annapolis, Maryland, 1695–1870*. Knoxville, TN: University of Tennessee Press.

Shackel, P. 1994: Town plans and everyday material culture: an archaeology of social relations in Colonial Maryland's capital cities. In P. Shackel and B. Little (eds), *Historical Archaeology of the Chesapeake*, Washington, DC: Smithsonian Institution Press, 85–96.

Shackel, P., and Little, B. 1994: Archaeological perspectives: an overview of the Chesapeake region. In P. Shackel and B. Little (eds), *Historical Archaeology of the Chesapeake*, Washington, DC: Smithsonian Institution Press, 1–15.

Shea, W. L. 1983: *The Virginia Militia in the Seventeenth Century*. Baton Rouge: Louisiana State University Press.

Shurcliff, A. A. 1929: Colonial Williamsburg Foundation Library, Volume 58.

Smith, J. 1986 [1624]: The Generall Historie of Virginia, New England, and the Summer Isles. In P. L. Barbour (ed.), *The Complete Works of Captain John Smith (1580–1631)*, vol. II, Chapel Hill: University of North Carolina Press, 25–478.

Tilley, C. 1994: *A Phenomenology of Landscape: Places, Paths and Monuments*. Oxford: Berg.

Turner, E. R. 1993: Archaeological manifestations of the Virginia Company period. In T. Reinhart and D. Pogue (eds), *The Archaeology of 17th Century*

Virginia, Richmond, VA: Dietz Press/Council of Virginia Archaeologists, 67–104.

Upton, D. (ed.) 1982: *Three Centuries of Maryland Architecture*. Baltimore: Maryland Historical Trust.

Upton, D. 1988: White and Black landscapes in eighteenth century Virginia. In R. B. St George (ed.), *Material Life in America 1600–1860*, Boston: Northeastern University Press, 357–70.

Wallerstein, I. 1974: *The Rise and Future Demise of the World Capitalist System: Comparative Studies in Society and History*. New York: Academic Press.

Wallerstein, I. 1980: *The Modern World System*, Volume II: *Mercantilism and the Consolidation of the European World Economy*. New York: Academic Press.

Walsh, L. 1988: Community networks in the early Chesapeake. In P. Morgan, L. Carr, and J. Russo (eds), *Colonial Chesapeake Society*, Chapel Hill: University of North Carolina Press, 200–41.

Wolf, E. 1982: *Europe and the People without History*. Berkeley: University of California Press.

Yentsch, A. 1990: Minimum vessel lists as evidence of change in folk and courtly traditions of food use. *Historical Archaeology*, 24, 24–53.

Yentsch, A. 1995: Culture is as culture does: examples of culture's impact on Chesapeake gardens. Paper presented at annual meeting, Society for Historical Archaeology, Washington, DC

4

Conceptual Landscapes in the Egyptian Nile Valley

Janet E. Richards

Introduction: Landscape, Memory, and Society

For both the archaeologist and the native dweller, the landscape tells —
or rather is — a story. It enfolds the lives and times of predecessors who,
over the generations, have moved around in it and played their part in
its formation. To perceive the landscape is therefore to carry out an act
of remembrance, and remembering is not so much a matter of calling
up an internal image, stored in the mind, as of engaging perceptually
with an environment that is itself pregnant with the past.

(Ingold 1993: 153)

With these evocative words, Tim Ingold has gracefully sketched key
aspects of a phenomenology of landscapes: that they are experienced,
that their extent and meaning are mutable through space and time,
and that they are created through a potent combination of people, history, and geographical emplacement. In this chapter, I take such a perspective on ancient Egyptian landscapes by calling on the concept of
"place" — what Feld and Basso have called "that most powerful fusion
of space, self and time" (1996: 9). Specific landscapes in the Egyptian
Nile Valley became and remained important because they contained
the sites of sacred events invested with cosmological and mythic significance, enacted by humans, making reference to symbolically potent
features of the natural topography within which these sites were
embedded (Tilley 1994).

Part of the power of place is its dynamism, its encouragement of
event and motion in its midst (Casey 1996: 23). Human bodies, moving within a place or between places, animate and impute meaning to
them through experience and perception, and in turn take away
seemingly "natural" images of social or cosmological order from the

structure of their movement in that place or landscape. An essential trait of these dynamic places is that they *gather* things in their midst: associations, experiences, and histories, becoming repositories of memory, concrete and complex arenas of common engagement over space and time (1996).

This temporality of place and landscape is highlighted in what John Barrett has called the "inhabitation" of landscape, the concept of social bodies being in, inhabiting a landscape of the past, and the process of assigning to that landscape – especially the natural, "unconstructed" parts of it – new or altered meanings (Barrett et al. 1991; Barrett, this volume). The past itself becomes a symbolic resource, and an essential component of the ritual impact of place, a dimension of meaning which can be manipulated to legitimize new political or social ideologies.

Our understanding of the meaning of ancient ideational landscapes, or their symbolically charged components, cannot therefore be extricated from the context of the people, history, or environment in which they were dynamically created. The discussion that follows considers the constitution of "place," landscape, and sacred geography in ancient Egypt from those viewpoints, and suggests why some sacred places outlasted others in temporal and symbolic terms.

"Symbols are only powerful repositories of meaning when the referents are familiar" (Kirsch 1997). Yet symbols drawn from ancient Egyptian sacred geography have been exported to the Western world for over three millennia now, beginning most intensively with the birth of tourism in the Ptolemaic–Roman era (332 BC–AD 5th century). Pylons lend an aura of stability to suspension bridges; and pyramids house casinos in Las Vegas, Nevada, or eccentric millionaires in small rural towns. These architectural forms are divorced from the system of belief within which they made specific and meaningful reference to features of the natural world, from the conceptual landscapes of which they were integral parts, and from the people who inhabited, experienced, and understood these landscapes.

In ironically similar fashion, sacred landscapes in the Egyptian Nile Valley have often been considered almost independently from their situation in the geophysical environment. As archaeologists studying the rise of the state or social organization, we more commonly assess the location and construction of these landscapes through the lens of political or economic motivation, giving limited consideration to the inherent qualities of the natural setting. But how did the ancient Egyptians, the inhabitants of these landscapes, perceive, use and interact with them? Why did they choose certain places over others for the development of important and persistent ceremonial places? What "natural signifiers" were most remarkable and potent? And how do textual and iconographic as well as environmental and archaeological data lend us insight into the logic governing their decisions, and the circumstances facilitating the longevity of one place over another?

My intent in this chapter is to examine the Egyptian conceptualization of the physical environment, and then to delineate a recurrent nexus of natural features in the desert which characterized what we might term "central" sacred places in the Upper Egyptian Nile Valley (figure 4.1). One such landscape developed at the site of Abydos in southern Egypt, which I would like to use as a primary example of a "persistent place," the kind of place Schlanger describes as "used repeatedly during the long-term occupation of a region" (1992: 92). A diachronic perspective on shifting access to portions of this landscape allows us to speculate on how sacred activity and the consequent marking of space reflected and negotiated social reality in this particular locale. A comparative look at a much shorter-lived landscape, the royal city of Amarna, offers a rare instance of the textually documented genesis and ideology of a place and conceptual landscape. Chosen at least in part because that same nexus of features was present, and deploying key elements of the same sacred vocabulary as seen at Abydos, Amarna as "place" anchored a far more restricted range of time, use and meaning, highlighting the importance of memory and history in the formation and dynamic persistence of key sacred places in Egypt.

Egyptian Conceptual Geography

The physical environment experienced by the ancient Egyptians presented a series of dramatic transitions: a life-giving river; a fertile alluvial plain created through annual inundation; a stark desert landscape (figure 4.2). In Lower (northern) Egypt, the floodplain widens to a vast delta whose northern border is the Mediterranean Sea. In Upper, or southern Egypt, the focus of this chapter, the limits of cultivable land resemble more closely a ribbon of oasis, flanked on either side by variably elevated desert. On the west, the low desert rises to the high cliffs of the Libyan plateau, and on the east, to the mountains and hills of the eastern desert, visibly highlighting the edges of the Egyptian world.

The Egyptians identified the fertile soil of the plain – *Kmt*, the Black Land – as the proper context for landscapes inhabited by the living, and located there cities, towns, and villages. The desert, on the other hand – *Dšrt*, the Red Land – was identified with chaos and death,

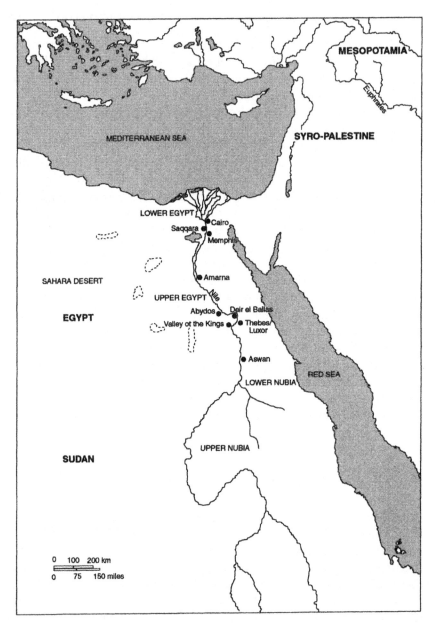

Figure 4.1 Map of Egypt showing key sites and places mentioned in the text.

Figure 4.2 Desert and alluvial plain in the Egyptian Nile Valley (photo: B. Baker, 1992).

being the place where the sun "died" each night in the western horizon; this was conceptualized as primarily the domain of the dead. However, in the Egyptian world view, the universe composed of these two lands – the Red Land of the desert, the Black Land of the floodplain – was shared by living humans, the king, the gods, and the dead. So, both landscapes were inherently sacred and dynamically interconnected in the daily quest to defend the cosmos against the forces of disorder which continually threatened it. The maintenance of order (or *ma'at*), the keeping of things in their place through careful adherence to established ritual procedures, was the chief ideological rationale and organizing principle of ancient Egyptian life, and was most exemplified in the development, meaning, and use of explicitly sacred landscapes.

These attitudes are documented in indigenous texts from the third millennium BC onward. What about iconographic and architectural representations of the natural world? Depictions of what we would

understand as natural, unmodified "landscapes" are rare in ancient
Egyptian art; no word for or concept of "landscape" *per se* existed. The
context of this art was mostly in temples and tombs, and it was produced in accordance with strict principles of decorum linked to the
global concept of order. In this idealized setting, features of the natural
world were reproduced as essentialized visual cues to the context of a
represented activity. The natural world, especially desert and, more
unexpectedly, the life-giving river, could be wild and unpredictable.[1]
So the desert was represented only in scenes where chaos was symbolically vanquished, as during the hunt; and similarly river scenes
depicted unruly fish in the process of being caught in a net. In both of
these genres, the strict conventions governing placement of elements
in art were relaxed when "chaotic" elements were represented (the
desert and its creatures; water and its inhabitants), to convey a sense of
turbulence and disorder.

More common are representations of fully domesticated space, like
pools in a garden, or fields under cultivation; or elements of the natural environment structured by the addition of architecture, or anthro-
pomorphized in some way. Such elements are named, and are
associated with central religious concepts. The sun itself, represented
for example as the god Re riding in his bark, is possibly the most ubiquitous and important "natural" element. Another example is a prominent desert peak on the west bank at Thebes, perceived to be a natural
pyramid. Pyramids evoked the primeval mound which emerged from
the inundation in the First Time, and on which the Creator God fashioned the perfect order of the universe. One of the several names of
this peak was "the Mistress of the West," and it was never depicted as
a simple physical or even natural feature (figure 4.3). Rather, it was
shown associated with the cow goddess Hathor, and embellished with
a pyramid-topped shrine, effectively taming it and keeping it in place
(figure 4.4).

The primary vocabulary of Egyptian sacred geography therefore
included the sun and its circuit; the eastern and western horizons and
the role they played in that daily journey, symbolizing the gates
between this world and the next; the primeval mound and its emergence from the waters of the first inundation; the river itself; and
finally the desert, as the embodiment of the chaos which must be held
off from the ordered world. These selected environmental features
found full architectural expression in the wholly constructed sacred
landscapes of Egyptian state temples. Gods' temples were conceived as
microcosms, where the god of the temple led a daily round parallel to
that of the sun. Demarcated by enclosure walls whose external faces

Figure 4.3 The "Mistress of the West" (photo: J. Richards, 1988).

Figure 4.4 Hathor emerging from the peak (© The British Museum).

graphically represented chaos lapping at the temple's boundaries, containing the domesticated waters of the sacred lake, and fronted by pylons symbolizing the horizon, these temples recalled the primeval mound and the first act of creation: the floor level from pylon to sanctuary gradually rose, in mimicry of the mound's emergence. In temples, the movement of human beings through sacred space was directed by walls and courts granting increasingly narrow access to increasingly narrow social groups as one progressed through the temple.

These constructed environments, built within the domesticated space of settlements, constituted major arenas where cosmic order was upheld. A community's direct experience of the temple's inhabitant occurred only when the deity exited from his microcosm at festival time; within the temples only cult specialists participated in the daily rituals necessary to maintain *ma'at*, and through it, the fabric of the universe itself. However, prior to the New Kingdom period (1570–1070 BC), as much if not more energy was devoted to the creation of potent ideational landscapes in the low desert, despite, or perhaps because of, identification of the desert with *isft*, the forces of chaos. Attention was focused away from the life-giving river within its fertile floodplain, and westward to the taming of the waterless, unpredictable Sahara. In contrast to the persistent restriction of access to temples, these desert arenas were experienced and in many cases eventually inhabited by much wider swaths of the Egyptian population.

Sacred places developed in the desert were for the most part mortuary landscapes, organized according to beliefs and practices relating to the disposal of the dead. Ideological emphasis here was on the defeat of individual annihilation, with the goal of gaining entry to the next world. The collective denial of death brought about through the construction of graves in a mortuary landscape and the practice of appropriate rituals was, in effect, another form of defeating chaos and thereby maintaining the cosmos at the level of the community. The unruly desert was colonized, domesticated, and ordered by its subordination to these activities. So in a sense these landscapes were functionally equivalent to temples, except that in these desert contexts a wider range of social groups played an active role. In the mortuary realm the ideologies of the state (or Great) religious tradition intersected with that of the domestic (or Little) traditions, in a unified concern with facilitating the dangerous transition to Afterlife. Additionally, the perceived connection to living landscapes made cemeteries arenas for social display, both between and among different social and economic levels.

Why were certain desert places chosen and maintained as especially sacred and powerful conceptual landscapes? The site of Abydos, in many ways, is the prototype for such places, pre-dating and outlasting most others in its coherence as a national ceremonial center, even through periods of decentralization. I suggest that, originally, it became an important place because of a potent co-occurrence of salient and suggestive features in the local physical environment. Furthermore, I suggest that its prominence as a conceptual landscape was sustained through a combination of political, mythological, and historical associations layered onto the physical symbolism of this place, as well as the broadening of social access over time to the ritual activities enacted there.

Abydos

> As surface the landscape is not passive; it is given a constitutive role as the stage set for the human drama itself. … The critical and enduring question concerns the bounds within which human life and action on the earth's surface should be defined.
>
> (Cosgrove 1993: 282)

Abydos (ancient *3bdw*) lies in one of the most agriculturally rich regions of Upper Egypt. The ancient site is several kilometers west of the Nile River at the junction between the floodplain and the low desert stretching back to the cliffs of the Nile gorge. The extent of these remains is more than 720 hectares, including a substantial town, temples, cemeteries, and royal installations (figure 4.5). Time depth at

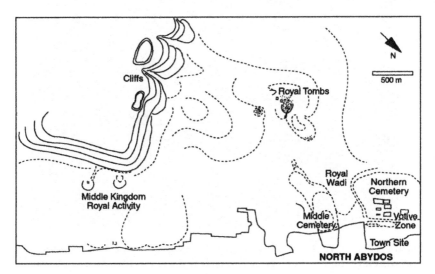

Figure 4.5 Map of Abydos (after Kemp 1975).

Abydos is also enormous: it was in use continuously as a conceptual landscape from about 5000 BC to around AD 400 in alternating areas of the site – a span of well over five millennia. I would like to focus on North Abydos, the longest-lasting core of this conceptual landscape.

North Abydos is set against the backdrop of a great bay of cliffs, which embraces a semicircular sweep of low desert (figure 4.6). This low desert rises as a steep western escarpment up to 20 meters above the ancient town, and is split by a broad, shallow *wadi* stretching out to the cliffs of the high desert. On either side of the *wadi*, the low desert also lifts in steep slopes to plateaus that we now call the Middle and Northern Cemeteries. The blank slate of this geophysical environment therefore provided a dramatic and theatrical setting: a stage high above the "audience" of the living, complete with different levels for display and demarcation of space, and a ready-made ceremonial path rising slowly out to an opening in the cliffs. This opening may well have signified to the earliest inhabitants of the area the quintessential gate to the next world. In *c.*3100 BC the first kings of politically unified Egypt laid claim to control of this otherworldly "gate," establishing their tombs at the southern end of an existing elite cemetery (figure 4.7). It was these kings who initially set a comprehensive North Abydos stage. Their tombs incorporated "back doors" oriented to the

Figure 4.6 Abydos: overall view of low desert and *wadi* looking west towards cliffs (photo courtesy of Pennsylvania–Yale–New York University Expedition).

Figure 4.7   Abydos: location of royal tombs and great opening in cliffs (photo courtesy of Pennsylvania–Yale–New York University Expedition).

cliff opening, with "front entrances" symbolically linked to ceremonial enclosures on the level plateau of the Northern Cemetery, by means of the natural "causeway" (what is now termed the Royal Wadi). Whatever the other reasons, economic or political, for selecting Abydos as an important place at the beginning of Egypt's history as a state, the natural topography surely suggested to these kings a majestic and symbolically charged setting for the enactment of politico-ritual events.

With the exception of water, the principal features of Egyptian sacred geography were all there: the desert, the rising gradient evoking the primeval mound, the setting of the sun through the gate of the western horizon. The only modification necessary to this physical landscape was the construction of the royal tombs and enclosures themselves, and the employment of water in ritual acts of purification. By structuring and eternally inhabiting the space in this way, the kings symbolically tamed and controlled the chaotic desert, while simultaneously monopolizing a highly sacred feature of cosmological geography – the entrance to the next world.

The absolute restriction of this entire landscape to royal participants lasted from approximately 3100 to 2500 BC, when the pattern of access began to widen. Even if the performance of rituals in this particular arena ceased when the location of royal mortuary complexes was switched to Saqqara in Lower Egypt, control over the space itself persisted. At first, only local elites appropriated or were granted cemetery space in the Middle Cemetery and visual access to the royal conceptual landscape of Northern Cemetery, *wadi*, and burial ground near the cliffs. The broadening of access accelerated 200 years later during a time of political decentralization. Then, around 2050 BC, in the late 11th dynasty, the Northern Cemetery was either opened or arrogated to private use as a burial ground for both elites and non-elites (J. Richards 1992). A 13th-dynasty decree of King Neferhotep, excavated from the Northern Cemetery, forbade use of the *wadi* but permitted widespread use of other areas (Leahy 1989); the orthography of the inscription may indicate that it is a later copy of an earlier Middle Kingdom decree (D. Silverman, personal communication). Whether access was granted or seized, 1,000 years of exclusively royal presence in that part of the landscape was ended. *Wadi* and cliffs were still set apart as a restricted place, but the significance of the site may have shifted at this time, from political and historical associations to more explicitly mythological meanings. Certainly by the 12th dynasty the location of the royal tombs became identified as the burial place of Osiris, king of the dead and mythical first king of Egypt, thereby merging the historical into the primordial (cf. C. Richards 1996: 194).

Around the same time, a zone for the dedication of votive stelae was initiated on a low desert ridge at the edge of the Northern Cemetery and referred to as the "terrace" or "stairway" of the Great God (Osiris), overlooking the Osiris temple in the town (O'Connor 1985; Simpson 1974). It is tempting to see this diversification of organization and function of the North Abydos conceptual landscape as reflecting the reorganization of social groups in the political and religious realms. If indeed this access to previously exclusive space was granted by elites, it might have been one materialization of their response to an increasingly complex social system.

Places anchor lives in social formations (Hirsch 1995: 7); and social order was still maintained through the partitioning of space. Royal ritual presence and activity moved to South Abydos at that time; recent work in the Middle Cemetery has established also that the boundaries of the most elite local cemetery initiated there in approximately 2400 BC were not challenged until nearly 1,600 years later. The sacred landscape seems still to have been conceptualized as a whole, the change being a new sharing among the different social groups: high national elites, regional elites, and non-elites. Boundaries in this shared landscape were implied by spatial distance and elevation, not by the erection of walls, and we can guess they were respected and reinforced by community tradition "sedimented into the deepest level of perception" (Casey 1996: 18), as much as by any element of elite control or regulation.

Throughout the next two millennia, the sacred landscape at Abydos was shared not only by central elites and by persons living in the adjacent town, but also by a national population making pilgrimages to the now firmly designated grave of Osiris, and using the Royal Wadi as a pathway to it. Osiris' description as the "eternal lord who presides in Abydos, who dwells distant in the graveyard, ... the great portals open for him" (Lichtheim 1975: 82) is explicit reference to the location and aspect of "his" tomb near the cliffs. Abydos had become a multidimensional arena transcending the local, embedded within an Egyptwide system of sacred spaces (cf. Lahiri 1996), imbued with complex and long-lived meaning and memory, identified as *wrt '3t hmhmt*, "ground great of fame" (Lichtheim 1988: 131), "seat blessed since the time of Osiris, settled by Horus [son of Osiris, incarnate in the living king] for the forebears" (1988: 110), "the birthplace," the place of rebirth of the dead (1988: 112). Over time, its landscape was conceived, and with very little actual building, constructed as representing the local and national social order. Thus the space "structure[d]... not only the group's representation of the world, but the group itself, which order[ed] itself in accordance" (Bourdieu 1977: 163, as quoted by Cresswell 1996: 8–9). These factors taken together could not have failed to facilitate the extreme longevity of Abydos as sacred place and ceremonial center.

Amarna

One site alone does not make a pattern of choice; other examples of the same felicitous nexus of prominent natural features seen at Abydos can be documented – and were mined conceptually – in other Upper Egyptian sites. Similar topographies existed at Deir el Ballas, location of an early 18th-dynasty city; Thebes, an important ceremonial and political center from the Middle Kingdom onward; and the very shortlived site of Amarna in Middle Egypt. Of these, I would like to explore the development of the Amarna landscape, for it provides the sharpest contrast to the ideology, population, and longevity of the North Abydos conceptual landscape (figure 4.8).[2]

The philosopher Edward Casey has said that "[s]tripping away cultural or linguistic accretions, we shall never find a pure place lying underneath – and still less an even purer Space or Time" (1996: 28). Yet Amarna seems to be precisely such a "pure place." It was established in the fourteenth century BC by the king Akhenaten, with the stated intent of providing a pure and perfect residence for his newly

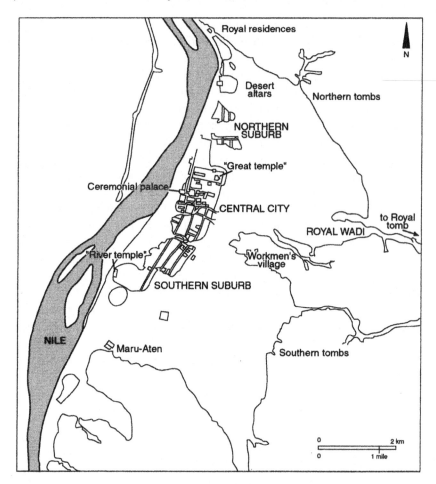

Figure 4.8 Map of Amarna (after Baines and Malek 1980).

paramount god Aten, the disc of the sun, and the evident intent of
providing himself with a clean stage for the enactment of a new
politico-religious ideology. The ancient name for this ideational landscape was Akhet-Aten, literally "horizon of the Aten." Contemporary
texts refer to the Aten having " chosen this place himself," precisely
because it was unsullied by the presence of any other god – linking its
choice therefore to a lack of memory and association with other sacred
beings, political entities or revered ancestors. The new landscape was
deliberately situated in a place divorced from history.

The scope and form of this landscape were defined by a series of royal
inscriptions over several years, on boundary stelae erected in the cliffs
surrounding the site. These inscriptions not only quantified the total

extent of the place to be inhabited, but described its natural components and its inhabitants. An excerpt from the later boundary stelae reads:

> Now within these four stelae, from the eastern mountain to the western mountain, is Akhet-Aten itself. It belongs to my father... who gives life forever, with mountains, deserts, meadows, new lands, highlands, fresh lands, fields, water, settlements, shorelands, people, cattle, trees and all other things that the Aten my father will let be forever.
>
> (Lichtheim 1975: 51)

In contrast to the situation at Abydos, this place in its totality explicitly straddled the Nile River, incorporating both its western and eastern banks. The most intensively developed and experienced portion of the landscape, however, was on the eastern side. An ideological rationale might be sought: that is, that Akhenaten was deliberately inverting the time-honored custom of symbolically domesticating the western desert and horizon (J. Baines, personal communication), stressing instead the rising or "birth" of the sun in the east, instead of controlling its setting or "death" in the west. However, his choice of the east bank may also have been influenced by the existence there of a topographical situation similar to that of Abydos and other important ceremonial sites. The east bank at Amarna features an immense bay of cliffs (the "mountains" of the inscription) encircling a broad swath of elevationally variable low desert, and a *wadi* stretching out to and beyond a great opening in the horizon, like the gate between this world and the next.

Taking advantage of this naturally prefabricated stage, Akhenaten built a unified city and desertscape, a giant open-air temple precinct showcasing his ideology of kingship. He imported a population, whose movements within the grand arena were structured and controlled by constructed roads and walls, and by the rhythmic passage of daily time. Here, Akhenaten mirrored the east–west passage of the sun in his own north–south movements within the landscape, and linked the arenas of life and death even more explicitly by situating the city itself on the low desert, normally the dangerous context of death and chaos. The non-royal inhabitants of the landscape, however, experienced it as spectators, not participants: observing Akhenaten's offerings to the god, whom only he and his family could worship directly; viewing Akhenaten's progress through the avenues of the city; mapping their own daily rounds on his emergence and withdrawal from the central core of the city.

The familiar symbolic raw material of a "special" natural landscape was therefore present and its vocabulary deployed, but the meanings assigned to it were Akhenaten's alone, inscribed upon a place divorced from history and from the wider spectrum of Egyptian mythology, meaningful only to a small political elite. This lack of a sense of memory, of connection with the activities of ancestors both human and mythic, and of a collective transformation of and relationship to the place and space, is perhaps what enabled Akhenaten's successors to so quickly and thoroughly destroy the place as a viable or re-usable – inhabitable – conceptual landscape. The temporality of Amarna as a dynamic arena amounted to barely 15 years.

Conclusion

In contrasting these two sites I have tried to identify and understand why some features of the Egyptian natural environment, when co-occurrent, encouraged the choice or development of these physical contexts as especially potent sacred places by the groups of people inhabiting them. The example of Amarna suggests that the raw physical parallels of that site with more traditional cosmological symbols and precedence were not enough to establish meaning and to prolong the temporality of this proclaimed "place." Given the deliberately historically and socially empty past of the ideational landscape there, the enduring aspects of place as "event," as motion by different players over different time periods, as gatherer, and as socially inhabited space, could not work together to build a compelling and long-lived "story."

What we have found in the landscape of deep temporality at Abydos, on the other hand, was an instance of "continuous and changing qualification of particular places: qualified by their own contents and qualified as well by the various ways these contents are articulated (denoted, described, discussed, narrated, and so forth)" (Casey 1996: 28) throughout millennia by different political, social, and economic beings. This mapping of individual, local, national, and mythical histories onto the low desert arena, the consequent articulation of the spatial and the social (cf. Alcock 1993), and the thickness of what Tilley has called "the layers of interwoven meaning and reference" (1994: 27) continually revitalized the perception and use of the Abydos low desert. The "story" experienced here was one of collective participation and gathered memory, a landscape "constantly oscillating between the 'foreground' of everyday lived emplacement, and a 'background' of social [and political] potential" (Feld and Basso 1996: 6; Hirsch and O'Hanlon 1995).

NOTES

1   Compare McEwan and van de Guchte on Inca attitudes to the world outside their territory and social universe: "a wild, unordered, and uncontrollable world that was at once ambivalent and potentially threatening" (1992: 368). Egyptian perceptions of the desert were also complicated by the residence there of nomadic groups who periodically wrought havoc on settled communities.

2   For detailed discussions of Amarna city, see Kemp (1989) and O'Connor (1989), without whose synthetic and critical discussions this analysis would not have been possible.

REFERENCES

Alcock, S. 1993: The sacred landscape. In S. Alcock, *Graecia Capta: The Landscapes of Roman Greece*, Cambridge: Cambridge University Press, 172–214.

Baines, J., and Malek, J. 1980: *Atlas of Ancient Egypt*. New York: Facts on File.

Barrett, J. C., Bradley, R., and Green, M. 1991: *Landscape, Monuments and Society: The Prehistory of Cranbourne Chase*. Cambridge: Cambridge University Press.

Bourdieu, P. 1977: *An Outline of a Theory of Practice*, R. Nice (transl.). Cambridge: Cambridge University Press.

Casey, E. 1996: How to get from Space to Place in a fairly short stretch of time: phenomenological prolegomena. In S. Feld and K. H. Basso (eds), *Senses of Place*, Santa Fe: SAR Press, 13–52.

Cosgrove, D. 1993: Landscapes and myths, gods and humans. In B. Bender (ed.), *Landscape: Politics and Perspectives*, Oxford: Berg, 281–305.

Cresswell, T. 1996: *In Place, Out of Place: Geography, Ideology and Transgression*. Minneapolis: University of Minnesota Press.

Feld, S., and Basso, K. H. 1996: Introduction. In S. Feld and K. H. Basso (eds), *Senses of Place*, Santa Fe: SAR Press, 3–11.

Hirsch, E. 1995: Introduction: landscape: between place and space. In E. Hirsch and M. O'Hanlon (eds), *The Anthropology of Landscape: Perspectives on Place and Space*, Oxford: Clarendon Press, 1–30.

Hirsch, E., and O'Hanlon, M. (eds) 1995: *The Anthropology of Landscape: Perspectives on Place and Space*. Oxford: Clarendon Press.

Ingold, T. 1993: The temporality of the landscape. *World Archaeology*, 25, 152–74.

Kemp, B. 1975: Abydos. In W. Helck and E. Otto (eds), *Lexikon der Agyptologie*, I, Wiesbaden: O. Harrassowitz, 28–41.

Kemp, B. 1989: *Ancient Egypt: Anatomy of a Civilization*. London: Routledge.

Kirsch, S. 1997: Changing views of place and time along the Ok Tedi. Paper presented at the conference "From Myth to Minerals," Wenner-Gren Foundation for Anthropological Research, Australian National University, Canberra.

Lahiri, N. 1996: Archaeological landscapes and textual images: a study of the sacred geography of medieval Ballabgarh. *World Archaeology*, 28, 244–64.

Leahy, A. 1989: A protective measure at Abydos in the Thirteenth Dynasty. *Journal of Egyptian Archaeology*, 75, 41–60.

Lichtheim, M. (transl.) 1975: *Ancient Egyptian Literature*, Volume 2: *The New Kingdom*. Berkeley: University of California Press.

Lichtheim, M. (transl.) 1988: *Ancient Egyptian Autobiographies Chiefly of the Middle Kingdom*. Friebourg, Sweden: Biblical Institute.

McEwan, C., and van de Guchte, M. 1992: Ancestral time and sacred space in Inca state ritual. In R. Townsend (ed.), *The Ancient Americas: Art from Sacred Landscapes*, Chicago, Munich: Art Institute of Chicago, Prestel Verlag, 359–71.

O'Connor, D. 1985: The "cenotaphs" of the Middle Kingdom at Abydos. In *Mélanges Gamal Eddin Mokhtar*, Cairo: Institut français de l'archéologie orientale, 162–77.

O'Connor, D. 1989: City and palace in New Kingdom Egypt. *Cahiers de Recherches de l'Institut de Papyrologie et d'Égyptologie de Lille*, 11, 73–87.

Richards, C. 1996: Monuments as landscape: creating the centre of the world in late Neolithic Orkney. *World Archaeology*, 28, 190–208.

Richards, J. E. 1992: Mortuary variability and social differentiation in Middle Kingdom Egypt. PhD dissertation, Ann Arbor, Michigan: University Microfilms.

Schlanger, S. 1992: Recognizing persistent places in Anasazi settlement systems. In J. Rossignol and L. Wandsnider (eds), *Space, Time and Archaeological Landscapes*, New York: Plenum Press, 91–112.

Simpson, W. K. 1974: *The Terrace of the Great God at Abydos*. New Haven and Philadelphia: Pennsylvania Yale Papers.

Tilley, C. 1994: *A Phenomenology of Landscape: Places, Paths and Monuments*. Oxford: Berg.

5

Buddhist Landscapes of East Asia

Gina L. Barnes

Introduction

The present volume is based on the conception of landscape as "a stage constructed in the mind to convey meaning to those who inhabit it" (Knapp and Ashmore, this volume). The editors specify that it is not necessary for a landscape to be "sacred" to be "ideational," a qualification allowing consideration of the total conception of the landscape – particularly how the mundane and the special or sacred aspects of that perceived landscape interrelate. However, there are two problems with these premises. First, any particular landscape feature may be attributed with different meanings by different viewers, or indeed by a single viewer at different moments, thus resulting in different "stages" in the minds of individual inhabitants. Waterfalls, for example, can be admired for their mundane beauty or valued for their energy potential (as in powering waterwheels); but within Buddhist ritual they are a locus for the practice of spiritual asceticism and are therefore accorded more attention within sacred realms of thought. Thus, a waterfall takes on a different meaning in the "stage constructed in the mind" depending on the viewer and the context of viewing.

Nevertheless, some landscape features may be intentionally and explicitly "marked" as to what their intended meaning is in specific systems of thought: if the waterfall above was clearly stated in writing at the site to be the locus of ascetic practices, anyone coming upon such written notice would have this notion added to their own preconceptions; if it were an orally transmitted marking, then one would have had to hear it to participate in that meaning and just visiting the location would not necessarily be enough. Explicit "marking" of landscape attributes is a method of extending meaning among inhabitants and contributes to the development of a shared acknowledgment of such meanings even if not all inhabitants adopt them as their own.

These concerns are important to a consideration of Buddhist landscapes, for a large part of their existence is the result of just such
"marking" activities.

There is no agreed definition of what constitutes a Buddhist landscape (cf. Barnes, ed. 1995). At minimum, we must recognize two
types of Buddhist landscapes: earthly and other-worldly. This chapter
examines the general outlines of both in order to understand a particular sub-category – that of the outdoor rock-cut sculptures that were
carved at sites from Afghanistan across north China into Korea and
Japan from the third and fourth centuries onwards (figure 5.1). The
creation of these sculptures on cliff walls or mountain boulders has
forever changed the visible landscape at that point from a natural to an
anthropogenic one with specific symbolic content. The sculptures, as a
form of "marking," draw the viewer into the particular meaning of the
Buddhist image through questions and comment. The result is knowledge created in the mind as guided by the anthropogenic landscape,
resulting in a widely shared meaning if not belief.

The physical presence of a *buddha* image in particular confronts the
observer more directly with the explicit religious message than does an
encounter with an architectural structure such as a temple, church or

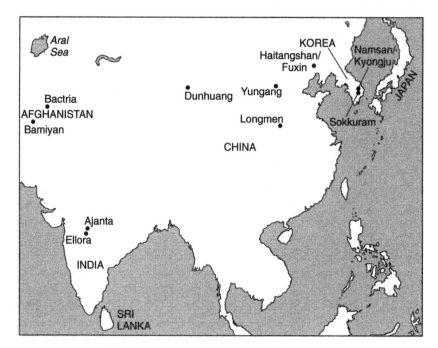

Figure 5.1 Map of sites and locations mentioned in the text.

mosque. To Christians, it would be like suddenly meeting an isolated crucifix sculpture placed on a mountainside, or perhaps an unexpected gravestone. The encounter automatically takes observers out of the mundane world and projects them into consideration of other worlds of existence, either past or future. The power of such physical objects to force a mental transcendence of the here-and-now concerns of personal sustenance and social obligations is indeed awesome, even for non-believers. That the Buddhist religion was able to take advantage of this power is due in part to its adoption of Hellenistic sculptural techniques and to a whole-hearted commitment to religious iconography. But the distinguishing attribute is that the practice of Buddhist sculpture was taken to the *out-of-doors*, so that parcels of landscape space are transformed by the existence of these images.

On the one hand, the sphere of power of such images is defined not only by the locus in which they reside but also by the viewing distance. Large *buddha* cliff sculptures such as at Bamiyan in present-day Afghanistan can be seen for several kilometers (Higuchi, with Barnes 1995; Klimberg-Salter 1989). By contrast, in modern Japan, roadside statues of Jizo images – the *bodhisattva* savior of travelers, women in childbirth, warriors, and children – are almost stumbled on before they are noticed; but when the images *are* noticed, the mental transcendence takes place. I would argue that this is a different result from the viewing of an architectural structure – an act which might force a mental categorization of religious activity ("Ah, a *Catholic* church"), but would not necessarily impact on the observer's consideration of their own mortality as might the viewing of a crucifix. Thus, the force of the Buddhist sculpture in the out-of-doors is only rarely paralleled in, for example, Christian monuments such as the figure of Christ overlooking Rio de Janeiro.

The congregation of many sculptures in one locality may further promote the designation of the entire area as sacred (figure 5.2). In these areas, the images might not be inter-visible (either one from another or all from an independent location), but the space between the sculptures – though falling outside the visual sphere – might also be designated as sacred. In such cases, we would have a sacred locale which would incorporate much mundane land area in addition to the religious monuments themselves. It is the development of such sacred park-like areas that is of interest here as a small subset of the numerous cases which are encompassed in the term "Buddhist landscapes."

The investigation undertaken here attempts to relate the physical landscapes of two mountain sites, Haitangshan in northeastern China and Namsan in southeastern Korea, to the historical development of

Figure 5.2 The mountainside of Haitangshan with carved *buddha* and deity panels on every boulder available (photo by author).

Buddhist landscapes in general and to their meaning within Buddhist cosmology. Each of these sites consists of a complex of temples built in mountainous terrain and accompanied by numerous outdoor Buddhist sculptures. It is hypothesized that the physical form of each site derives from melding the Buddhist cosmological principle of the axial mountain with Chinese folk beliefs concerning sacred mountains. In the ensuing investigation, the shift from caves to mountains as sites suited to temples will be documented in the historical section, followed by a description of the actual sites under question and a discussion of the theology propounding sacred mountains and paradises.

Earthly Buddhist Landscapes

Among many variants, the earthly landscapes of Buddhism include (1) the locations of activities of the historical Buddha and King Asoka across north India – many of which have become destinations of pilgrimage (Finegan 1952; Law 1932), and (2) the historical distribution of early Buddhist establishments and institutions as the religion took root in South Asia and then expanded along three routes: Mahayana Buddhism west into Afghanistan and then northeast into China, Korea and Japan; Theravada Buddhism east into Southeast Asia; and then Esoteric (Tantric) Buddhism northeast into China, Japan, Tibet, and Mongolia (cf. Zürcher 1962; 1972).

Buddhist landscapes date from the lifetime of the historic Buddha, Siddhartha Gautama or Sakyamuni ("Sage of the Shaka clan") as he was often called, in the mid-sixth century BC (see Barnes 1995 and Bechert and Gombrich 1984 for background). After Sakyamuni's death, several generations of his disciples lived as itinerant beggars or hermits while teaching the Buddha's doctrines. Finally in the third century BC, monks began to congregate into permanent monasteries established through the donations of lay people, both rich and poor, who intended through such donations to improve their *karma*. Between the third century BC and third century AD, Buddhism was patronized by powerful kings and wealthy merchants, resulting in monumental reliquaries (*stupa*), worship halls (*chaitya*) and monasteries (*vihara*) being built across the Buddhist homeland of the Indian sub-continent (Chakrabarti 1995). Brick or brick-and-stone structures became the monastic architecture of the north – often located in or near contemporary cities. In south India, the hermit tradition influenced the choice of siting of the monasteries in remote locations of intense natural beauty, where temple plans were carved out as caves in huge ranges of natural cliffs. The famous sites of Ajanta and Ellora, in the western Deccan, can still be visited today to experience the majestic rock faces into which whole worship halls and temple complexes have been cut.

It is important to note that the early rock-cut monasteries of India are devoid of any sculptures of the Buddha himself, since the sculptural tradition did not develop until later and in an area outside India. Sculptural representations of the Buddha were a product of one of the mature sects of Buddhism, Mahayana, being transmitted from India into the western regions of modern Afghanistan, Pakistan and Uzbekistan. These areas were at the time under the rule of the Hellenistic states of Bactria and subsequently the Kushan. When the religion met with the Hellenistic tradition of statuesque representation, the result was the Buddha himself depicted in the full iconography of contemporary Hellenism, including classical Greek facial structure and garments of draped cloth. Such sculptures and statues were then reproduced in sizes ranging from the miniature to the monumental all across Eurasia to the east in conjunction with the spread of Buddhism from Central Asia through China to Korea and Japan. The other major sect of Buddhism, Theravada, which is distributed mainly throughout

Southeast Asia, also eventually adopted the sculptural tradition in the Medieval period. In addition to the Buddha, *bodhisattva* figures are common in Mahayana Buddhist sculpture, representing individuals who have achieved enlightenment but have declined entering *nirvana* in favor of turning back to help fellow human beings on the path to enlightenment. *Bodhisattvas* can almost always be identified by the heavy jewelry they wear – in contrast to the Buddha, who has forsaken all worldly luxuries. Often we encounter a triad formation of the Buddha flanked by two *bodhisattva* as a sculptural focus for worship.

The early Buddhism of the Deccan and Afghanistan, then, bequeathed two traditions which have contributed to the establishment of historic Buddhist landscapes across northern Asia: those of rock carving and of iconic representation. These traditions have combined and splintered in interesting ways at different times and places to produce individual Buddhist landscapes with distinct characters, including the carving of cave temples, the sculpting of *buddha* images out of cliffs or incising of images on rock faces, and finally the sculpting of *buddha* images on boulders. The well-known cave sites of Dunhuang (Akiyama and Matsubara 1969; DRA 1981; Gray 1959; Mizuno 1950), Longmen and Yungang (Anonymous 1977; Juliano 1980; 1984) in China are in this tradition yet begin to show evidence of local accommodations (Ma 1995). At Dunhuang, the *buddha* sculptures occur inside the caves instead of outside on the rock cliffs, and they are not carved in rock but are modeled with mud plaster over wooden frames. Many of the cliff caves are faced with wooden temple architecture of traditional Chinese form. And further on in Korea, an artificial grotto was built at Sokkuram to house a *buddha* sculpture in an area where there were no natural caves or carveable rock cliffs (Harrell 1995). It is in this eastern area of the Manchurian basin and Korean peninsula that we also begin to see the shift in focus from the cave to the mountain as the favored locus for outdoor Buddhist sculpture, even though caves might continue to be used for meditation purposes, as shown in the story of the siting of Haitangshan, below.

Haitang Mountain Forest Park

Haitang Mountain near Fuxin, Liaoning province,[1] is a good example of the new practice of exhibiting Buddhist images on a mountainside instead of in a rock cliff cave site. Here, a mountainside full of boulder outcrops sports many which have been adorned with the carving of a *buddha*, *bodhisattva* or one of many other guardian warriors, deities etc.

The sculptures are adjuncts to a large temple site, now defunct, located on adjoining land; moreover, they sit in juxtaposition to natural rock formations that have been named for the images they conjure up: Coiled Dragon Rock, Toad Rock, Mountain Eagle Rock and Hat Rock. The legend of the founding of the adjacent Pu'an Temple early in the Qing period (AD 1644–1912) gives an insight into the selection criteria for its location (Lu and Luo n.d.: 10–11):[2]

> According to tradition, around the 12th year of Kangxi (1681) in the Qing Dynasty, E'erdemutu became the Prince of Zhasakeduoluodaerhan in Tumoteqi. In order to build the second largest temple in the area, he sent Damulin to the [Qing] capital and to Tibet to pay his respects to the emperor and high-ranking lamas. He took a memorial containing the choice of location for the temple and the specifications of the building. Later, an imperial edict specified that it should be built at a place with excellent *fengshui* with "two scenes and one object" whose names begin with the [sound] "A." The government of Tumoteqi received the order and began searching for a suitable spot in their area. ...
>
> One day the government sent men to the slopes of Lama Cave Mountain, and they prevented a farmer from going on his way to the mountain. The farmer asked to be allowed to pass so he could get to Abusigai (Mongolian for "Coffin Rock") to chop wood. ... The government men ... followed him to inspect the place. ... Reaching the southern slope, they saw a young man who pointed forward and said, "I want to go and dig for medicinal drugs near Abusilang (Mongolian for 'Lion Rock')." The government men followed where the young man had pointed and saw a large rock on the mountain slope which truly resembled a lion. Just as the government men reached the bottom of the mountain, they met a lama chanting sutras in front of a cave. They asked, "Is there an object here which begins with 'A'?" The lama pointed to the cave and said, "Inside there is an *alatanxiri* (Mongolian for 'gold table', in fact a stone table)." ... So they had found "two scenes and one object" beginning with "A." After the results of the government men finding a site was reported to the Qing court and Tibet, they approved the financing of the construction of the second largest temple in the district. ...

Other aspects of this story are extremely interesting. First, the original *lama* exploiting the "cave" at the site is said to have been a Mongolian who had followed the Qing army into Manchu territory when he was 13 years old. At age 50 he became a hermit monk and secluded himself in the mountain cave, which was only 1 *zhang* wide and 1 *zhang* deep (3.3 × 3.3 m). There he meditated and carried out the observances of Tantric Buddhism, which was then popular in both

Mongolia and Tibet. Thus, the presence of this tiny cave was the first determinant of the mountain being exploited for religious purposes. Secondly, if the focus on the three "A" names in the legend is taken as apocryphal, then perhaps a second factor – besides the cave – determining the siting of a large temple there was the presence of large boulders on the mountain suitable for sculpting. A third factor was the excellent siting of the area according to *fengshui* geomantic principles. Fourthly, it is notable that Haitangshan sits at the north end of the Yiwulü mountain range, one of the five sacred mountains in China as discussed below. As recorded in the *Fuxin County Gazetteer* in 1683 (Lu and Luo n.d.: 3), these factors encouraged a "living Buddha" to lead his followers to this location to begin construction of the Pu'an temple, affiliated to the Yellow Sect of Tibetan Tantric Buddhism.

Construction carried on for some 200 years until 1883, by which time there were several complexes of buildings on the slope and at the foot of the mountain. These included a Great Hall; the Faxiang temple for the study of Buddhist philosophical logic; the Micheng temple for the study of cultivating Tantric chanting of the True Word and Tantric sayings; the Shilun temple for the study of astronomy, calendrics and meteorology; a Living Buddha palace; a meditation hall; a white pagoda; and several other named temples. The complex extended over 4.7 ha with 26 large-scale buildings, 1,500 towers and halls, and 8 km of preaching paths; over 400 monks' quarters occupied another 5.3 ha. The population exceeded 1,600 people in the temple's heyday. Today, only the foundations of the temple complex remain.

In addition to the architectural constructions, the carving of images on the boulder outcrops was carried out over this time "through communal subscription as a way of showing the accumulation of virtue, belief in the Buddha and the carrying out of good works" (Lu and Luo n.d.: 3). The Haitang Mountain carvings range from 30 cm to 5 m in height and number more than 200 (see figure 5.2). Many are accompanied by inscriptions in the Mongolian, Manchu, and Tibetan languages. Several are colored in the Tantric tradition – not a common attribute of other rock art sites. Even after 200–300 years of open-air existence, the colors are bright, especially after rain. The carvings are distributed over the boulder faces wherever they can be squeezed in, sometimes with three or four abutting each other. The styles are mainly full frontal images, some executed in a soft, flowing style, others stiff and formal. New stone stairways and paths wind over the mountainside between the boulders to give good close-up views of each collection.

Namsan

"Southern Mountain" is a sacred mountain forming the southern border of the Kyongju Basin, the home of the archaic Silla state from
the third to tenth centuries. Its oval shape extends *c*.13.5 km (N–S) ×
3.25 km (E–W) – much larger than Haitangshan – and houses innu-
merable examples of monumental Buddhist sculpture (figure 5.3) and
former temple sites in 40 different mountain valleys (Hwang 1979;
MKY 1992; Whitfield 1993; Yun 1994). Like Haitangshan, Namsan
is a mountain of granite boulder outcrops affording few cave sites and
was thus exploited for its scattered stone boulders of limited surface
area. These determined the nature and style of Buddhist representations, and it is hypothesized here that they also acted as a major determinant (after water availability) as to exactly where in Namsan's
valleys temples would be built. A further consideration was the geomantic quality of the location: it is claimed that nearly all the temple
sites conform to standard Chinese principles of geomancy, having
ridges bordering their sides and two mountain peaks – a guardian
mountain and an opposing mountain – at opposite ends of the site
(Yun 1994: 42–3, 173). Often these considerations dictated that temples would be erected on architecturally unsuitable terrain: steep slopes

Figure 5.3 The *haut-relief* and *bas-relief* sculptures on the southern face of
Pulmu-sa Buddha Rock at Namsan (photo by author).

or very uneven ground. Thus, one of the most common archaeological features of this sacred mountain complex is the dry-stone walling of terraces built to provide level foundations for the wooden temple buildings perched on the slopes.

Some of these temples have remained active, such as Pori-sa, which has recently had a new Buddha Hall, Mountain Spirit Hall and Bell Pavilion built. But most are now archaeological sites whose terrace features can sometimes be related to names of temples existing in the historical literature. For buildings which did not require a terraced foundation, clues to their former existence are provided by surface scatters of ceramic roof tiles and/or pieces of brick. Stone pagodas and stone lanterns also dot the mountainsides, often tumbled over into their composite parts during the historic periods; some have been recently re-erected, either *in situ* or in the grounds of the nearby Kyongju National Museum. A total of 63 pagodas, 19 lanterns, and 113 temple sites are attributed to Namsan (Yun 1994: 410).

The main Buddhist use of Namsan dates from the sixth century AD, but it may have had some sacred functions prior to that date. One of its low foothills is called the *todang*, "a site where one gives offerings to the spirits who protect the village," and some scholars believe it was the locus of succession ceremonies for the polity called Saro, a chiefly forerunner of the great state of Silla (AD 300–935) (Yun 1994: 24). At other points on the mountain, shamanist rain dances are reported to have been conducted (1994: 326). Some of the valleys of Namsan house dolmen burials of the earlier Bronze Age (first millennium BC), and others are populated by rocks resembling animals and objects that could well have attracted spiritual devotion throughout the ages. Such figurative rocks abound particularly in the Yongjang valley, where they bear such names as Fierce Tiger, Lion, Big Bear, Old Man, Boar, Cat, Python and the natural outcome of all these beings, Dung Rock. Recall that the existence of suggestively shaped rocks on Haitangshan was, as noted above, one of the legendary causes of choosing it for a temple site; the same propensity might have operated on Namsan as well. The transformation of Namsan into a sacred Buddhist mountain was achieved through the belief of the new Silla converts that this mountain was the home of many *buddhas* and *bodhisattvas* who had descended from heaven to reside in the rocks, the trees and the mountain itself (1994: 20, 261).

This *buddha* homeland was tangibly manifested in the many *buddha* images found on Namsan: 38 statues and at least 50 rock carvings (see figure 5.3). There are three major if overlapping categories of representations: (1) independent stone statues of *buddhas*, sculpted in standing

Figure 5.4 Diagram of the paradise of Sakyamuni, with Mt Sumeru rising up through the lower corners of the picture, the levels of existence keyed to its slopes, and entryways from the multiple worlds below with their rings of seas and central pillar of their own Mt Sumeru (after Ishida 1987: fig. 17).

or sitting postures; (2) high- and low-relief carvings on granite boulders; and (3) intaglio incising of figures on the boulder faces. Some of the more interesting overlaps are a large *buddha* figure 8.6 m high at Chebiwon, incised on the surface of a tall granite outcrop with its head formed by an independent small boulder sitting on the top of the outcrop and carved in the round; a *buddha* figure on Sangsa Rock, carved in high relief for the head but continued below in intaglio; and niches such as at Puch'o valley, carved into the boulders leaving *haut-relief* statues in their hollows.

The largest boulder is Buddha Rock in T'ap valley; its surface measurements are 5.7 m wide × 9 m high on the north face, a narrow west face, 2.7 m high × 6 m wide on the south face, and 10 m high × 13 m wide on the eastern face. Each face has several carved images drawn from the Buddhist Pure Lands of the Four Directions (see below), but they form neither coherent scenes in the sense of separate landscapes nor stories with integral storylines. They are not meant to be fully representational but objects of worship for use in transcending reality. Such carvings occur on the rocks where the surfaces are most amenable; they include multi-story pagodas, lion figures, celestial maidens, and many *buddhas* and their *bodhisattvas*. Most are carved in low relief, but the southern face is hollowed out to form a shallow niche in which a triad arrangement is depicted in higher relief. In front of the southern face stands an independent stone *buddha* statue 2.2 m tall carved in two parts: the square low pedestal and feet, and the body from the ankles up. The majority of sculptures and carvings on Namsan were made between the seventh and ninth centuries, and an evolution in style can be seen, from the stiff folds of Three Kingdoms–Six Dynasties style (AD 220–581) to the soft drapery of the Tang dynasty (AD 618–907), as these modes of depiction were diffused from China.

The uses of Namsan in the heyday of Buddhism were quite diverse, as revealed by the histories recorded in the *Samguk Sagi* (written in 1145; Kim 1983) and *Samguk Yusa* chronicles (compiled by Ilyon between 1274 and 1308; Ha and Mintz 1972). The carvings and sculptures as well as the temples may have been frequented by travelers on the road south from the Silla capital to the coast, with devotional offerings being made for safe journeys. Some temples were patronized by aristocrats seeking cures for chronic illnesses, and others hosted devotees praying for the ruler's health and for peace and prosperity. Still others, or just the *buddha* images themselves, were founded by kings and nobles in thanks for, or to ensure, good fortune or as an apology to the great deity. The Ch'ilburam hermitage was sponsored and managed by the state, while some small temples were merely the structures of hermit monks devoted to isolated meditation. Ch'onnyong-sa had the distinction of being visited by a Tang Chinese envoy (Yun 1994: 183). However, all the temples on Namsan were overshadowed by the great temple of Hwangnyong-sa, built directly on the Kyongju plains within the gridded capital city. As the main state temple, Hwangnyong-sa was the most politically important Silla temple, but Namsan was the source of spiritual solace and support for both the people and the state.

In order to understand this shift in focus from cave and rock cliff to the mountainside, it is necessary to examine the theological constructions of Buddhist landscapes and their interactions with local Chinese forms of thought at the time Buddhism was introduced in the Han Dynasty (206 BC–AD 220). Thus, considerable space below will be devoted to the different branches of Buddhism and how they conceived the present world in relation to heavens and hells. It is my hypothesis that these philosophical systems contributed greatly to this major shift in the form of iconic display in the later and eastern areas of Buddhism.

Other-worldly Buddhist Landscapes

In addition to the historical landscapes such as Haitangshan and Namsan produced by Buddhist activity on this earth of ours, there are many Buddhist landscapes of the mind that have no objective reality except in the artistic products of different sects. Each major branch of Buddhism has a cosmological system and traditional means of describing or illustrating the topography of the cosmos. Each of these will be described in turn, and then the traditional Chinese attitude to mountains will be examined before we conclude with an integrated view of the relative importance of caves and mountains in Buddhist landscapes.

Theravada Buddhism

Buddhist cosmography according to the earliest form of Buddhism is extremely complex. As described by Haldar (1977, condensed here from pp. 1–15), the universe is composed of countless world-systems grouped into three kinds of cosmos, respectively containing one thousand, one million, and one billion world-systems. In addition, there are three kinds of fields associated with the Buddha: the field of his birth (entailing ten thousand world-systems), the field of his authority (comprising the one billion world-systems of the large cosmos), and the field of his sphere (unlimited in size). Each of these world-systems has a sun, moon, nine planets, and a multitude of stars; and each world-system center is occupied by the mountain known as Meru, Sumeru, Sineru or numerous other names (Werner 1932: 315). This cosmic, central mountain is encircled by seven ranges of mountains, which decrease in height by half in each succeeding peripheral ring (figure 5.4). Between every two ranges lies an ocean where the Nagas (snake-like spirits) live; and the innermost ocean between the central mountain and first mountain range hosts four continents, each surrounded by five hundred smaller islands. In this world-system of ours, one of those four continents includes India, where *buddhas* and righteous rulers are born.

From the summit of Mt Sumeru to under its base, there are 31 levels of existence ranked from bottom to top according to merit of their inhabitants; the realm of human beings is fifth from the bottom, while the top four are spheres of conception of infinite space, infinite consciousness, nothingness, and neither consciousness nor unconsciousness. The intermediary levels are heavens of various classes of gods and supreme or beautiful beings, each of which has its own geography, populace, and pantheon. The objective of rebirth, of course, is to work one's way up through these levels of existence until finally one has such great merit as to escape rebirth itself and attain *nirvana*. Within the world-systems, not only are living beings subject to the cycle of birth and death, with *karma* determining in which level of existence rebirth takes place; the whole universe is cyclically destroyed and re-created. The forces of destruction are the familiar earthly ones: fire, water, and wind.

This description of Buddhist worlds is a fractal-like conception of never-ending compartmentalization of variations on the known world. Many features, such as Mt Sumeru itself, can be seen in the previous Hindu cosmology (Finegan 1952: 168–9; Werner 1932: 315), and Mt Sumeru was again transferred on to other religions like Jainism at a later date (Finegan 1952: 203). Werner states that it "would seem to be some mountain north of the Himalayas" (Werner 1932: 315), and some think it appears in Chinese mythology as Mt Kunlun – a cosmic mountain west of China on which dwells the Queen Mother of the West (Munakata 1991: 33). Needless to say, both the Himalayas and the real Kunlun range in western China are very good role models for mountains which pierce the heavens, provide the route of communication between heaven and earth, and support the home of the gods.

Our concern here is primarily with the role of the sacred mountain and how it was made manifest on earth. Theravada Buddhism gives little scope for visual illustration, since the emphasis is upon the monastic lifestyle and individual enlightenment of monks through good deeds and meditation. The other two forms of Buddhism which developed subsequently put much more attention on the salvation of the masses whether they follow an ascetic lifestyle or not. In both Mahayana Buddhism and Esoteric or Tantric Buddhism, visual aids for helping the masses achieve enlightenment led to two-dimensional representations of Buddhist worlds. These were very different between the Mahayana and Tantric traditions, meriting some basic discussion before returning to sacred mountains.

Mahayana Buddhism

The northern Mahayana branch of Buddhism envisioned many different *buddhas* and *bodhisattvas*, each reigning over its own paradise. These *buddhas* and future *buddhas* "could bring believers to be reborn in their

Buddha-lands and guide them thus to Awakening" (Ishida 1987: 183). The most popular, Amida, presides over the Land of Pure Beryl or Lapis Lazuli in the west. The historic Buddha himself, Sakyamuni, presides over "Vulture's Peak near Rajagrha in Magadha, the imaginary site of the preaching of the Lotus Sutra" (Okazaki 1977: 29). Maitreya, *buddha* of the future, presides over Tusita heaven; and Avalokitesvara, the *bodhisattva* of compassion (Chinese: Kwanyin; Japanese: Kannon), reigns over Mt Potalaka in the southern seas, a paradise on earth. Finally, Mount Sumeru, "the mythical 'world mountain' that rises through the center of the Buddhist universe," supported the heaven of 33 other gods on its summit (ten Grotenhuis 1977: 187). Jizo (Sanskrit: Ksitigarbha) is a *bodhisattva* associated with this heaven of 33 gods. Other lesser deities also had their own paradises, all of which are described in the *sutras* of Mahayana Buddhism.

The Western Paradise is described in the smaller Sukhavativyuha *sutra* from India as modeled on all good things in the earthly world (Okazaki 1977: 15):

> the gorgeous palaces, parks, and gardens; the gem trees made of gold, silver, crystal, and coral; the fragrant flowers and luscious fruits; the rivers and lotus lakes with their perfumed water that is either hot or cold for bathing as desired; the delightful, soothing sounds of birds and angelic singers.

Illustrations of these lands occur in various forms. Visions-of-Paradise paintings provided visual access for believers who couldn't follow the complex and technical *sutras*. The Dunhuang Caves in northwestern China were filled with frescoes which pictured the Pure Land paradises (Whitfield 1995). Other representations of the *buddha* paradises exist as *mandalas*, which owe their more geometric visual organization to the esoteric Buddhist sects. In Japan, a medieval tradition of painting focused on the descent of Amida to welcome believers into the Western Paradise (Okazaki 1977). In such paintings, the descent and return of Amida are assisted by clouds, often accompanied by a setting sun, and the view of the earth is from above — all of which suggest that the Western Paradise is located somewhere in the heavens, particularly in the westerly direction. A selection of these paintings show a path between earth and the Pure Lands with rivers of anger and greed each flowing alongside. Thus devotees on the path were in danger of being caught in the flow and carried back to their starting point on earth.

Judging from these various examples, earthly imagery supplied the models for envisioning paradise, and the same applied to the various Buddhist hells. Pure Land Buddhism taught that if one did not enter paradise, one was condemned to rebirth in the "Six Realms," again a fractal-type conception of hellish subdivisions of existence – for example, the "sixteen subhells within the great hell of screams" (Okazaki 1977: 177). In paintings depicting these hells, not only was earthly topography employed, but seasonal referents such as cherry blossoms or maple leaves indicated the fragility, transience, and never-ending cycle of life (Okazaki 1977: 172–3).

Tantric Buddhism

In contrast to these approachable pictures of paradises whose architecture, gardens, and ponds resemble those of the known world, the Buddhist universe of the esoteric sects is much more abstract, less representational, and more cosmographical. For example, the Japanese Shingon form of esoteric Buddhism, as described by Saunders (1977: 19–21), has as its basis the Mandalas of the Two Worlds: the Womb Mandala ("innate reason") and the Diamond Mandala ("knowledge"). These mandalas have at their center the solar deity Vairocana, and they represent the entire universe while encompassing the six natural elements: earth, fire, water, air, and ether (all belonging to "innate reason"), and conscience (belonging to "knowledge"). However, in their graphic form, Two World Mandalas are usually represented as a hierarchy of deities who are organized into "courts" in the four directions around the "central world of enlightenment," with "east" and "west" clearly specified. The courts of the Womb World are organized as strips around the center with only the outer border including referents to the real world in the form of animals, constellations, and buildings. The courts of the Diamond World are organized as nine cells with specific deities occupying the four directions.

Thus the esoteric mandalas show a "universe" or "world" that is far less substantive than their constituent "elements" would lead us to believe. Instead, they seem to operate with prime reference to the cosmos – with directionality, framework, and stellar symbols being more common than earthly topographic features such as mountains, rivers, and oceans. The one exception to this is that when the historical Buddha, Sakyamuni, is depicted, he is often shown "seated on a golden disk on the peak of Mount Sumeru, the cosmic, axial mountain"

(Ishida 1987: 54, 63). The tantric mandalas are a "place" only in the sense that the picture itself is a place for the eyes to rest while contemplating the *buddha*-nature and searching for enlightenment. They are not maps to a specific locus functioning as a paradise or heaven, as we find in Amida Buddhism or in Theravada cosmology.

Chinese Sacred Mountains

The concept of the "sacred mountain" in China was not attributable to Buddhism alone but was well developed long before Buddhist influence, in the first millennium BC. The development of the sacred mountain in Chinese art is discussed thoroughly by Munakata, who states that from the Zhou period (*c*. eleventh century through 221 BC) onwards Chinese kings and emperors offered prayers to mountains to ensure the prosperity of the state – based on the idea that mountains, as the source of rivers and the clouds above them, provided the water necessary for crops to grow (Munakata 1991: 2, 4). The *Zhou Li* (written in the Warring States period, 403–221 BC) lists Five Sacred Mountains and Four Garrison Mountains of particular significance in the imperial rites. One function of the Five Sacred Mountains was to "act collectively or individually as intermediaries between earth and heaven, where the Supreme Heavenly Sovereign resided" (1991: 4). In later thought, they were conceived of as the pillars which connected the celestial dome of Heaven with earth, and mountains in general were considered to provide the route of passage for the soul after death.

Not included among these sacred mountains, however, is Mt Kunlun – the mythological home of the Queen Mother of the West; the concepts of the mountain and the goddess were apparently developed independently but became associated with each other in the first century BC. Munakata is of the opinion that this is an entirely fictional or imaginary mountain that evolved from a shamanistic trip between heaven and earth, but he notes that others have tried to equate it with Mt Sumeru, the cosmic mountain of Buddhism (Munakata 1991: 10–11). The *Huai Nan Zi* (compiled in the second century BC) describes Mt Kunlun as having several layers of peaks: Kunlun itself, "Cool Breeze," "Hanging Garden," and "Upper Heaven" (1991: 80; cf. also Major 1973); these are reminiscent of the many "levels of existence" of Mt Sumeru.

In Early Han times (*c*. mid-second century BC), a new item of material culture made its appearance: a cast bronze incense burner consisting of a mountain-shaped lid covering a pedestaled bowl base (figure 5.5).

Figure 5.5 Two bronze mountain-lid censers, the left with a highly sculpted mountainside and the right standing in a basin to be filled with water (after Erickson 1989: 152, 176).

The censer lids were often deeply sculpted with valleys and peaks, and sometimes they bore images of wild animals in early versions – with men and "immortals" added to later versions under the influence of Taoism. Erickson (1989: 97) believes the mountain shape is not strictly representational but refers to one or any of the Five Sacred Mountains or the Taoist "mountainous Isles of the Immortals."

It is interesting to note that many pedestaled mountain censers were designed to stand in a basin filled with water, which Munakata suggests represented the "life-supporting water flowing from the sacred mountain" (1991: 73) and Erickson (1989: 92) reports as equivalent to the Taoist barrier which must be crossed to achieve immortality. However, the similarity of arrangement with the primary location of the Buddhist Mt Sumeru encircled by the first of seven oceans is uncanny. Given the timing of this object's development and the advent of Mt Kunlun into the repertoire – coinciding very closely to Han Wudi's expansion to the northwest, possibly encountering South Asian philosophies en route – it is difficult to ignore possible cross-fertilization in cosmological thinking between the two philosophical systems. This is especially the case since the mountain censer appeared in Early Han without precedent but with full-blown iconography (Erickson 1989: 122). By Tang times, the censer had entered Buddhist usage but had lost the imagery of the mountain, becoming instead more associated with the lotus bud and acting as a reliquary (1989: 65).

To Taoists, mountains were "havens for those who sought to attain supernatural powers or spiritual enlightenment," and they eventually became "associated ... with the theological concept of the realms of the immortals" (Munakata 1991: 2). Munakata notes that "individual seekers of immortality started to visit mountains in order to discipline themselves; to receive divine revelations and attain immortality, or at least certain magical powers; and, in some cases, to prepare elixir by their own hands" (1991: 34). Chinese Buddhists followed this practice; one monk, Huiyuan (AD 334–416), built a temple at sacred Mt Lu. "His Buddhism, which sought cosmic revelation in the mountains, is sometimes called 'landscape Buddhism'" (1991: 118). The Guoqing Temple, headquarters of the Tientai (Japanese: Tendai) sect, was built in AD 598 at sacred Mt Tientai, a mountain already important in Taoism and which subsequently became known as a Buddhist mountain (1991: 122).

During the 3 Kingdoms–6 Dynasties period (AD 220–581), lay people began making trips to mountains for their own spiritual renewal (1991: 112); and by Tang times, the mountains had became destinations of mass pilgrimage. Rather than the fearful, wild, and unknown places of yore, they became familiar places for monks and lay people alike. Many of these sacred mountains and their temples came to be subjects of Chinese landscape painting in the thirteenth to sixteenth centuries; but unlike mandalas and other Buddhist paintings, these paintings were not in and of themselves religious objects.

Caves and Mountains as Buddhist Landscape Anchors

Caves were important to early Buddhists because the historical Buddha is said to have sequestered himself in one for meditation and reflection (Finegan 1952: 289). This became a pattern in the hermit monk tradition that is still alive in some Buddhist areas such as Sri Lanka (cf. Coningham 1995). The monks who established the Ajanta and Ellora cave temples were elaborating on this tradition by carving their own caves in a place of intense natural beauty and rock cliff majesty. This tradition was continued at Bamiyan with the addition of iconic sculpture, and at Dunhuang, Longmen, Yungang, and many other rock cliff sites in China. Yet Buddhists were not the only ones to use caves for ritual purposes in China. Taoists often escaped to mountain caves in order to mix their elixirs for immortality. Chinese Buddhists followed in their footsteps.

The shift from rock cliff caves to mountain caves was the first step in re-addressing earthly Buddhist landscapes from cliff sites to mountainsides. Once the mountains themselves became destinations for ritual activities, their innate resources began to be exploited in traditional manner. In fact, certain mountains may have been sought out for their abundance of boulder outcrops in order to carry out the iconic sculpture that had become so important for worship purposes. More often granite than other materials, these boulders proved much more difficult to sculpt, and their limited size constrained the types of art that could be represented. Few were large enough to be hollowed out to provide a worship hall; a deep niche containing a *buddha* figure was the maximum possible. Most boulders, therefore, sported panels carved in low or high relief – like those found at Haitangshan, and a few boulders were in themselves shaped into three-quarter round sculptures or independent statues – for example, at Namsan.

The resulting effect of a mountainside full of boulder sculptures is virtually a life-size replication of the imagery on a mountain censer: hills and valleys studded with images – but rather than men and immortals, these images were now *buddhas* and *bodhisattvas* among which humans could wander, pay obeisance and work towards the release from the cycle of life. One could also argue that the mountains themselves became the earthly representatives of Mt Sumeru, providing the potential of working one's way up through the levels of existence to the summit and thus hoping to gain entrance to the heaven of the gods.

The step from boulder sculpture gardens as at Haitangshan to the independent occurrence of *buddha* and *bodhisattva* sculptures in the secular landscape is again a short step. Throughout present-day Mongolia and northern China, one might happen upon a boulder outcrop and be confronted with a brightly painted *buddha* carving. Again, along the roadside in Japan, sculptures of Jizo *bodhisattvas* stand as saviors to passing travelers and memorials to traffic deaths. These represent the final stage in the evolution of the Buddhist landscape and the intrusion of sacred elements into the every-day scenery. The movement of Buddhist imagery from the mountains back into the urban setting completes the logical utilization of materials (moveable stone) and exploits to the fullest the potential power of Buddhist images as they are visualized not just by the pious in select settings but by as many lay persons as pass through their sphere. In so doing, they make every landscape of their occurrence a Buddhist landscape, facilitating a metaphysical awareness as persons go about their daily business.

NOTES

1 Information about this site is all drawn from the site leaflet in Chinese (Lu and Luo n.d.), translated by Sarah Dauncey into English.
2 Translated by Sarah Dauncey, with minor modification by the present author.

REFERENCES

Akiyama, T., and Matsubara, S. 1969: *Arts of China: Buddhist Cave Temples, New Researches*. Tokyo: Kondansha International.

Anonymous 1977: *The Yunkang Caves*. Beijing: Cultural Relics (in Chinese).

Barnes, G. L. (ed.) 1995: Buddhist Archaeology. *World Archaeology*, 27 (2, whole issue).

Barnes, G. L. 1995: An introduction to Buddhist archaeology. *World Archaeology*, 27, 165–84.

Bechert, H., and Gombrich, R. 1984: *The World of Buddhism*. London: Thames and Hudson.

Chakrabarti, D. K. 1995: Buddhist sites across South Asia as influenced by political and economic forces. *World Archaeology*, 27, 185–202.

Coningham, R. A. E. 1995: Monks, caves and kings: a reassessment of the nature of early Buddhism in Sri Lanka. *World Archaeology*, 27, 222–42.

DRA (Dunhuang Research Academy) 1981: *The Art Treasures of Dunhuang*. Hong Kong, New York: Joint Publishing Co. and Lee Publishing Group.

Erickson, S. N. 1989: *Boshanlu* mountain censers: mountains and immortality in the Western Han period. PhD dissertation, University of Minnesota.

Finegan, J. 1952: *The Archeology of World Religions*. Princeton: Princeton University Press.

Governor General of Chosen 1939: *Buddhist Relics in the Region South of Keishu*, Chosen Hobutsu Koseki Zuroku 2. Keishu: Chosen Sotokufu (in Japanese).

Gray, B. 1959: *Buddhist Cave Paintings at Tun-Huang*. London: Faber and Faber.

Ha, T. H., and Mintz, G. 1972: *Samguk Yusa: Legends and History of the Three Kingdoms of Ancient Korea*. Seoul: Yonsei University Press.

Haldar, J. R. 1977: *Early Buddhist Mythology*. New Delhi: Manohar.

Harrell, M. 1995: Sokkuram: Buddhist monument and political statement in Korea. *World Archaeology*, 27, 318–35.

Higuchi, T., with Barnes, G. L. 1995: Bamiyan: Buddhist cave temples in Afghanistan. *World Archaeology*, 27, 282–302.

Hwang, S. 1979: *Korean Buddhist Art: Hanguk oe Mi*, vol. 10. Seoul: Chung'ang Ilbo and Dongyang Broadcasting (in Korean).

Ishida, H. 1987: *Esoteric Buddhist Painting*. Tokyo: Kodanasha International.

Juliano, A. L. 1980: Buddhist in China. *Archaeology*, 33 (3), 23–30.

Juliano, A. L. 1984: New discoveries at the Yungang Caves. In N. S. Steinhardt, X. Fu, E. Glahn, R. L. Thorp and A. L. Juliano, *Chinese Traditional Architecture*, New York: China Institute in America, 79–90.

Kim, P. 1983: *History of the Three Kingdoms*, 2 vols. Seoul: Eul-yoo (in Korean and Chinese).

Klimberg-Salter, D. 1989: *The Kingdom of Bamiyan: Buddhist Art and Culture of the Hindu Kush*. Naples, Rome: Istituto Universitario Orientale and Istituto Italiano per il Medio ed Estremo Oriente.

Law, B. C. 1932: *Geography of Early Buddhism*. London: Kegan Paul, Trench, Trubner.

Lu, Z., and Luo, X. n.d.: *Tibetan Buddhist Art Treasures and the Cliff Statues of Haitang Mountain*, Pamphlet. Liaoning: Fuxin Mongolian Autonomous District Publishing Bureau (in Chinese). Translation into English by Sarah Dauncey, available at University of Durham Library.

Ma, S. 1995: Buddhist cave-temples and the Cao family at Mogao Ku, Dunhuang. *World Archaeology*, 27, 303–17.

Major, J. 1973: Topography and cosmology in early Han thought: chapter four of the Huai-nan-tzu. PhD dissertation, Harvard University. [This dissertation was unavailable to the present author but is included here for completeness' sake.]

Mizuno, S. 1950: Archaeological survey of the Tun-kang grottoes. *Archives of the Chinese Art Society of America*, 4, 39–60.

MKY. 1992: *Kyongju Namsan-oe pulkyo yujok* [Buddhist sites of Namsan, Kyongju]. Seoul: Munhwajae Kwalliguk Yonguso (MKY) (in Korean).

Munakata, K. 1991: *Sacred Mountains in Chinese Art*. Urbana: University of Illinois Press.

Okazaki, J. 1977: *Pure Land Buddhist Painting*, Japan Arts Library. Tokyo: Kodansha International and Shibundo.

Saunders, E. D. 1977 [1964]: *Buddhism in Japan, with an Outline of its Origins in India*, Reprint. Philadelphia: University of Pennsylvania Press.

ten Grotenhuis, E. 1977: Introduction; Glossary. In J. Okazaki (ed.), *Pure Land Buddhist Painting*, Japan Arts Library, Tokyo: Kodansha International and Shibundo, 13–28, 183–8.

Werner, E. C. T. 1932: *A Dictionary of Chinese Mythology*. Shanghai: Kelly and Walsh.

Whitfield, R. 1993: The monuments of Kyongju Namsan. *Transactions of the Oriental Ceramic Society*, 58, 89–92.

Whitfield, R. 1995: *Dunhuang: Caves of the Singing Sands: Buddhist Art from the Silk Road*. London: Textile and Art Publications.

Yun, K. 1994: *Namsan: Discovering the Ancient Wonder of Kyongju's Mt Namsan*. Seoul: Buddha Land.

Zürcher, E. 1962: *Buddhism: Its Origin and Spread in Words, Maps and Pictures*. London: Routledge and Kegan Paul.

Zürcher, E. 1972: *The Buddhist Conquest of China*, Reprint, with additions and corrections. Leiden: Brill.

6

Mountains, Caves, Water: Ideational Landscapes of the Ancient Maya

James E. Brady and Wendy Ashmore

Introduction

For the Maya, landscape is firmly linked to powerful supernatural domains. The night sky is a dynamic map of events in the mythic realm of creation, and trees, birds, and other wildlife are key players in the retelling of these events. It is the terrestrial landscape, however, that frames and shapes the world's re-creation on literally a daily basis. Many scholars have explored elements of the Maya landscape, their symbolism and their relation to ancient art, architecture, and society. In this chapter, we focus on mountains, caves, and water as features which jointly orient and actively order the Maya world (figure 6.1). Although we concentrate on the lowland Maya of the Classic period (AD 250–900), we draw relevant material from other locales, periods, and peoples of Mesoamerica. Highlighting recent field research on Maya caves, especially the Petexbatún Regional Cave Survey, we note growing recognition of the strength, antiquity, pervasiveness, and organizing role of material reference to this conceptual complex.

Landscapes and Maya Archaeology

Studies of human spatial orders have burgeoned dramatically in recent years, and the literature on "space and place" is now enormous, across many disciplines (e.g., Lawrence and Low 1990). Topographic features anchor memory (e.g., Basso 1996; Schama 1995); key geographic elements and assemblages, whether actual, or idealized in imagination, provide models for architectural mimicry (e.g., Miller 1986: 84; Tuan 1977). "Landscape," loosely considered as the environs perceived by

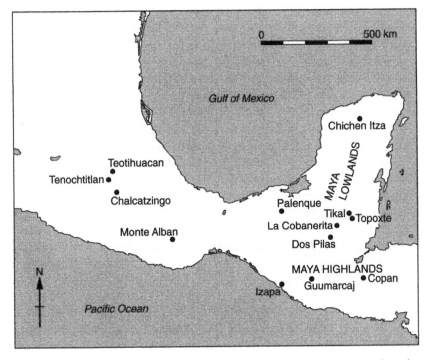

Figure 6.1 Map of the Maya area, showing sites and localities noted in the text.

particular individuals or groups, is contingent on specific experience (e.g., Bender 1992; Fowler 1995). In Bernard Knapp's words, landscape

> is not to be viewed as a ready-made, naturally given substrate on which a cultural design or mental template is imposed. It is never "complete," nor is it "built" or "unbuilt"; rather it is a "social expression," perpetually under construction.
>
> (1997: 17)

Maya archaeologists have begun to recognize more explicitly the contingency, temporality, and fluidity in ancient landscapes, and to acknowledge more effectively that our landscape is not necessarily that of the Maya (e.g., Stuart and Houston 1994). Even now, however, investigation tends to objectify the whole and to decouple the forms of Maya settlement from their surroundings, often treating buildings, plazas, and whole sites as if perched statically on a physiographic stand from which they were largely distinct. For the Maya, however, as for other peoples, architecture and engineering have frequently mimicked and accentuated but seldom, if ever, replaced the characteristically Maya natural world (e.g., Andrews 1975; Stone 1992; Tuan 1977). As argued below, we view these as positions on a conceptual continuum, rather than disjunctive categories. Moreover, built and unbuilt – constructed and conceptualized – Maya landscapes are far from passive arenas or stage sets; then as now, they have played tangibly active roles in constant creation and shaping of Maya life.

We focus here on the complex of mountains, caves, and water in ancient Maya and Mesoamerican society, and on the roles these played in localized strategies for living. Recognizing continuities between built and unbuilt landscapes, we argue that the whole is a nearly seamless extension of world view, manifest in domestic, civic, and wider spatial scales (e.g., Hanks 1990; Stone 1992; Vogt 1981). In living with the land, Maya and neighboring peoples continually re-create and renew the world; their material legacy bears witness to repeated or recrafted strategies for acknowledging the earth, for honoring and harnessing its vital forces.

Modern Maya Landscape Concepts

Like other Mesoamerican peoples, the Maya today hold the earth to be sacred and animate, often personified as an "Earth Lord." The deity is known to the Q'eqchi' Maya as the *Tzuultaq'a*, which means "hill-valley," an expression found in many other Maya languages as well (e.g., Tedlock 1992). Although the term *tzuultaq'a* can serve as a simple geographical referent in everyday speech, the concept retains strong supernatural connotations. Moreover, this focus on Earth seems to be a generalized Mesoamerican, even pan-American, phenomenon (e.g., Miller 1992: 161; compare van de Guchte, this volume).

Mountains and caves figure prominently in ethnographic accounts (e.g., Vogt 1981). Mountains are thought to be hollow, and caves are their entries. The "heart of the mountain" is said variously to contain the home of the Earth Lord, the corrals where he keeps wild animals, or repositories of valued resources, including maize, treasure, and – significantly – water. Among the Q'eqchi' Maya, each of 13 sacred mountains is home to an important Tzuultaq'a, and for each, a cave is the most honored and appropriate location for rites to this lord. Indeed, while the Q'eqchi' speak of going to Xucaneb, the most sacred mountain, their actual destination is the cave. The same is true for Tzotzil Zinacantan, where "crosses" mark the portal, even without direct link to an actual cave (Vogt 1981). Artificial caves may equally be the destination of pilgrimage, as indicated by the reported discovery of the "Cross of the Black Christ" at Esquipulas in an artificial cave (Brady and Veni 1992), or the appearance of Chan Kom's patron saint in an abandoned *sascab* (limestone) mine (Redfield and Villa Rojas 1962: 109). Thus it appears that mountains and caves are linked in indigenous thought; taken together, they epitomize the earth and its powers, and their existence is sufficiently critical that artificial features may substitute for natural ones to complete the landscape whole.

"Cave" here glosses the Maya word, *c'en*, which designates a hole or a cavity penetrating the earth. What lies beyond the break is the Underworld, a realm inhabited by powerful supernaturals. As mouths of the Earth Lord and portals to the Underworld, caves have rich symbolic significance (e.g., Bassie-Sweet 1991; 1996; Bonor 1989). Not surprisingly, their depiction in public art throughout Mesoamerica endows authority, largely shamanic, on individuals framed by the mouth of a cave (e.g., Brady 1989; Grove and Gillespie 1984; Stone 1995).

The Maya Underworld is characterized as watery, which is also a physical attribute of limestone caves. That is, in karst environments like that of most of the Maya lowlands, caves are geological conduits for movement of ground water. Caves are created and scoured by moving water; seepage then constructs their internal architecture, the stalactites, stalagmites, and related formations known collectively as speleothems (Bassie-Sweet 1991; Brady, Scott, Neff, and Glascock 1997; Heyden 1981: 27–8). *Cenotes* appear when surface bedrock collapses, exposing the subterranean water table. Within caves, water may form pools, often of great majesty, as well as rivers and streams which vary seasonally in water volume and velocity. Water in caves is considered ritually pure, and is designated by its own name, *zuhuy ha* (e.g., Thompson 1975: xv–xxii). Caves thus physically incorporate water and the earth's interior in a complex of powerful animate forces.

A cave may also serve as *axis mundi*, as when the center of a Maya village is marked by a cave or *cenote* (Redfield and Villa Rojas 1962: 114; compare Eliade 1979: 335). In an individual house, the "center" may be marked as a small pit in the floor (Vogt 1976). "Center," in turn, is cross-culturally the place of human creation, and is here consistent with Native American myths tracing origins to emergence from beneath the earth's surface, commonly from a seven-chambered cavern (e.g., Heyden 1981). Modern Tzeltal Maya communities take their names from particular nearby caves, and contemporary Tzotzil Maya settlements cluster around water holes or caves from which inhabitants take their surnames (e.g., Vogt 1976: 25). In this way, caves, pits, and water holes are conceptual counterparts, linking the living community simultaneously with ancestors and with the earth.

Mountains, caves, and bodies of water are today important foci for ceremonies, settlement and social organization. Comparable observances were documented by the Spanish early in the conquest period (García-Zambrano 1994). Not surprisingly, such focus seems detectable much earlier, as well, in the archaeologically tangible remains of ritual and in the location and orientation of architecture. Indeed, material reference to an ideational landscape is inferred in a range of settings, from mundane domestic contexts through civic and wider arenas. In the case study that follows, we show how situating architecture within an ideational landscape illuminates the observed form of one particular Maya site, Dos Pilas, offering insights into a range of ancient behavioral strategies and meanings there. We then place the phenomena observed at Dos Pilas in larger cultural and interpretive contexts.

Maya Landscapes at Dos Pilas

The Petexbatún Regional Cave Survey was the first archaeological attempt to investigate specifically and systematically the role of caves in the ancient Maya ideational landscape (e.g., Brady 1991; 1997; Brady and Rodas 1992; Brady, Scott, Cobb et al. 1997). As a subproject of Vanderbilt University's Petexbatún Regional Archaeological Project (Demarest 1997), the four-year cave survey documented some three dozen caves, the longest – the Cueva de Sangre – explored for 3.5 km. Collectively, more than 11 km of cave chambers were mapped, all in the immediate area of the site of Dos Pilas. Time limits, combined with the logistical exigencies of cave investigation, precluded complete survey of even the Dos Pilas core area, let alone the entire Petexbatún region. Nevertheless, the project documented a far more pervasive relationship than expected between architecture, cave location, and ritual use of caves. We believe that the purpose of the relationship was to embed individual lives as well as civic history among active, tangible reminders of people's ties to the earth, and to do so with daily, seasonal and more attenuated frequencies.

Architecture and caves at Dos Pilas were strongly linked at multiple levels of architectural elaboration and sociopolitical integration, including royal courts and commoner compounds, as well as the city itself. At the highest level, the Dos Pilas kings placed two of the three largest public architectural complexes in direct association with caves and their expression as springs. According to Stuart and Houston

(1994: 84–5), the largest complex, today called El Duende, was known in ancient times as *K'inalha'*, a name acknowledging the springs to which it orients (figure 6.2; Brady 1997: 605). Another of the three largest complexes also may be aligned with springs, with possibly a cave extending below the architecture (1997: 608). The third complex is the royal palace, whose central axis was determined by location of a cave entrance.

The royal palace complex also provides a dramatic seasonal assertion of the earth's power, expressed with clamoring fervor. Just below the palace platform lies the Cueva de Murciélagos, which serves as the outlet for an entire drainage system. After heavy rains, water discharges from this cave (figure 6.3) with such force that the roar can be heard more than a half kilometer away. This was a predictably repeating hierophany, a manifestation of the sacred, surely on a par aurally with the public visual hierophany of the dying sun's winter solstice descent into Pacal's tomb at Palenque (Schele 1977), or the effect of light and shadow transforming staircase to serpent on Chichen Itza's Castillo at equinox sunset (Carlson 1981).

The sound hierophany at Dos Pilas is a transformative call, a metronome of the seasons. It specifically signals the onset of the rainy season, and thereby the advance of the crop cycle. Because the king

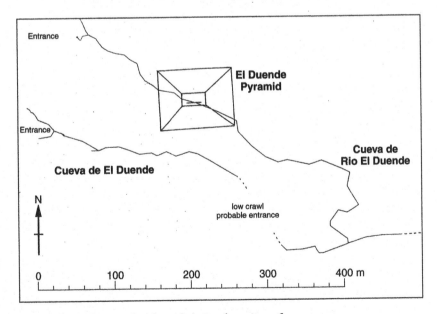

Figure 6.2 El Duende plan, showing location of cave entry.

Figure 6.3   Water issuing from palace-complex cave (photo: George Veni).

was responsible for crop productivity and quality, identifying his palace with this dramatic water source seems hardly coincidental and, in fact, a conscious political strategy, re-expressed every year. The landscape itself thus loudly proclaimed the king's control over water, and presumably over rain-making and fertility. Interestingly, and not coincidentally, that is exactly the claim made in the first millennium BC by a non-Maya king on Chalcatzingo's "El Rey" panel, where wind issues from the mouth of a cave portal, on whose wall a ruler is shown seated in a cave mouth, and next to which ancient artificial channeling concentrates the mountain's rainwater run-off into a seasonal torrent (figure 6.4; Grove 1984: 426).

At lesser spatial and social scales as well, Dos Pilas architectural complexes reinforce links and encounters with caves and the earth. In even the humblest domestic milieus, compounds or individual house structures are associated with very small natural chambers in bedrock, all of which yield evidence of use. Generally, a house platform was

Figure 6.4   Chalcatzingo Monument 1, "El Rey" (drawing by Frances Pratt, courtesy of Akademische Druck- und Verlagsanstalt, Graz).

placed just in front of the cave entry and the tunnel extended under the structure. The regularity in placement suggests widely shared norms. In other cultural settings, sacred landmarks and symbols shape even the most mundane spaces (e.g., Bourdieu 1973; Douglas 1972; Rapoport 1969; Tuan 1977); the same was doubtless true for Dos Pilas, where household residents would be reminded on a daily basis of their connection with the earth.

Archaeological excavations have demonstrated that cave use long preceded adjoining construction at Dos Pilas. Whereas the major civic center emerged only in the Late Classic period, after the arrival of an intrusive elite in the seventh century AD (Demarest 1997), all five major known caves yielded ample Preclassic ceramic assemblages, thereby implying their ritual importance to local people a millennium before florescence of the city. It is clear that the massive and rapid Late Classic construction program respected and incorporated a centuries-old system of sacred landmarks. Indeed, one suspects that for their newly established capital, the initial kings of Dos Pilas were particularly anxious to appropriate symbols with which to invoke a deeper, and preferably mythic, past (see below, and e.g., Ashmore 1998; Bradley 1993).

Orienting architecture to sacred landmarks implies that the civic center was established and perceived to grow in a cosmically ordained pattern, and assured continued encounter with the supernatural realms the constructions mark. Because caves share with the cosmic "center" the distinction of being the place of human creation, converting the highest locally available hill into the El Duende pyramid with its watery cave plausibly served to "center" the whole of Dos Pilas. The more pervasive pattern of appropriating prominent sacred landmarks into public architecture reflects a larger strategy to sanctify and legitimize the city and, by extension, its leaders. Reciprocally, these acts humanized the landscape, bringing primordial powers more firmly into the realm of accountable human action and control.

Given the marked prominence of water, hills, and caves at places like Dos Pilas, then, the inhabitants were surrounded on all sides with landmarks of enormous power and deep meaning. Within nested scales of space, time, and architectural metaphor, families could ritually lay claim to continuity with the earth and its primordial past, and kings literally positioned their claims to rulership within the most majestic and awe-inspiring centers of once-and-future, perpetual creation.

Ancient Maya and Mesoamerican Landscapes

Archaeological finds at Dos Pilas comprise the most intensively considered instance of wider material reference to mountains, caves, and water. The importance of the natural landscape is prominent at Dos Pilas precisely because builders attempted to incorporate but could not outdo such dramatic natural elements as the 3.5-kilometer-long Cueva de Sangre, the massive bulk of the El Duende hill, or the aquatic eruptions of the Cueva de Murciélagos. The mountain–cave–water complex detailed at Dos Pilas captures a fundamental paradigm for understanding Maya landscapes elsewhere. The close relationship, even metaphorical interchangeability, between natural and constructed forms becomes evident in multiple contexts.

Evon Vogt (1981, 1992) has long since argued persuasively that ancient Mesoamerican temple-pyramids represent sacred mountains, and not solely for the Maya. Construction may even incorporate substantial mass from natural hills, essentially terracing a natural feature, and once again blurring distinctions between built and unbuilt. Although this strategy surely required less material and labor input than did the alternative, the motive was as plausibly ideational as economic. A decade ago, David Stuart (1987: 17ff) offered epigraphic and iconographic corroboration that Maya pyramids were specifically labeled *wits*, or mountain. More recently, Stuart and Houston have isolated a category of Classic Maya glyphs identifiable as place names, and remark that what

> is perhaps most striking is that...the idiom for referring to human construction is often a metaphor for "hill." The geography of the Classic Maya apparently involved a conceit in which there existed substantial overlap between natural and artificial categories.
>
> (1994: 86)

Interestingly, the same authors note only a "small" overlap between names referring to physical locations and those defining a mythic landscape (1994: 80), a point to which we will return.

Beyond the Maya area, pyramid-mountains are recognized as marking the *axis mundi* of a range of civic centers, from the fourteenth-century Aztec Templo Mayor in Tenochtitlan, back more than two millennia to Olmec sites and Izapa (e.g., Coggins 1982; Schele 1995; Townsend 1982). As with Teotihuacan's Cerro Gordo or the Aztecs' Mount Tlaloc, physiographic mountains were often identified — especially iconographically — as sources of water, whether through caves' disgorging water from within the earth, or as places triggering the storm clouds to release their precious rain (e.g., Berlo 1992: 147; Townsend 1992).

Artificial mountains and the open courts adjacent to them were sometimes marked further, with sculpture explicitly identifying them as aquatic realms and linking them thereby to supernatural underworld domains. Two examples are the Feathered Serpent Pyramid at Teotihuacan and, in the Maya area, the West Court of Copan's Acropolis (e.g., Miller 1984; Sugiyama 1993). Both of the watery mountains and courts cited have been argued as well to be situated metaphorically in the Underworld, reinforcing their aquatic setting within their respective cities' overall plans (e.g., Ashmore 1991; Miller 1984; Sugiyama 1993). Both complexes have similarly been identified as the sanctum of central authority for their respective polities; their invocation of mountain, cave, and water seems hardly coincidental.

Caves are also abundant in Mesoamerican built landscapes. Temples atop the pyramid-mountains are commonly understood as symbolic caves (e.g., Benson 1985), and the interior shrines of temples in Palenque's Cross Group (figure 6.5) are expressly labeled as *pib na*, or "underground house" (Schele and Freidel 1990: 239, 470). That "temples" and other buildings are effigy caves is made quite explicit when a doorway is sculptured to represent the open mouth of the earth monster (e.g., Miller 1992: 161–2). Furthermore, the playing alleys of ballcourts signify clefts in the earth, inviting players to enter the Underworld to re-enact primordial contests with supernatural opponents (e.g., Gillespie 1991; Miller and Houston 1987).

The most obvious caves fully within pyramids are the tombs in or under these artificial mountains. Discovered half a century ago, the seventh-century tomb of Lord Pacal in Palenque's Temple of the Inscriptions is perhaps the best known from Maya Classic times (figure 6.6; Ruz L. 1954), although abundant, other royal mountains have yielded cave-tombs in recent years, across the Maya world (e.g., Chase 1992; Demarest 1997; Sharer 1997; Trik 1963). These tombs constitute direct material linkage of caves, mountains, and ancestors. Freidel and Schele (1989) have portrayed the Classic-period development of such tombs as a convergence of Preclassic traditions, wherein the burial of lineage leaders under house floors, the locus of familial authority,

Figure 6.5(a)

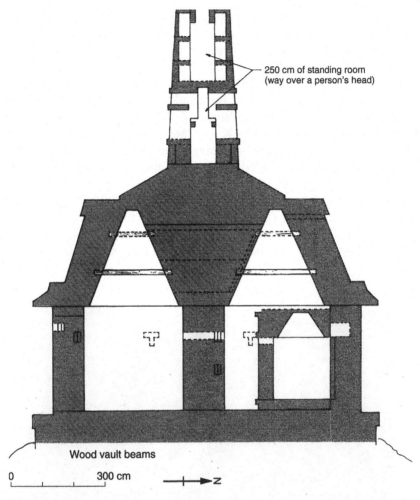

250 cm of standing room
(way over a person's head)

Wood vault beams

0   300 cm   N

Figure 6.5(b)

Figure 6.5 Palenque Temple of the Cross: (a) pyramid-mountain; (b) *pib na* shrine within temple building ([a] photo by Wendy Ashmore; [b] Greene Robertson, Merle, *The Sculpture of Palenque,* volume IV, © 1991 by Princeton University Press; reprinted by permission of Princeton University Press).

was linked to termination rituals and rededication for civic arenas. Successive entombment and re-creation of stages for the public rituals of authority both drew on and publicly enhanced the authority vested in hereditary leaders. Marshall Becker (1988) argues that burials, caches and all deliberate interments are variant forms of earth offering;

we see them as variant forms of caves, as well. Their earliest direct antecedents may be burials in natural caves, such as the ossuary of La Cobanerita cave, of Middle Preclassic age, in the mid-first millennium BC (Brady, Ware et al. 1997).

The abundance of artificial caves beyond those in pyramid-mountains further underscores the fundamental importance of these features for a proper local landscape. At Guumarcaj, or Utatlan, the fifteenth-century capital of the K'iche' Maya, Brady (1991) has argued that the 100-meter-long artificial cavern beneath the central plaza represents the seven-chambered cave of origin of the K'iche' people, whose construction sanctifies the location and legitimizes local rule. Constructed caves have also been discovered elsewhere in the volcanic Guatemalan highlands (e.g., Termer 1957: 178), and even in prime *natural* cave country of the karstic lowlands, as on Topoxte Island (Hermes 1993). Beyond the Maya world, in Central Mexico, caves at

Figure 6.6 Cutaway view of tomb location in Palenque's Temple of Inscriptions (first published 1962 by Penguin Books Ltd; new impression by Yale University Press, copyright © George Kubler 1962, 1975, 1984, 1990).

Teotihuacan, Xochicalco, and Malinalco are also artificial, including the famous cave beneath Teotihuacan's Pyramid of the Sun (e.g., Manzanilla et al. 1994). If a civic center lacked a natural cave, considerable effort might well be expended to create one (but see also Heyden 1981: 14, n. 1, 38). Even where no caves are documented directly, they often persist in legend (e.g., Smith 1955).

Vernon Scarborough's pathbreaking research on ancient Maya water management further reveals the extent of material allusion to caves, mountains, and water. Specifically, Scarborough has documented huge, hydraulically engineered watersheds in numerous Maya civic locales, intricately worked landscapes whose practical results were both an augmented water supply and enhanced control of the latter by a city's leaders (e.g., Scarborough and Gallopin 1991). Not coincidentally, reservoirs for water catchment are prominent and focal features in the civic landscape, and at Tikal, the four largest are "located roughly in the cardinal directions from the epicenter" (Scarborough 1996: 305; 1998: 141), an arrangement consistent with widespread Native American spatial symbolism (e.g., Ashmore 1989). Although his earlier emphasis was largely economic, Scarborough (1998) has begun to consider as well the symbolism and ritual embodied in these reservoirs. Certainly Maya rituals and sacrifice made at bodies of water are well known, the most famous evidence being offerings documented from Chichen Itza's Cenote of Sacrifice (e.g., Coggins 1992).

Moreover, the surface of the exposed water may have been considered a mirror, an object whose reflective qualities were appreciated throughout Mesoamerica. Mirrors had multiple meanings in pre-Columbian society (e.g., Saunders 1988; Scarborough 1998; Taube 1992). They were symbols of shamanic power, and often emblems of royal authority. Karl Taube notes that, in both "Mesoamerica and the American Southwest, the reflective surface of water-filled bowls is frequently used for divinitory scrying" (1992: 189). He goes on to show that mirrors were also widely equated with supernatural caves (1992: 194–7). Both caves and mirrors were thus portals to another world, another reality; one can hardly imagine a more evocative or sacred combination than water forming a mirror on the mouth of a reservoir-cave – one portal upon a second and set within a third.

Water management was also prominent at Teotihuacan. Within the extent of what became a 20-km^2 city in the first centuries AD, both the San Lorenzo and the San Juan rivers were channelized and rerouted, the latter for a distance of more than 2.5 km (Sugiyama 1993: 110). Indeed, Saburo Sugiyama views the plan of the entire city as "water related," the two modified watercourses serving as "principal elements" in the whole city layout. He believes that they may have determined the locations of the major pyramid-mountains early in the city's history, and that the San Juan marked the opening to the Underworld, with all of the city south of its course lying in that watery domain (1993). The Ciudadela and its Feathered Serpent Pyramid, rich with aquatic imagery, lay just south of that river, within the metaphorical Underworld. A small canal extended under the north side of the Ciudadela to a pit (cave?), by means of which Teotihuacan's priests or other officials may have actualized the watery setting on specified occasions (Sugiyama 1993: 111–12). Façade sculpture marks this spatially pivotal pyramid-mountain specifically as the watery place where time began; the massive human sacrifice attendant on its erection simply underscores the political and ritual importance of the locality (1993; López A. et al. 1991). And once again, the fundamental signficance is materialized in a combination of mountain, water, and cave.

While the interweaving of natural and constructed landscape is most notable with public architecture, mountains, caves, and water are also widely evident on a more intimate scale, within domestic compounds. At Dos Pilas, both natural and artificial caves oriented and presumably centered such compounds. The most abundant artificial earth openings found in lowland Maya domestic sites, generally, are *chultuns*. Sometimes these were wholly artificial; at other times, they were modified natural caves, or served as entry to natural chambers. In Yucatan, *chultuns* were lined, watertight, and demonstrably used as cisterns, domestic caves as receptacles of precious water (e.g., Thompson 1897; Zapata P. 1989). In the southern lowlands, however, *chultuns* are not watertight, and probably had varied roles. At times their careful, centered positions suggest ritual roles, and some were used for human burial. We are reminded again of Becker's (1988) arguments that all interments were earth offerings – and by extension, all actively acknowledged chambers were perhaps earth shrines. Puleston (1965: 26) estimated that every residential group at Tikal had at least one *chultun*. Each such chamber could plausibly be an artificial cave, next to the domestic mountain of a house platform, and suggested earlier to mark the *axis mundi* for the household. Creation, use, and maintenance of these features would involve household residents repeatedly with shaping the earth and being shaped by its forms. This would be a more intimate variant of the less frequent occasions when the larger populace engaged in observances marking creation, use, and maintenance of civic landscapes. If the hundreds of house compounds are considered to replicate the mountain, cave, and water complexes of Tikal, Dos Pilas, and other civic centers, it takes little reflection to see how fundamentally our appreciation of Maya and Mesoamerican cities' ideational landscapes would change.

Stuart and Houston's distinction, cited earlier, between mythic and lived landscapes in Classic Maya place names may expand the arguments beyond local references. Citing Dennis Tedlock, those authors suggest that the seemingly distinct class of named "mythic" locales may simply be places more distant and "only rarely visited by humans" (Stuart and Houston 1994: 80). Among others, Mary Helms (e.g., 1988) has repeatedly linked the derivation of social power to recognition of an extraordinary ability to control the distant, whose remove could be measured not only geographically but also across time (e.g., by reference to ancestry) and across states of existence (e.g., by intervention with the supernatural, especially as with shamanism or altered states of consciousness). In households, one draws authority locally from ties to one's own landscape, home and kin, and does so on a daily basis (e.g., McAnany 1995). In civic centers, kings and their subjects participate in public observances, invoking authority from mountains, caves, and water resources on a monumental civic scale. The "mythic" place names identified epigraphically may refer, in turn, either to mythic places or to multi-polity, region-wide landmarks visited with less frequent regularity, and perhaps by a relatively select few, who thereby acquire even greater authority. Perhaps pilgrimages to the relatively isolated but extraordinary Naj Tunich cave mark experiences and consequent prestige of this sort (e.g., Brady 1989; Stone 1995). The seeming disjunction between "mythic" and "real" places in Classic Maya allusions, then, may again reflect degrees along a continuous dimension of conceived and constructed landscapes, rather than referring to discrete or even minimally overlapping domains.

Conclusion

At a variety of scales, from household to civic center and perhaps beyond, the ancient Maya and their neighbors referred to and replicated the key elements of an ideational landscape: mountains of earth and stone, water lying within the earth, and caves linking them all together. Leaders of family and polity alike took hold of the critical anchoring complex, and created domestic, public, and mythical landscapes in which the continuities of human existence were verified by material reference to primordial landscape assemblages. Recent investigations of caves at Dos Pilas underscore the interpretive productivity of inquiries positing closer relations between "built" and "unbuilt" landscapes. Like other peoples of the world, the Maya have situated themselves at the heart of the universe. The ways in which they have used the landscape to do so were and are nearly universal in strategy, even as they remain distinctively Maya in form.

There is still much to do, to pursue more fully the potentials in examining Maya ideational landscape. We agree with Stuart and Houston when they conclude that what "remains for the future is an integration of... emic geographical concepts with the etic patterns documented by settlement pattern archaeology" (1994: 95). Although a good bit is yet to be done to reach this goal, we believe the process will illuminate successive ancient strategies for living, manifest as palimpsest expressions of an ideational landscape perpetually under construction.

ACKNOWLEDGMENTS

Portions of this essay grew from Brady's work in the Petexbatún Regional Cave Survey, especially from the report published in the *American Anthropologist* (1997). The Petexbatún field research was conducted under permit to Arthur Demarest from the Guatemalan Instituto de Antropología e Historia; Brady's cave research was made possible through their sponsorship and with generous support from the National Geographic Society. We would like to thank Bernard Knapp, Robert Preucel, Cynthia Robin, Jeremy Sabloff, and Vernon Scarborough for helpful comments.

REFERENCES

Andrews, G. F. 1975: *Maya Cities: Placemaking and Urbanization*. Norman: University of Oklahoma Press.

Ashmore, W. 1989: Construction and cosmology: politics and ideology in lowland Maya settlement patterns. In W. F. Hanks and D. S. Rice (eds), *Word and Image in Maya Culture: Explorations in Language, Writing and Representation*, Salt Lake City: University of Utah Press, 272–86.

Ashmore, W. 1991: Site-planning principles and concepts of directionality among the ancient Maya. *Latin American Antiquity*, 2, 199–226.

Ashmore, W. 1998: Monumentos políticos: sitios, asentamiento, y paisaje por Xunantunich, Belice. In A. Ciudad Ruiz, Y. Fernández M., J. M. García C., M. J. Iglesias P., A. L. García-Gallo, and L. T. Sanz C. (eds), *Anatomía de una Civilización: Aproximaciones Interdisciplinarias a la Cultura Maya*, Publ. no. 4, Madrid: Sociedad Española de Estudios Mayas, 161–83.

Bassie-Sweet, K. 1991: *From the Mouth of the Dark Cave: Commemorative Sculpture of the Late Classic Maya*. Norman: University of Oklahoma Press.

Bassie-Sweet, K. 1996: *At the Edge of the World: Caves and Late Classic Maya Worldview*. Norman: University of Oklahoma Press.

Basso, K. H. 1996: *Wisdom Sits in Places: Landscape and Language among the Western Apache*. Albuquerque: University of New Mexico Press.

Becker, M. J. 1988: Caches as burials, burials as caches: the meaning of ritual deposits among the Classic period lowland Maya. In N. J. Saunders and O. de Montmollin (eds), *Recent Studies in Pre-Columbian Archaeology*, BAR International Series, 421, Oxford: British Archaeological Reports, 117–42.

Bender, B. 1992: Theorising landscapes, and the prehistoric landscape of Stonehenge. *Man*, 27, 735–55.

Benson, E. P. 1985: Architecture as metaphor. In M. Greene Robertson and V. M. Fields (eds), *Fifth Palenque Round Table, 1983*, San Francisco: Pre-Columbian Art Research Institute, 183–8.

Berlo, J. C. 1992: Icons and ideologies at Teotihuacan: the Great Goddess reconsidered. In J. C. Berlo (ed.), *Art, Ideology, and the City of Teotihuacan*, Washington, DC: Dumbarton Oaks, 129–68.

Bonor V., J. L. 1989: *Las Cuevas Mayas: Simbolismo y Ritual*. Madrid: Universidad Complutense de Madrid.

Bourdieu, P. 1973: The Berber house. In M. Douglas (ed.), *Rules and Meanings*, Harmondsworth: Penguin, 98–110.

Bradley, R. 1993: *Altering the Earth: The Origins of Monuments in Britain and Continental Europe*, Monograph Series, 8. Edinburgh: Society of Antiquaries of Scotland.

Brady, J. E. 1989: An Investigation of Maya Ritual Cave Use with Special Reference to Naj Tunich, Peten, Guatemala. PhD dissertation, University of California at Los Angeles, Los Angeles.

Brady, J. E. 1991: Caves and cosmovision at Utatlan. *California Anthropologist*, 18 (1), 1–10.

Brady, J. E. 1997: Settlement configuration and cosmology: the role of caves at Dos Pilas. *American Anthropologist*, 99, 602–18.

Brady, J. E., and Rodas, I. 1992: Hallazgos recientes y nuevas interpretaciones de la cueva de El Duende. In J. P. Laporte, H. L. Escobedo A., and S. Villagrán de Brady (eds), *V Simposio de Investigaciones Arqueológicas en Guatemala*, Guatemala City: Ministerio de Cultura y Deportes, Instituto de Antropología e Historia, Asociación Tikal, 185–94.

Brady, J. E., Scott, A., Cobb, A., Rodas, I., Fogarty, J., and Urquizú Sanchez, M. 1997: Glimpses of the dark side of the Petexbatún Project: The Petexbatún Regional Cave Survey. *Ancient Mesoamerica*, 8, 353–64.

Brady, J. E., Scott, A., Neff, H., and Glascock, M. D. 1997: Speleothem breakage, movement, removal, and caching: an aspect of ancient Maya cave modification. *Geoarchaeology*, 12, 725–50.

Brady, J. E., and Veni, G. 1992: Man-made and pseudo-karst caves: the implications of subsurface geologic features within Maya centers. *Geoarchaeology*, 7, 149–67.

Brady, J. E., Ware, G. A., Luke, B., Cobb, A., Fogarty, J., and Shade, B. 1997: Preclassic cave utilization near Cobanerita, San Benito, Peten. *Mexicon*, 19, 91–6.

Carlson, J. 1981: A geomantic model for the interpretation of Mesoamerican sites: an essay in cross-cultural comparison. In E. P. Benson (ed.), *Mesoamerican Sites and World-Views*, Washington, DC: Dumbarton Oaks, 143–215.

Chase, A. F. 1992: Elites and the changing organization of Classic Maya society. In D. Z. Chase and A. F. Chase (eds), *Mesoamerican Elites: An Archaeological Assessment*, Norman: University of Oklahoma Press, 30–49.

Coggins, C. C. 1982: The zenith, the mountain, the center, and the sea. In A. F. Aveni and G. Urton (eds), *Ethnoastronomy and Archaeoastronomy in the American Tropics, Annals of the New York Academy of Sciences*, 385, 11–23.

Coggins, C. C. 1992: Artifacts from the Cenote of Sacrifice, Chichen Itza, Yucatan. *Memoirs of the Peabody Museum of Archaeology and Ethnology*, 10, 3.

Demarest, A. A. 1997: The Vanderbilt Petexbatún Regional Archaeological Project 1989–1994: overview, history, and major results of a multidisciplinary study of the Classic Maya collapse. *Ancient Mesoamerica*, 8, 209–27.

Douglas, M. 1972: Symbolic orders and the use of domestic space. In P. Ucko, R. Tringham, and G. W. Dimbleby (eds), *Man, Settlement, and Urbanism*, London: Duckworth, 513–22.

Eliade, M. 1979: *Tratado de Historia de Las Religiones*. Mexico City: Biblioteca Era.

Fowler, P. J. 1995: Writing on the countryside. In I. Hodder, M. Shanks, A. Alexandri, V. Buchli, J. Carman, J. Last, and G. Lucas (eds), *Interpretive Archaeology: Finding Meaning in the Past*, London: Routledge, 100–9.

Freidel, D. A., and Schele, L. 1989: Dead kings and living temples: dedication and termination rituals among the ancient Maya. In W. F. Hanks and D. S. Rice (eds), *Word and Image in Maya Culture: Explorations in Language, Writing and Representation*, Salt Lake City: University of Utah Press, 233–43.

García-Zambrano, A. J. 1994: Early Colonial evidence of pre-Columbian rituals of foundation. In M. Greene Robertson and V. M. Fields (eds), *Seventh Palenque Round Table, 1989*, San Francisco: Pre-Columbian Art Research Institute, 217–27.

Gillespie, S. D. 1991: Ballgames and boundaries. In V. L. Scarborough and D. R. Wilcox (eds), *The Mesoamerican Ballgame*, Tucson: University of Arizona Press, 317–45.

Grove, D. C. 1984: Comments on the site and its organization. In D. C. Grove (ed.), *Ancient Chalcatzingo*, Austin: University of Texas Press, 420–33.

Grove, D. C., and Gillespie, S. D. 1984: Chalcatzingo portrait figurines and the cult of the ruler. *Archaeology*, 37 (4), 27–33.

Hanks, W. F. 1990: *Referential Practice: Language and Lived Space among the Maya*. Chicago: University of Chicago Press.

Helms, M. W. 1988: *Ulysses' Sail: An Ethnographic Odyssey of Power, Knowledge, and Geographical Distance*. Princeton: Princeton University Press.

Hermes C., B. 1993: La secuencia cerámica de Topoxté: Un informe preliminar. *Beiträge zur Allegemeinen und Vergleichenden Archäologie*, 13, 221–51.

Heyden, D. 1981: Caves, gods, and myths: world-view and planning at Teotihuacan. In E. P. Benson (ed.), *Mesoamerican Sites and World-Views*, Washington, DC: Dumbarton Oaks, 1–39.

Knapp, A. B. 1997: Settlement archaeology and landscapes. In *The Archaeology of Late Bronze Age Cypriot Society: The Study of Settlement, Survey and Landscape*, Glasgow: Department of Archaeology, University of Glasgow, 1–18.

Kubler, G. F. 1984: *The Art and Architecture of Ancient America*, 3rd edn. Harmondsworth: Penguin.

Lawrence, D. L., and Low, S. M. 1990: The built environment and spatial form. *Annual Review of Anthropology*, 19, 453–505.

López Austin, A., López Luján, L., and Sugiyama, S. 1991: The Temple of Quetzalcoatl at Teotihuacan: its possible ideological significance. *Ancient Mesoamerica*, 2, 93–105.

Manzanilla. L., Barba, L., Chávez, R., Tejero, A., Cifuentes, C., and Peralta, N. 1994: Caves and geophysics: an approximation to the Underworld of Teotihuacan, Mexico. *Archaeometry*, 36, 141–57.

McAnany, P. A. 1995: *Living with the Ancestors: Kinship and Kingship in Ancient Maya Society*. Austin: University of Texas Press.

Miller, M. E. 1984: The meaning and function of the Main Acropolis, Copan. In E. H. Boone and G. R. Willey (eds), *The Southeast Classic Maya Zone*, Washington, DC: Dumbarton Oaks, 149–94.

Miller, M. E. 1986: *The Art of Mesoamerica: From Olmec to Aztec*. New York: Thames and Hudson.

Miller, M. E. 1992: The image of people and nature in Classic Maya art and architecture. In R. F. Townsend (ed.), *The Ancient Americas: Art from Sacred Landscapes*, Chicago, Munich: Art Institute of Chicago, Prestel Verlag, 158–69.

Miller, M. E., and Houston, S. D. 1987: The Classic Maya ballgame and its architectural setting: a study in relations between text and image. *Res*, 14, 47–66.

Puleston, D. E. 1965: The chultuns of Tikal. *Expedition*, 7 (3), 24–9.

Rapoport, A. 1969: *House Form and Culture*. Englewood Cliffs, NJ: Prentice-Hall.

Redfield, R., and Villa Rojas, A. 1962: *Chan Kom: A Maya Village*. Chicago: University of Chicago Press.

Ruz L., A. 1954: La pirámide-tumba de Palenque. *Cuadernos Americanos*, 74, 141–59.

Saunders, N. J. 1988: Anthropological reflections on archaeological mirrors. In N. J. Saunders and O. de Montmollin (eds), *Recent Studies in Pre-Columbian*

Archaeology, BAR International Series, 421, Oxford: British Archaeological Reports, 1–39.

Scarborough, V. L. 1996: Reservoirs and watersheds in the central Maya lowlands. In S. L. Fedick (ed.), *The Managed Mosaic: Ancient Maya Agriculture and Resource Use*, Salt Lake City: University of Utah Press, 304–14.

Scarborough, V. L. 1998: Ecology and ritual: water management and the Maya. *Latin American Antiquity*, 9, 135–59.

Scarborough, V. L., and Gallopin, G. G. 1991: A water storage adaptation in the Maya lowlands. *Science*, 251, 658–62.

Schama, S. 1995: *Landscape and Memory*. New York: Knopf.

Schele, L. 1977: Palenque: the house of the dying sun. In A. F. Aveni (ed.), *Native American Astronomy*, Austin: University of Texas Press, 42–56.

Schele, L. 1995: The Olmec mountain and tree of creation in Mesoamerican cosmology. In G. Griffin (ed.), *The Olmec World: Ritual and Rulership*, Princeton, NJ: The Art Museum, in association with Harry N. Abrams, 105–17.

Schele, L., and Freidel, D. A. 1990: *A Forest of Kings*. New York: William Morrow.

Sharer, R. J. 1997: Political and ideological power and the origins of the Acropolis, ECAP [Early Copan Acropolis Project], Paper 1. Philadelphia: University of Pennsylvania Museum.

Smith, A. L. 1955: *Archaeological Reconnaissance in Central Guatemala*, Publication 608. Washington, DC: Carnegie Institution.

Stone, A. 1992: From ritual in the landscape to capture in the urban center: the recreation of ritual environments in Mesoamerica. *Journal of Ritual Studies*, 6, 109–32.

Stone, A. 1995: *Images from the Underworld: Naj Tunich and the Tradition of Maya Cave Painting*. Austin: University of Texas Press.

Stuart, D. 1987: *Ten Phonetic Syllables*, Research Reports on Ancient Maya Writing, 14. Washington, DC: Center for Maya Research.

Stuart, D., and Houston, S. D. 1994: *Classic Maya Place Names*, Studies in Pre-Columbian Art and Archaeology, 33. Washington, DC: Dumbarton Oaks.

Sugiyama, S. 1993: Worldview materialized in Teotihuacan, Mexico. *Latin American Antiquity*, 4, 103–29.

Taube, K. A. 1992: The iconography of mirrors at Teotihuacan. In J. C. Berlo (ed.), *Art, Ideology, and the City of Teotihuacan*, Washington, DC: Dumbarton Oaks, 169–204.

Tedlock, B. 1992: The role of dreams and visionary narratives in Mayan cultural survivals. *Ethnos*, 20, 453–76.

Termer, F. 1957: *Etnología y Etnografía de Guatemala*, Publication 5. Guatemala: Seminario de Integración Social Guatemalteca.

Thompson, E. H. 1897: *The Chultunes of Labná, Yucatan*, Memoirs of the Peabody Museum of Archaeology and Ethnology, 1. Cambridge, MA: Harvard University.

Thompson, J. E. S. 1975: Introduction. In H. C. Mercer, *The Hill-Caves of Yucatan*, Norman: University of Oklahoma Press, vii–xliv.

Townsend, R. F. 1982: Pyramid and sacred mountain. In A. F. Aveni and G. Urton (eds), *Ethnoastronomy and Archaeoastronomy in the American Tropics*, *Annals of the New York Academy of Sciences*, 385, 37–62.

Townsend, R. F. 1992: Introduction: landscape and symbol. In R. F. Townsend (ed.), *The Ancient Americas: Art from Sacred Landscapes*, Chicago, Munich: Art Institute of Chicago, Prestel Verlag, 29–47.

Trik, A. S. 1963: The splendid tomb of Temple I, Tikal, Guatemala. *Expedition*, 6 (1), 2–18.

Tuan, Y. F. 1977: *Space and Place: The Perspective of Experience*. Minneapolis: University of Minnesota Press.

Vogt, E. Z. 1976: *Tortillas for the Gods: A Symbolic Analysis of Zinacantan Ritual*. Cambridge, MA: Harvard University Press.

Vogt, E. Z. 1981: Some aspects of the sacred geography of highland Chiapas. In E. P. Benson (ed.), *Mesoamerican Sites and World-Views*, Washington, DC: Dumbarton Oaks, 119–42.

Vogt, E. Z. 1992: The persistence of Maya tradition in Zinacantan. In R. F. Townsend (ed.), *The Ancient Americas: Art from Sacred Landscapes*, Chicago, Munich: Art Institute of Chicago, Prestel Verlag, 60–9.

Zapata P. 1989: *Los Chultunes: Sistemas de Captación y Almacenamiento de Agua Pluvial*, Colección Científica. Mexico, DF: Instituto Nacional de Antropología e Historia.

Part II

Protohistoric/Ethnohistoric Cases

7

The Inca Cognition of Landscape: Archaeology, Ethnohistory, and the Aesthetic of Alterity

Maarten van de Guchte

Introduction

The epistemological problems of writing across cultural boundaries are distinctly evident when dealing with a non-western cognitive system, such as Inca ideas about the landscape. Natural features were often points of great ritual importance in the spatial organization of the Inca empire (*c*. AD 1200–1532) in southern Peru. As often, these features lacked any overt human markings, such as architectural structures or carved decorations. Had these landscape features not been reported in the ethnohistorical literature, they would have been extremely difficult to recognize as focal points of Inca ideology. In the following pages, I draw on ethnohistorical and archaeological data as evidence of pronounced Inca interest in alterity, defined as irregularity or difference, to highlight what I see as distinctly Inca in the cognition and manipulation of the Andean natural world (figure 7.1).

I begin by asking whose concepts we use when we seek to analyze ancient landscapes, and argue that both ethnohistoric texts and our own observations of the material world are required, paired with due critical attention to each. Consider, for example, the landscape implications of 15 entries from an early seventeenth-century Quechua dictionary, all providing descriptions of various types of noses – flat noses, broad noses, split noses, and so on – articulating a highly expressive description of the Quechua face as human landscape (Gonzalez Holguin 1952 [1608]). One entry, *cencca*, is given as "nose, or the crest of the mountain." Twenty-five similarly detailed entries for the concept "eye" can be found in the same dictionary, again with explicit metaphorical links to landscape features. Some argue that bodily

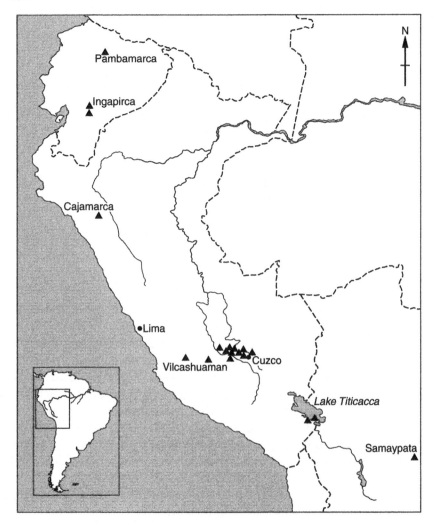

Figure 7.1   Map of Peru, locating places mentioned in the text.

features, human as well as animal, were crucial tools for the Inca in thinking about their world, whether one deals with the sky above (Urton 1981) or the mountain one cultivates (Bastien 1978; Classen 1993). But must one therefore analyze Inca cognition of landscape by using body metaphors?

Michel de Certeau writes of seeking a "science of singularity," looking for those phenomena that separate a culture from its neighbors in time and space (Certeau 1984). Such a science would, in Certeau's words, link "everyday pursuits to particular circumstances. ... The characteristically subtle logic of these 'ordinary' activities comes to light only in the details" (1984: ix). Much is left to the individual author in determining what constitutes singularity in Inca society. Would body metaphors qualify, or the 385 different names for potatoes, or an equally complex inventory of sacrificial animals, their colors, and calendric associations? Or consider cloth, frequently accorded economic and symbolic primacy in Andean culture (e.g., Murra 1975; Stone-Miller 1992a). But can one base a "science of singularity," which would demonstrate "the subtle logic" for the whole of Inca culture and society, simply on the art of weaving or a taxonomy of potatoes? After all, textiles and tubers have been prevalent in Peruvian prehistory from earliest times on.

In contrast, the Andean landscape as constructed and conceptualized during Inca times seems an apt domain for isolating some form of "singularity" as a diagnostic and analytical instrument. Land use, settlement patterns, and ritual attention to nature in the lands controlled by the Incas seem to have a different character when compared with Huari (Wari), an earlier state (c. AD 500–800), and most definitely when compared with post-Conquest practices in the same general area. Here I will argue that the Inca cognition of landscape was embedded in a state-controlled practice, blending mythology, geophysical reality, political ambitions, and alterity or difference, the latter being the pivotal principle of an Inca aesthetic. It resulted in a world view which, as a structuring process, did not produce a hieratic and static grid of fixed positions, but rather a flexible pattern of overlapping and shifting cognitive strategies in the social management of Andean space.

Consider the Huari state, and inference of a Huari "state aesthetic." Stone-Miller and McEwan (1990/91) regard post-Conquest Spanish documents concerning the Inca temporally too remote to be of use in the study of Huari culture. Comparing the site plan of Pikillacta with textile designs on Huari tunics, however, they argue that the "representation of the Huari state" can be detected in each medium, through four structural traits: atopographic positioning, generalized framework, modular construction, and formal regularity broken by intentional anomalies. The first trait is highly pertinent here, for "both architecture and tapestries are state imposed and positioned atopographically within their respective 'environments,' whether natural or human. They are laid down with little or no regard to the irregularity of the ground, in the case of Pikillacta, or to the human form, in the case of the tunics" (1990/91: 76).

Anyone even remotely familiar with Inca settlement planning or site location will note the contrast. Pikillacta's layout and physical appearance "is almost perfectly rectangular, and it rests on the terrain as if the architect had given no particular consideration to topographic irregularities. Thus Pikillacta appears not to have been adapted to the terrain, but rather imposed on, or built in spite of the terrain" (1990/91: 57). This description is a far cry from the character of well-known Inca sites such as Machu Picchu or Pisaq, which have been described by a variety of travelers and archaeologists as adapting to and integrating prominent natural parts of the mountain side (Bingham 1979 [1930]; Hyslop 1990; Niles 1992). Adaptation to the constraints and challenges of a particular topographic setting seems to have been the *sine qua non* of Inca settlement planning (figure 7.2). Terrace construction was used "to sculpt existing hillocks or open areas into new forms and [as such, was] conceptually intermediate between obeying the contours of a valley and imposing a pleasing form on the landscape" (Nickel 1982; Niles 1987: 163). In his comprehensive study of Inca settlement planning, Hyslop (1990: 300) notes that

[g]iven the importance Inkas associated with the sacred, animate land-scape, [royal] settlements ... appear to be places where Inka architects created a synthesis between environment and settlement, not only by accommodation to natural features, but also by modifying the landscape.

Figure 7.2 View of Inca terracing at Pisaq (photo: M. van de Guchte).

Elsewhere he writes:

> No two Inka state settlements are identical. There were no universal principles followed in selecting a location and planning the layout of major Inka settlements. Rather, a complex set of concepts was used, based on the major activities to be carried out in the settlement, its topography, the distance and amount of local labor, and local cultural influences.
>
> (1990: 306)

And he adds

> Inka settlements are ... not precise physical replications of [the capital] Cuzco. ... Inka social, religious, and political concepts developed in Cuzco are spread to diverse parts of the state via the design and specific features of the larger state settlements. This was done in part by *the flexible use of spatial divisions*.
>
> (1990: 305; emphasis added)

The studies by Stone-Miller and McEwan and by Hyslop clarify the differences and correspondences between Huari and Inca settlement planning. For both societies, the cited authors stress state-control of the planning process. But the expressed results are quite different, with Huari imposition of a blueprint on the landscape, regardless of physical obstacles, while the Incas employed flexible, locally adaptive strategies in their civic planning. Planners and artisans of both cultures, according to these different authors, were very conscious of the mandate to make the respective sites "representations" of state ideology. Where the Huari case evinces parallels between architecture and textiles, such correspondences have been suggested only tentatively, as yet, for the Inca (Hyslop 1990: 309). Although Inca art has been generally thought of "in limited and limiting terms," and "termed awkward, repetitive and dull," at least one author has argued that Inca artists "produced the new, the interesting, the experimental – oftentimes the misshapen – but always the most progressive artforms of that fabled [16th] century" (Jones 1964: 5).

What consequences does this contrast between the Huari and the Inca have for understanding the Inca approach to landscape? To what extent is it possible to articulate an ideology and cognitive matrix based on these discontinuities and dissimilarities between Inca and Huari landscapes? In itself, such a comparison is inconclusive. Ethnohistory offers additional, critically important insights, however. Post-Conquest Spanish chroniclers provide observations which are eminently applicable to the Inca materials due to their temporal proximity, enabling a "thick description" of the Inca cognition of landscape. Ethnohistory thus complements, contrasts, complicates, and occasionally contradicts the material record.

An articulate example is the Jesuit author Bernabé Cobo who wrote that "these Indians of Peru worshipped the works of nature [that were] unaltered by human contrivance" (Cobo 1990 [1653]: 44). The priest expands on this observation saying that

> it must be pointed out that these people customarily worshipped and offered sacrifices to any natural things that were found to differ somewhat from others of the same kind because of some oddity or extraordinary quality found in them. ... They worshipped exceptionally large trees, roots and other things that come from the land. They also worshipped springs, rivers, lakes, and hills which were different in shape or substance from those nearby, being formed of earth or sand, where the rest were rocky, or vice versa. Also included was the snow-capped mountain range and any other sierra or high peak which had snow on it, boulders or large rocks, cliffs and deep gorges, as well as the high places and hilltops called *apachitas* (places of rest).
>
> (1990 [1653])

Difference is the crucial notion in Cobo's writing about the Inca's ritual attention to landscape. Without going into the Derrida-inspired literature on "difference" and "deference" (Derrida 1976), it is appropriate and useful to ask how the Incas noted difference in nature and whether this difference generated deference for any such feature. How did the Incas see, use, and think about the land they inhabited? Is it possible to interpret the Inca interest in difference as a building-block if not for a science of singularity, then for an aesthetic of alterity? If correctly surmised, the Inca interest in alterity can be compared with a peculiar trait in Huari weaving practices. A characteristic, if not diagnostic, feature of the Huari aesthetic is articulated by one scholar as: "One of the design rules was to break the rules. ... What makes the Huari aesthetic system so fascinating and culturally reflective is that most tunic compositions intentionally break this rigid formal repetition through deviation in color and shape" (Stone-Miller 1992b: 344). These observations beg the question whether "rupture" or "chaos" in the weaving of a Huari textile and "difference" in the perception of an Inca landscape feature could be integrated into a pan-Andean aesthetic and cognitive system in which alterity is a defining element.

Inca Ethnohistory and the Identification of *Huacas*

Before exploring this further, it is important to consider to what extent the ethnohistorical data shape and sharpen our perception of the Andean environment. The Incas had a special relationship with the land they inhabited, which expressed itself in their perception and interpretation of that land. In this way, the Inca resemble other Andean people preceding them in time. However, the Inca case is more complex for a number of reasons, primarily because of the increased complexity and diversity of the interpretive sources available to us. The "fit" between the material expressions of Inca culture and the natural environment appears the result of careful observation and selection. Landscape features such as rocks, carved as well as uncarved, lakes, springs, and hills were perceived by the Inca as instruments in the collective memory of origins and interrelationships with the supernatural, and as tools in the creation of their empire and the replication of icons of power in conquered territories. Many of these landscape features are commonly referred to in the ethnohistorical and archaeological literature as *huacas*.

As an element of Inca theory and praxis, *huaca* covers a field encompassing ancestral cults and death, genealogical and ethnic associations, oracular capacities and shamanic activities. For clarity, I define the concept *huaca* here as "a material object or location which received ritual attention, and the 'force' which inhabited that object or location." An additional caveat is that a *huaca* could become a non-*huaca*. An itinerant official in the Inca empire was in charge of determining which *huacas* were still in force and which ones were *atisqa*, that is, 'conquered *huacas*' or *huacas* that had lost their power. It is not clear from the ethnohistorical documents if a *huaca atisqa* was subject to mutilation or defacement. Whether that "powerless" *huaca* became anonymous, so to speak, or continued to receive some form of ritual attention is also unknown. In brief, *huaca* and *huaca atisqa* are the crucial actors in the Andean dialectic of power and non-power. Reasons for these conceptual distinctions may be found in the intellectual foundations of the process of the classification of *huacas*. Selected landscape features in Tahuantinsuyu – the Inca empire, land of the four quarters – were sacralized by a class of Inca officials following specific ritual prescriptions and concerns (van de Guchte 1990). These *huacas* can be distinguished, *grosso modo*, in three categories: cosmological markers, markers of mediation, and markers of identity.

Huacas as cosmological markers

In this category *huacas*, very often in the form of rocks, carved as well as uncarved, act as markers of places of ancestral origin, of sites where legendary feats of culture-heroes took place, and of spots where humans and animals were transformed in stone. At places where cosmogonic events, the metamorphosis of ancestors and culture-heroes, and acts of creation and supernatural death were supposed to have taken place, rocks acted as lithic testimony to the involvement of metaphysical beings with the world of humans. In brief, *huacas* act as focal points in the collective art of Inca memory. The stones, known as *huanca* (field stone), *pururauca* (ancestor and warrior stone) and *sayhua* (marker) in the Quechua classificatory system, can be considered sub-categories in the overarching concept of *huaca*.

Huacas as markers of mediation

In this second category *huacas* act as instruments of mediation and communication between mortals and the supernatural. They act as places for libations or as altars for sacrificial offerings, where an attempt is made at establishing contact with a cosmic entity. Equally, selected rocks in close proximity to caves function as instruments facilitating the descent into the underworld. Some *huacas* in this category can be interpreted as steps to heaven, or, inversely, as tools for celestial bodies to descend from the sky. A mediating function of *huacas* is the visualization of Inca presence and power. Finally, certain *huacas* act as markers of mediation in a system of visual bonding, such as a "seat" from which a particular mountain-peak can be observed. Stones known as *chanca* (resting place) should be placed within this category. Other Inca objects and concepts, such as *tiana* (seat) and *usnu* (throne), share similar characteristics.

Huacas as markers of identity

This third, overarching category groups *huacas* that, through their physical presence, indicate certain modes of identity. The most immediate and arresting modality of a *huaca* is its designation of the "Incaness" of a certain place. The distinctiveness of a carved *huaca*-stone as "Inca" addresses the nucleus of concepts contained within the "science of singularity." Rocks and other landscape features also functioned as markers of kin, gender, or personal identity. Certain *huacas* were associated with particular kin groups. Other landscape features were reportedly exclusively affiliated with women, with young male nobles, with the health of the Inca king, or with the cult of the Earth Goddess, the Pachamama (Cobo 1990 [1653]: 51ff).

One aesthetically revealing practice should be noted at this point, that in Inca times ritually significant landscape features were covered with textiles. The *huacas* were thus not immediately visible, but obscured from the eye by richly colored weavings. As important for subsequent study, however, the location and existence of a *huaca* would have been far more obvious then than now. The chronicler Albornoz describes this peculiar fact, when he describes a class of *huacas* called *pacariscas* (places of origin of a particular ethnic group). First he mentions that the Indians always carried a piece of cloth, which belonged to their *huaca pacarisca*. This piece of textile was handed to them by the priest of the *huaca* of origin (*huaca de descendencia*) and served as a token of identification. Subsequently Albornoz writes: "When their *pacarisca* is a stone they put the piece of cloth on top of it and bring it to another stone" (Albornoz 1984 [1585]: 199). I interpret this fragment to signify that the stones, which were held to be stones of origin, were known and venerated by means of the superimposed textiles. A member of a particular ethnic group or kin-group would establish a link between the mythical or historical place of origin of that group and their actual residence by means of a particularly designed textile. The textile or its decoration served as a memory-aid in the field of ethnic identity and personal alliance. This is confirmed in an Inca myth of origin, which narrates how people emerged from caves, mountains, springs, lakes, and trees. As the people multiplied, they made *huacas* and temples in those places, as memorials to their origins. And, it is added: "In commemoration of the first of their lineage, every ethnic group wears and shows with pride the textile garment, with which they clothed their *huaca*" (Molina 1943 [1574]: 9).

This particular custom of covering carved stones with textiles, recorded from oral traditions less than a century after the Spanish Conquest, strikes me as especially important in making features already conceived as different stand out from their surroundings even more clearly. Although it is not clear from Molina's account whether both carved and uncarved (unaltered or non-manipulated) rocks were covered, another chronicler, Martín de Murua, documents that covering houses and streets with finely colored textiles, and likewise the walls of agricultural terraces surrounding the city, was widespread in Inca and early Colonial times. Murua writes that when the corpse of the Inca king Huayna Capac was brought back to Cuzco from

Tumibamba (in modern-day Ecuador), where he had died victim of an attack of smallpox, the city of Cuzco and its surroundings were made ready for a royal reception, reminiscent of a Roman triumphal entry:

> The Inca king Huascar Ynga ordered that to make the triumph and entry of his father more grandiose and sublime, that all the streets of Cuzco and the terraces around it, their fronts which looked towards Cuzco, that all these were to be covered with tapestry and clad with fine colored textiles and that the houses and towers of Cuzco were to be covered with *cumbi*-cloth [highly prized weavings], with silverwork of gold and silver, as rich and splendid as possible.
>
> (Murua 1962–4 [1590–1611]: 115).

This image of an Incaic town and its surrounding mountains, covered with red and black and orange textiles, calls to mind a landscape composed of infinite colored cultural elements, a huge Incaic quilt spread out over the valley and its mountains.

Memory and Maps: Alterity among *Quipus*, *Ceques*, and Metaphorical Kin

What were the tools for memorizing and controlling these practices? How did the Inca bureaucracy keep track of these different *huacas* and other landscape features? The planning of these mental and practical activities was the domain of specialists within the Inca state, who produced and controlled instruments such as maps and *quipus* (counting devices). With the aid of these mnemonic devices, these *quipucamayoc* (masters of the *quipus*) structured various cognitive fields such as the *ceques* (sight lines), *huacas*, and Inca kinship terminology.

Data on maps in pre-Columbian Peru are relatively abundant. An eye-witness report details a map-like device, as seen by the author Garcilaso de la Vega, el Inca, before he left Peru in the year 1560:

> With geography they were well acquainted, in order to paint and make a model and drawing of their villages and provinces. ... I myself saw the model of Cuzco and part of its surroundings, with its four principal roads, made of clay and small pebbles and sticks, designed as precise as possible, ... Similarly it was admirable to see the countryside with its high and low mountains, plains and ravines, rivers and streams with their turns and counter-turns, so that the best cosmographer could not have put it better.
>
> (Garcilaso de la Vega, el Inca 1965 [1609], II: 77)

Other reports, as written down in chronicles and legal documents, confirm the existence of models in clay, or *pinturas* (paintings), which gave the particulars of a certain village or valley, often used in legal disputes, as in the following case:

> In July 1567, in the public court of justice the two defendants were notified that both parties should exhibit clay models of their lands. The chief of Quivi said he had used such a model on a previous occasion to explain in a general way the disposition of the lands that had been stolen. For their part, the other party [in the village of Chaclla] showed paintings, but they also were asked to show a clay model of the valley. They pleaded that they could not do so, because although they had formerly brought such a model it had since fallen to pieces.
>
> (Rostworowski de Diez Canseco 1988: 63)

A map of a different sort is contained in an extraordinary document, one which stands out among all ethnohistorical writing about Peru and the Incas. This occasionally bizarre document, commonly known as the "List of Ceques and Huacas," suggests that the Incas elaborated a very complex, logically coherent and unifying conceptual scheme which served as an ordering framework for the social organization of the capital of their empire (Cobo 1990 [1653]). This body of native knowledge details the Inca mental activity of drawing lines on the landscape. The "gridding" of this cognitive map and the rituals through which this endeavor was pursued are described in an account, recorded in the sixteenth century but surviving in a seventeenth-century chronicle, which may be the only truly indigenous and native body of materials handed down to us in written form (Cobo 1990 [1653]). This unique and complex corpus of sightlines, place names, sacrifices, and indications of genealogical alliance is recorded as a long list of names of every rock, spring, hill, and craggy ravine in the valley of Cuzco. This list not only constituted a geographical map and ritual calendar, but also became a mental map that provided the Incas with a way of flexibly organizing social relationships to accommodate constantly shifting alliances, opportunities, and mythico-historic events.

Radiating out from the Temple of the Sun in Cuzco were a set of 41 lines called *ceques* (figure 7.3). Located on them or near them were 328 *huacas*. The lines are grouped into a number of divisions, such as two halves, and four *suyus* or quarters. Furthermore the lines running from the center to the horizon formed by mountains surrounding Cuzco are divided into three parts, ranked hierarchically as *collana* (upper, Inca), *payan* (middle, Inca and non-Inca) and *cayao* (lower, non-Inca) (Wachtel 1973; Zuidema 1964). Originally analyzed and interpreted

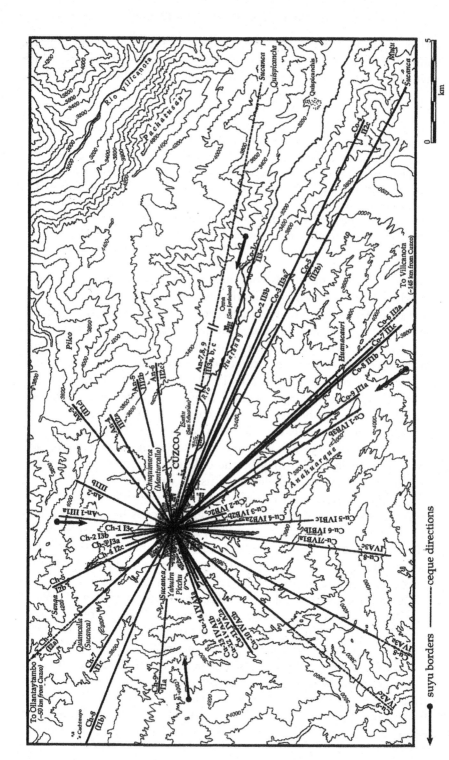

Figure 7.3 Diagram of *ceque* system in the Valley of Cuzco (courtesy of R. T. Zuidema).

● ━━━ suyu borders ━━━━ ceque directions

as a model of social organization, the *ceque* system has more recently yielded insights on Inca astronomy (Zuidema 1992), ritual (Zuidema 1978), irrigation (Sherbondy 1986), and architectural planning (Hyslop 1990; Niles 1987). The *huacas* on the *ceque* lines are for the greater part features in the landscape such as rocks, springs, hills, and ravines (258 out of 328), although fields and buildings also are named. With great complexity they demarcate the ritual topography of the valley of Cuzco. Water, stone, houses that evoke the memory of a king or queen, and flat places are all salient attributes in selecting sites and marking the landscape. Each town and valley in southern Peru and Bolivia is thought to have possessed comparable topographical information about its surroundings.

The "List of Ceques and Huacas" must have been memorized and transferred to paper with the aid of a *quipu*, an indigenous counting device characterized as a cord, from which hung smaller strings with groups of simple knots at intervals (Zuidema 1989). *Quipus* could be used to account for practical matters, such as numbers of animals, people, liturgical matters, and the order and associations of *huacas*. A special class of officials, called *quipucamayoc*, was in charge of these tools. Their duty was "to memorize the statistical, historical, and liturgical material accumulated by the government and to be prepared at all times to repeat it for the benefit of officials who desired to refer to it" (Rowe 1944: 326; Ascher and Ascher 1981). The numbering system in the *quipu* was probably standardized, but the interpretation of that information could be flexible to a degree, because, as Rowe stated, "the *quipu* had to be accompanied by an oral comment" (Rowe 1944: 325). If the "reader" does not know whether the knots refer to llamas or to *huacas*, the instrument becomes incomprehensible. Devoid of its context, the narrative based in the knots could become highly personal and discursive. Important for our understanding of the use of *quipus* in the organization of ritual space is that *quipus* can be assigned both horizontal and vertical direction and have different levels, depending on the use of color and the distancing between the various knots (Ascher and Ascher 1981: 17). Seen from above, the spatial distribution of *huacas* in the valley of Cuzco is reminiscent of a *quipu* being spread over the mountainous landscape. Instead of knots on different strings, *huacas* function as markers in this mental map.

To maintain coherence in the production and reproduction of mental maps, Incas used kinship terminology to suggest interdependence between points in this conceptual network. Terms like "brothers" and "sisters" were used to designate relations between mountains, between rocks and mountains, and between mountains, sculptures, and human beings. Inca kings, for instance, were accompanied by a stone brother called *huauque*, which received the same reverence as the living king (van de Guchte 1997). The most sacred mountain in the valley of Cuzco, Huanacauri, was said to be a brother of the first Inca king Manco Capac. Equally important were relations of descent. In this manner, the mythological relations between different points in the landscape were expressed in a system of geographical relations, organized along generational lines. It appears that *huacas* functioned as commemorative features in the landscape linking people spatially with their temporal past (Poole 1984). A ritual network positing symbolic or mythological connections between distant social groups, political-economic subsystems, and ecological zones was brought to life through the movement of ancestors and supernatural beings. Sacred places and *huacas* identified with specific mountains, lakes, rocks, or other prominent landmarks provided the basis for the elaboration of complex rituals and mythologies in Inca times (see figure 7.4).

Considering the integration of natural phenomena as cultural elements within Inca symbolic practice, I suggest that the Incas conceived of an animate landscape, parallel and similar to their own social fabric. In this parallel physical world, stones were put in the same mental categories that ruled the human world. This parallelism included the attribution of kinship categories to stones, made stones

Figure 7.4 Stone at Sayhuite carved to show a landscape (photo: M. van de Guchte).

capable of moving, dancing, and speaking, and embraced the belief that stones could be transformed into human beings and human beings into stones (van de Guchte 1984). Apparently this mineral world was ruled by the same practical regulations prevalent in the human world. Ritually significant landscape features received tribute in the form of the produce of agricultural fields and animals, particularly camelids. As such, these features clearly function in a network of economic relations. Relating these sacred places to conceptual lines (*ceques*) radiating out from Cuzco and to the kin-groups which were in charge of these *ceques*, provided a territorial organization for the Inca empire as a whole which was capable of focusing the power of distant places on Cuzco as its supreme political and religious center.

How can the "List of Ceques" and other devices be utilized in the study of the Inca cognition of landscape? Do they provide answers to the questions of how *huacas* were selected and how they were memorized and transferred from one generation to the next? Certain *huacas* were selected on the basis of their location on the horizon as crucial elements in a system of astronomical alignment. Others were selected due to their visibility from the Temple of the Sun, the center of this radial system. However, it appears that the crucial factor for the selection of a *huaca* was its state of difference, an arresting visual characteristic or peculiar feature in an Inca aesthetic of alterity. For instance, a stone wall is mentioned as a *huaca*, due to its curious form ("like a bulging belly") which attracted the attention of the Incas. A stone is marked for its resemblance to a human being, and another for a shape "in the manner of a falcon." Difference becomes an operational element in this process of selection and marking. Reading the *huacas* in the "List of Ceques" as a text, certain patterns do emerge. However, some of the qualities mentioned in the list of *huacas* defy facile classification. One stone is said to have jumped from one mountain to another. For that reason the Incas venerated it. The "otherness" of these statements suggests that the ethnohistorical source contains a core which is not yet contaminated by post-Conquest Spanish doctrines.

But how valid is the ethnohistorical documentation in the interpretation of the archaeological record? A curious disjunction between material remains and mental categories in the valley of Cuzco exemplifies the issues. The cultural geography of the valley was marked by the opposition between *hanan* (upper) and *hurin* (lower) as spatial and social categories. To what extent is that opposition visible in the archaeological record of the valley of Cuzco? All the carved rock complexes are found, without exception, in the higher, or northern, part of the valley (Astete Victoria 1984; Hemming and Ranney 1982;

Niles 1987). The explanation for this phenomenon appears quite straightforward. The geology of the northern part of the valley is dominated by limestone formations with occasional diorite intrusions. In contrast, the southern part of the valley is characterized by much softer sandstone formations (Gregory 1916). If interpretation were based exclusively on the material remains and the geological record, no problems would be evident. One would see a clear-cut dualism, expressed in *huacas* as carved stones and important irrigation districts in the *hanan* or upper part of the valley as contrasted with the *hurin* or lower part of the valley, firmly anchored in the geological characteristics of the area.

But the moment we turn to the ethnohistorical record, the picture becomes more complex. Of the 328 *huacas* described for the valley of Cuzco, 108 are stone, an equal number on each side of the valley, and equally divided over the four *suyus* or quarters. Moreover, descriptions do not differ substantially between upper and lower Cuzco. How can this apparent discrepancy between the archaeological record and the ethnohistorical document be explained? There are at least three possibilities, not mutually exclusive. The stone-*huacas* in the southern part of the valley might have disappeared, due to the porous nature of the sandstone in that area. Or perhaps stone-*huacas* in the southern part of the valley were movable stones, carried to other places, according to needs of the ritual calendar or for *ad hoc* reasons. In one case this hypothesis can be confirmed: the stone-*huaca* of Huanacauri was said to have been carried into war, as far north as Quito (Ecuador). When the Spaniards finally discovered this stone, it was hidden in a house of an Inca noble, back again in Cuzco, but in the northern section of the city. A third possibility is that the majority of the *huacas* in the northern and southern parts of the valley of Cuzco were natural features, rocks and stones without any cultural alterations, and for that reason are not evident in the archaeological record.

These explanations may be partially valid, but I would like to suggest here a fourth possibility. In a sense, the archaeological record conforms to a model of diametric oppositions, supported by geological contrasts, by the presence versus absence of carved rocks, and by the higher elevation of the northern part relative to the southern part of the valley of Cuzco. On the other hand, the ethnohistorical record indicates an equal distribution of stone-*huacas* over the four *suyus*, with a harmonious balance between rocks in the northern and the southern parts of the valley. These data can be read as conforming to a concentric model. In this concentric model stone-*huacas* are situated in a series of concentric rings around the city of Cuzco, arranged like nodes on the strings of a *quipu*. The fact that the diametric model does not parallel the concentric model may be due to the different nature of the sets of data generating these models. In other words, the diametric model remains close to perceptual elements of the natural world, while the concentric model is a representation of ideal concepts interposed by the Incas. The tension between these two models brings to mind the well-known discussion of similar dichotomies in Winnebago and Bororo social systems by Claude Lévi-Strauss. He wrote:

> The important point is that the dualism is itself twofold. It seems in some cases to be conceived as the result of a balanced and symmetrical dichotomy between social groups, between aspects of the physical world, or between moral or metaphysical attributes; that is, it seems to be a diametric type of structure. And according to a concentric perspective it is also conceived in terms of opposition, with the one difference that the opposition is, with regard to social and/or religious prestige, necessarily unequal.
>
> (Lévi-Strauss 1963: 139)

Inca Landscape: The Singularity of Alterity

It was necessary to articulate the foregoing problems in order to demonstrate the tension between the archaeological and ethnohistorical records and to emphasize the demand for complex explanations in response to complex problems, such as those found in studying a highly bureaucratic state like the Inca empire. Traditionally, archaeologists look for artifacts which, as material culture, constitute the exclusive text on which cultural analysis is based. But in dealing with a more dialectic research topic such as the cognition of landscape, we must ask how unaltered landscape features and spaces are recognized? In brief, how do we evaluate the absence of pattern and regularity as integrative aspects of our understanding of culture?

Some archaeologists have argued that similarities and differences can be identified at many levels. As Hodder notes: "They may occur in terms of underlying dimensions of variation such as structural oppositions, notions of 'orderliness,' 'naturalness' and so on." And he adds: "It can be argued that archaeologists have concentrated too much on similarities and too little on differences" (Hodder 1986: 127). The Inca case suggests that alterity, as irregularity and difference, is highly significant to cognition and manipulation of the Andean landscape. The possibility of alterity as an alternative and often crucial component should be included in any archaeological search for pattern and

regularity in the past. The relative indifference of contemporary scholars to elements of "difference" in non-western societies and cognitive
systems may well have led to the under-recognition of alterity in the
study of material culture and mental structures.

With respect to the complex state bureaucracy of Inca society, Niles
(1987: 1) argues that "the architecture of empire included the creation
of a state aesthetic with little tolerance of variation from official stan-
dards, which resulted in a recognizable and seemingly uniform architectural style distributed throughout the Inca domain." To this
conceptualization should now be added an additional component: an
Inca "aesthetic of alterity," which attributed great significance to "the
works of nature unaltered by human contrivance" (Cobo 1990 [1653]:
44). The Inca interest in "difference," "idiosyncrasy," and "anomaly"
has to be included in any assessment of settlement planning, *ceque* system, taxonomy of noses or potatoes, astronomical lore, and, specifically
here, the cognition of landscape. The Inca "aesthetic of alterity" may
correspond on an abstract and conceptual level to the Huari strategy
"of presenting the state as a human order mediating the chaos of
nature" (Stone-Miller 1992b: 336). As demonstrated in the analysis of
Huari tunics mentioned in the beginning of this chapter, manifestations of chaos are apparent in the variety, unpredictability, and idiosyncrasy of textile design. The absence of similar studies for Inca textiles
prevents the presentation of a corresponding hypothesis for Inca art
and society. However, it is suggestive to think of the Inca interest in
alterity in nature as a continuation of the Huari preoccupation with
"chaos." Within a system of rigid state control, the possibility of "difference" and "chaos" introduced a necessary degree of flexibility.
Mnemonic devices such as the *quipus* and mental topography such as
the *ceque* lines can be seen as valuable instruments in this program of
mediating the demands of land, life, and belief.

ACKNOWLEDGMENTS

I gratefully acknowledge very useful and much appreciated editorial
comments made by Wendy Ashmore, Clark Erickson, and Margaret
van de Guchte.

REFERENCES

Albornoz, C. de 1984 [1584]: La instrucción para descubrir todas las guacas
del Peru. *Revista Andina* 2 (1), 169–222.

Ascher, M., and Ascher, R. 1981: *Code of the Quipu: A Study in Media, Mathematics, and Culture*. Ann Arbor: University of Michigan Press.

Astete Victoria, J. F. 1984: Los sistemas hidráulicos del Valle del Cusco (prehispánicos). Tesis de Bachillerato, Universidad Nacional San Antonio Abad del Cusco.

Bastien, J. W. 1978: *Mountain of the Condor: Metaphor and Ritual in an Andean Ayllu*. St Paul: West Publishing Company.

Bingham, H. 1979 [1930]: *Machu-Picchu: A Citadel of the Incas*. New Haven: Yale University Press.

Certeau, M. de. 1984: *The Practice of Everyday Life*. Berkeley: University of California Press.

Classen, C. 1993: *Inca Cosmology and the Body*. Salt Lake City: University of Utah Press.

Cobo, B. 1990 [1653]: *Inca Religions and Customs*, R. Hamilton (transl.). Austin: University of Texas Press.

Derrida, J. 1976: *Of Grammatology*, G. C. Spivak (transl.). Baltimore: Johns Hopkins University Press.

Garcilaso de la Vega, el Inca 1965 [1609]: *Obras Completas*, 4 vols, P. Carmelo Saenz de Santa Maria, S. I. (ed.). Madrid: Biblioteca de Autores Españoles.

Gonzales Holguin, D. 1952 [1608]: *Vocabulario de la Lengua General... Llamado Quichua*, R. Porras Barrenachea (ed.). Lima: Instituto de Historia.

Gregory, H. E. 1916: A geological reconnaissance of the Cuzco valley, Peru. *American Journal of Science*, 41, 1–100.

Hemming, J., and Ranney, E. 1982: *Monuments of the Incas*. Boston: New York Graphic Society.

Hodder, I. 1986: *Reading the Past: Current Approaches to Interpretation in Archaeology*. Cambridge: Cambridge University Press.

Hyslop, J. 1990: *Inka Settlement Planning*. Austin: University of Texas Press.

Jones, J. 1964: *Art of Empire: The Inca of Peru*. New York: Museum of Primitive Art.

Lévi-Strauss, C. 1963: *Structural Anthropology*. New York: Basic Books.

Molina "el Cuzqueño," C. 1943 [1574]: *Fábulas y Ritos de los Incas*, F. A. Loayza (ed.), Series I, vol. IV. Lima: Los Pequeños Grandes Libros de Historia Americana.

Murra, J. V. 1975: *Formaciones Económicas y Políticas del Mundo Andino*. Lima: Instituto de Estudios Peruanos.

Murua, M. de. 1962–4 [1590–1611]: *Historia General del Perú, Origen y Descendencia de los Incas*, 2 vols, M. Ballesteros-Gaibrois (ed.). Madrid: Instituto Gonzalo Fernández de Oviedo, Consejo Superior de Investigaciones Científicas.

Nickel, C. 1982: The semiotics of Andean terracing. *Art Journal*, Fall, 200–3.

Niles, S. A. 1987: *Callachaca: Style and Status in an Inca Community*. Iowa City: University of Iowa Press.

Niles, S. A. 1992: Inca architecture and the sacred landscape. In R. Townsend (ed.), *The Ancient Americas: Art from Sacred Landscapes*, Chicago, Munich: Art Institute of Chicago, Prestel Verlag, 347–58.

Poole, D. A. 1984: Ritual-economic calendars in Paruro: the structure of representation in Andean ethnography. PhD dissertation, University of Illinois, Urbana–Champaign.

Rostworowski de Diez Canseco, M. 1988: *Conflicts over Coca Fields in XVIth-Century Perú*. Memoirs of the Museum of Anthropology, 21. Ann Arbor: University of Michigan.

Rowe, J. H. 1944: Inca culture at the time of the Spanish conquest. In J. H. Steward (ed.), *Handbook of South American Indians*, vol. 2, Bulletin 143, Washington, DC: Bureau of American Ethnology, 183–330.

Sherbondy, J. 1986: Los ceques: código de canales en el Cusco Incáico. *Allpanchis*, 18 (27), 39–74.

Stone-Miller, R. 1992a: *To Weave for the Sun: Andean Textiles in the Museum of Fine Arts*. Boston: Museum of Fine Arts.

Stone-Miller, R. 1992b: Camelids and chaos in Huari and Tiwanaku textiles. In R. Townsend (ed.), *The Ancient Americas: Art from Sacred Landscapes*, Chicago, Munich: Art Institute of Chicago, Prestel Verlag, 335–46.

Stone-Miller, R., and McEwan, G. F. 1990/91: The representation of the Wari state in stone and thread: a comparison of architecture and tapestry tunics. *Res*, 19/20, 53–80.

Urton, G. 1981: *At the Crossroads of the Earth and the Sky: An Andean Cosmology*. Austin: University of Texas Press.

van de Guchte, M. 1984: El ciclo mítico andino de la piedra cansada. *Revista Andina*, 2, 539–56.

van de Guchte, M. 1990: Carving the world: Inca monumental sculpture and landscape. PhD dissertation, University of Illinois, Urbana-Champaign.

van de Guchte, M. 1997: Sculpture and the concept of the double among the Inca kings. *Res*, 29/30, 256–69.

Wachtel, N. 1973: *Sociedad e Ideología. Ensayos de Historia y Antropología Andinas*. Lima: Instituto de Estudios Peruanos.

Zuidema, R. T. 1964: *The Ceque System of Cuzco: The Social Organization of the Capital of the Inca*. Leiden: Brill.

Zuidema, R. T. 1978: Lieux sacrés et irrigation: tradition historique, mythes et rituels au Cuzco. *Annales, Économies, Sociétés, Civilisations*, 3, 1037–57.

Zuidema, R. T. 1989: A quipu calendar from Ica, Peru, with a comparison to the ceque calendar from Cuzco. In A. Aveni (ed.), *World Archaeoastronomy*, Cambridge: Cambridge University Press, 341–55.

Zuidema, R. T. 1992: De Inca Kalender. In E. de Bock (ed.), *De Erfenis van de Incas*, Rotterdam: Museum voor Volkenkunde, 15–19.

8

The Ideology of Settlement: Ancestral Keres Landscapes in the Northern Rio Grande

James E. Snead and Robert W. Preucel

The Santa Ana Indians know what the universe is like; they know its shape and nature. They are acquainted with all the gods and spirits; they know where they live and what they do. They know how and where mankind originated and what has happened to them since the beginning. And they know how they, the Tamayame, have acquired their social organization, their ceremonies and their paraphernalia.

(White 1942: 80)

Introduction

The natural and cultural landscapes of the North American Southwest present a compelling vista. Rugged topography characterized by harsh beauty and extremes of climate provides the setting for contemporary indigenous communities with extraordinarily intricate social and ideological systems. From the beginning, Southwestern archaeologists, like Adolph Bandelier, relied upon ecological arguments to understand the adaptations of past and present native peoples, since survival in a place with low rainfall, limited arable soil, and a short growing season was held to be the critical factor. This perspective still underlies much of the current ecosystems focus on agricultural strategies, residential mobility, storage practices, diet breadth, and food-processing technologies. These studies suggest that patterns of resource exploitation have had considerable impact on fuel wood availability, soil fertility, and game abundance. Variability in the land as a productive resource is seen as providing a fundamental context, albeit changeable and complex, for the organization of human society.

Recently, Southwestern archaeologists have begun to expand the standard ecosystems approach by studying the ways in which indigenous societies have conceptualized the land. There appear to be two distinct directions of research developing. The first of these considers architecture as a social process which both constrains and enables social acts. For example, John Stein and Stephen Lekson (1992), writing about ritual architecture in sites associated with the Chaco system, argue that concepts expressed within site-level architecture were replicated in community design and in the organization of the Chacoan landscape as a whole. The second approach examines the agricultural landscape as an integral part of the built environment. Kurt Anschuetz (1995) has explored variability in prehistoric agricultural technologies in the Chama district, many of which involve extensive modifications to the landscape. When the constitutive roles of ideology are considered and the constructed nature of landscape is acknowledged, the complexity of indigenous conceptions of self and world can begin to be appreciated. Land, as the setting for social interaction and as a warrant for belief, becomes a resource of a different kind, one invested with multiple and changing meanings by its human inhabitants.

This new landscape perspective has several methodological implications. Most standard archaeological surveys have been organized according to complex spatial sampling schemes or narrow pipeline rights-of-way. The basic assumption is that the data produced by these surveys can be aggregated in order to reveal patterns of culture process over long periods of time. However useful this approach has been and continues to be, it has had the unfortunate consequence of disembedding archaeological sites from their social contexts. Sites obtain their meaning by virtue of their relations to other sites and physical features in a pre-existing social landscape. Landscape cannot be fully understood without reference to a world view which integrates place and space in the production of meaning. This is true whether one wishes to look at culture from the inside using its own logic, as it were, or whether one is interested in modeling general principles of decision making in non-market contexts. In recognition of this fact, transect surveys are now being supplemented by the recording of smaller areas in greater detail, a "microscale-regional" approach which documents the richness and diversity of the cultural landscape (e.g., Preucel 1990; Snead 1995). This method allows for the reconstruction of the local context, which was previously unavailable.

In this chapter, we discuss the construction and maintenance of ideological landscapes by the ancestors of the modern Keres people of the northern Rio Grande region of New Mexico.[1] Using two case studies drawn from our current research, we examine some of the ways in which the Ancestral Keres people perceived the land around them and used this knowledge to structure their own communities and social practices. Integrating archaeological, ethnographic, and ethnohistorical data, we develop an argument for strong continuities in distinctive Keres ideological landscapes for a period of over half a millennium. We attribute this stability to a process of "place making" which involves both the "domestication of the physical" and the "naturalization of the social." While not denying that the process of settlement has a distinct ecological component, the shift in interpretive emphasis towards an ideological approach has the advantage of placing Ancestral Keres communities in a broader social context. New insights, both for relationships between people and the land and for the history of the Keres people themselves, are the result.

The Ideology of Settlement

The study of indigenous perceptions of the countryside was an important goal of Boasian anthropologists in the first two decades of the twentieth century. Ethnogeographies were produced which were based on linguistic data, place names, and patterns of land use (e.g. Boas 1934; Harrington 1916; Loud 1918). In recent years, these ethnogeographies have gained new favor, and several new studies of hunter-gatherers (Munn 1970; Myers 1986; Tonkinson 1991) and sedentary agriculturalists (Bloch 1995; Bonnemaison 1994; Dillehay 1990; Lee 1989; Toren 1995) have reinserted history into culture by looking at social agency and perceptions of land. Collectively, this work illustrates the diverse ways in which meaning is ascribed to place and how these meanings transcend simple economics, suggesting approaches that can be used to inform archaeological research.

The "assignment of meaning" to land and landmarks described by the modern ethnogeographies and evident cross-culturally can be understood as a way of structuring the landscape along lines which relate existing social principles to lived experience. Australian Aboriginal landscapes, for example, are crossed by Dream Tracks marking the wanderings of totemic ancestors, a process through which the world was "socialized" (Myers 1986: 54). Nancy Munn describes the significance of this process for the Pitjantjatjara people:

> The importance of these sacred countries is not economic in the sense that the sites do not define the limits of the region over which those in residence may forage for food. Rather, the home country must be seen as a symbol of stability, a spatial and temporal anchorage conceptualized

in terms of specific place names and the originating ancestors found within it.

(Munn 1970: 146)

Another perception of the relationship between society and landscape is described by Maurice Bloch for the agricultural Zafimaniry in the eastern highlands of Madagascar. In the Zafimaniry world view, permanency, represented by nature, is a desirable characteristic, in contrast to the transitory human state. Individuals aspire to attain permanence in various ways, such as through the establishment of families and the construction of houses, which as material symbols of social success are often inhabited for generations. A further movement toward permanence is the construction of stone monuments to honor the dead. These monuments mark the complete merging of the human and the natural, through which people attach themselves "most totally to the unchanging land" (Bloch 1995: 74), since the monuments remain features of the countryside long after their association with particular individuals is forgotten. The Zafimaniry landscape, with its houses and monuments, is thus an oblique reflection of the society which created it (1995). A similar process has been documented for the Dogon people of Mali, whose fields, villages, and homesteads are constructed as cosmological models of great complexity (Griaule and Dieterlein 1954: 99).

The assignment of meaning in these, and other examples, involves two complementary strategies. One is a process of "domestication," the reconfiguration of nature by placing it within a cultural frame of reference. The areas commonly used by members of a community are filled with familiar places, structures, and landmarks, and these are all known by their corresponding names and associations. Occasionally places are renamed to commemorate a remarkable event or particular happening. But there are also dangerous places in the world and once defined these can be negotiated or avoided. The more distant regions of the world are often regarded as unfamiliar and dangerous places. For example, Mary Helms (1988: 85) has documented cross-cultural perceptions of travel as a dangerous and liminal activity, in part, because it removes the individual from "known" territory to the unknown. The organization of space through the imposition of a system of place names and corresponding references can be seen as a widespread cultural response to living within an otherwise uncontrollable world.

The second, and related process, is "naturalization," the establishment of the legitimacy of social action by linking it to nature. The rising and setting of the sun, the seasons, and the topography of the home range are observable and essentially permanent phenomena from the human perspective. Human existence, in contrast, is comparatively ephemeral with issues of life transition particularly important in generating meaning. Death, for example, is a traumatic event for both family and community and it requires acknowledgment usually through proscribed social acts. Similarly, specific transitions and rites of passage within an individual's lifetime are often marked by ritual theater in which different social identities are established and played out. Connecting the social with the natural, then, is a means through which the human can be made part of the permanent or natural order. In this way existing circumstances and social relations can be defined as traditional, historical, and proper.

The creation of landscape thus involves manipulating the dialectic between society and nature in which the "natural becomes social" and the "social becomes natural." As the product of social acts, these changing definitions of "place" can be manifested in various media: " ... myth, prayer, music, dance, art, architecture and, in many communities, recurrent forms of religious and political ritual" (Basso 1996: 109). The resultant ideological landscapes are never static, however, since the social groups which create them are themselves constantly undergoing change. Perceptions of the land are continually constructed and contested by different social groups in the formation of cultural identities. This discourse is often expressed in debates over the use rights to land, water, game animals, ritual materials, and sacred places. The "invention of tradition," as documented by Eric Hobsbawm and Terence Ranger (1983), is thus a continuous social activity which legitimizes contemporary practices and power relations.

The interface between the natural landscape and the built environment holds special promise for archaeological study. As Bloch argues for the Zafimaniry, the permanence of architecture is a means through which society connects itself with the perceived natural order and, unlike place names, one which may be detected archaeologically. This is a process which involves both the construction of artificial features and the organization of the features as they are distributed across space. The material remains of such systems, dramatic or ephemeral, can thus provide an unique window onto the landscapes and world views of the societies which created them.

Research on ideological landscapes in antiquity has tended to emphasize so-called "complex" society, for which detailed records or historical accounts are often available (e.g., Farrington 1992; Wheatley 1971). The ethnogeographic record, however, indicates that concern for the organization of the built environment as a referent to the landscape is widespread among indigenous societies at many different levels of integration. A considerable amount of archaeological research, particularly in Europe, has begun to analyze archaeological data for landscape organization among hunter-gatherer and Neolithic societies, analyzing features from monuments to rock art (Bradley 1997; Bradley et al. 1994; Fleming 1988; Thomas 1991; Tilley 1994).

Early Southwestern archaeologists recognized the potential of the rich archaeological record for studying the cultural landscapes in Ancestral Pueblo society. In 1906 Edgar Lee Hewett, in a discussion of the archaeology of New Mexico's Pajarito Plateau, remarked that

> The village sites of the ancient inhabitants, with all the accessories of village life, such as kivas, shrines, burial places, fields, irrigation works, lookouts, stairways and trails...preserve a complete picture of the ancient life of the Southwest.
>
> (Hewett 1906: 52)

While some aspects of the "complete picture" which Hewett described have received their fair share of attention, others have not. In particular, elements of the archaeological record which pertain specifically to social and ideological aspects of society remain under-studied. Shrines, for instance, have long been recognized as basic architectural components of ancestral pueblo society (e.g., Douglass 1912; 1917; Hewett 1953; Jeançon 1923; Nelson 1914; Wendorf 1953), but only recently have they been systematically incorporated into archaeological discussions (Anschuetz 1996; Snead 1995; Steen 1977). While the interpretation of shrines can be problematic on many levels, the ethnographic and ethnohistoric record provides extensive documentation for their historic use and significance and this can provide a productive backdrop for further study. Similar promise is offered by the analysis of relationships between the landscape and components of the built environment, such as domestic architecture. Looking at shrines and architecture in a landscape context offers significant potential for understanding continuity and change in indigenous Southwestern society.

The Keres World

The Northern Keres people today live in five villages distributed along the Rio Grande and the Rio Jemez between Albuquerque and Santa Fe, New Mexico (figure 8.1). The communities of Cochiti (*Kotyiti*), San Felipe (*Katishya*), Santa Ana (*Tamaya*), Santo Domingo (*Kewa*), and Zia

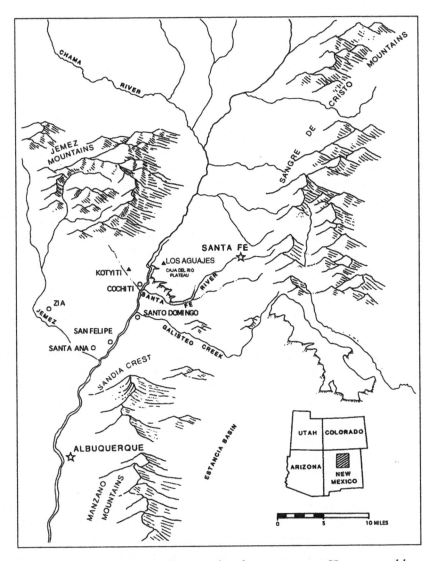

Figure 8.1 Location map of ancestral and contemporary Keresan pueblos discussed in the text (map based on Habichte-Mauche 1993: figure 1).

(*Tsia*) are united by language, but are otherwise autonomous. The Southern Keres inhabit Acoma (*Aku*) and Laguna (*Kawaika*) to the northeast. While the Keres share many cultural attributes with other neighboring Pueblo people in the region, such as the Tewa and Tiwa, their distinctive language and close spatial proximity has led to them being considered a cultural "group" of their own, a distinction probably originating with Spanish identification of a group of communities along the Rio Grande which they called Queres (sometimes also known as Quires).[2] The five northern villages are linked by a shared migration narrative in which the people entered the region from the north, after emergence from the ceremonial opening called *shipap*, some time prior to the Spanish *entradas*. The Keres landscape, thus, includes not only areas encompassed by their present villages and experience, but lands with which they have long-standing historical associations.

The Keres world view is known largely due to the pioneering ethnographic work of Franz Boas, Elsie Clews Parsons, and Leslie White.[3] Boas recorded aspects of the Keres language and world view at Laguna (Boas 1928). Parsons studied ceremonialism at Laguna, San Felipe and Santo Domingo (Parsons 1920; 1923). White carried out research on social organization, economics, and religion at Acoma (White 1932b), Santo Domingo (White 1935), San Felipe (White 1932a), Santa Ana (White 1942), and Zia (White 1962). The most comprehensive synthesis of the Keres world is that provided by White, which uses the cosmology of Santa Ana Pueblo as a model (White 1960). The following discussion, which relates cosmology to built environment in the construction of the Keres ideological landscape, is derived largely from White's work and supplemented with additional ethnographic information where appropriate. The reader is cautioned that this description is a composite and not intended as an accurate depiction of the world view of any individual Keres pueblo.

Like the Tewa (cf. Ortiz 1969), the Keres people conceptualize their world as a series of nested, but interrelated, regions containing mountains, lakes, springs, hunting grounds, agricultural fields, and mineral resources, all of which focus on a central village (figure 8.2). The farthest, and most dangerous, region consists of the places at the edge of the world inhabited by powerful supernatural beings. Significantly, the world is divided in half along gender lines with the deities of the northwest and southwest being female, and those of the northeast and southeast, male. The female deities are frequently mentioned in oral narratives, and Thought Woman, also called Yellow Woman, is regarded as the creator who "thought people into being." Her house, known as House of Leaves, is located in the northwest corner. Spider Grandmother is the consistent helper of people in trouble, and her house, called Lumber House, is in the southwest corner. The male deities appear to be associated with the movements of the Sun. Butterfly is a protector of the *cacique*, an important leadership position within the Keres communities. Butterfly lives at Turquoise House, in

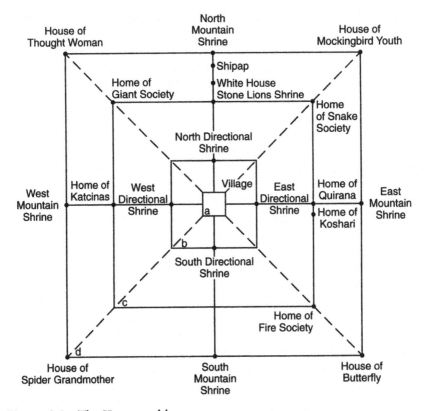

Figure 8.2 The Keres world.
Key: a=village and plaza shrines; b=directional shrines; c=society shrines; d=mountain shrines.

the southeast corner. Mockingbird Youth lives in his house in the northeast. These latter two corners are associated with the summer and winter solstices respectively. At Santa Ana, the war chief is the designated sunwatcher, and he determines the date of the solstice ceremonies by marking where the sun rises on the eastern horizon (White 1942: 205).

In the six directions (the four cardinal directions plus the zenith and nadir) are the sacred mountains. At each of these places live pairs of male and female deities who bear special responsibility for the weather and the seasons. Each of these mountains is also associated with its own color, animal, and tree. The names of these mountains appear to be shared by most of the Keres pueblos, although their physical referents vary depending on the location of the pueblo. For example, Mt Taylor is the West Mountain for Laguna, but it is the North Mountain for Acoma (White 1935: 32). These natural features are further sacralized by the construction of shrines. The mountain shrine on top of Mt Taylor is a shallow pit about three feet in diameter with short trails leading out in the directions of Laguna, Acoma, Zuni, Jemez, and Navajo country (Boas 1928: 298). Ritual practitioners visit these shrines at specific times of the year in order to pray for good crops and success in hunting.

The next region, somewhat closer in, is defined by the homes of the supernatural deities associated with the medicine societies so prominent in Keres ceremonialism. At certain times in the summer, members of different societies go on retreat to visit the homes of the Fathers of their societies and pray for rain for the crops. These homes are often located in mountain caves and springs (White 1962: 234). Similarly, members of the Hunting Society make pilgrimages to hunting shrines where certain animal deities dwell in order to pray for success in the hunt. The best known of these shrines are the two Stone Lions shrines. The northernmost of these, located in Bandelier National Monument, is called *Yapashi* and is associated with the prehistoric pueblo of the same name. The shrine consists of a large circle of loosely piled stones enclosing two couchant lions carved from volcanic tuff with an opening to the southeast (Bandelier 1892: 152–3; Prince 1903; 1904). The southern shrine is sited on a mesa in the Cañada de Cochiti and most likely associated with *Kuapa*, a nearby ancestral Cochiti village. It is also formed by an enclosure of stones and once contained two crouching lions, only one of which is still extant (Bandelier 1892: 161; Dumarest 1919: 207).[4]

Immediately outside the pueblo are the village directional shrines. These shrines mark the symbolic boundaries of the village. They are located in the four cardinal directions, and are typically keyhole-shaped stone structures with openings facing the north or east (Boas 1928: 299; Dumarest 1919: 169, 207). Access is not restricted and they can be visited by anyone from the pueblo wishing to pray for something (Boas 1928: 299; Goldfrank 1927: 70). Such directional shrines were noted by the Spanish during the *entradas*. Antonio de Espejo wrote that "just as the Spaniards have crosses along the roads, these people set up, midway between pueblos, their artificial hillocks built of stone like wayside shrines, where they place painted sticks and feathers" (Hammond and Rey 1966: 220). During the period of the Spanish Reconquest (1680–94), they were observed at Alameda, Puaray, Sandia, San Felipe, Santo Domingo and Cochiti (Testimony of Lucas de Quintana, in Hackett and Shelby 1942: 286; Testimony of Josephe, in Hackett and Shelby 1942: 240). Some of these shrines were apparently surrounded by wattle enclosures to keep out animals possibly indicating a sacred/profane distinction (Testimony of Diego Lopez Sambrano, in Hackett and Shelby 1942: 292).

Finally, there is a series of shrines within each village, the most important being the plaza shrines. These shrines define and consecrate the pueblo. At Zia, there are important shrines in the north and south plazas; the shrine in the north plaza is the home of Whiteman, while the two in the south plaza represent the mountain lion and the twin war gods and their helpers (White 1962: 49). These shrines protect the village against witches and diseases. Similar, but not identical shrines were located in the plazas of all the Keres villages and were places where offerings of maize and tobacco were made. These shrines were present in almost all Pueblo villages at the time of Otermin's reconquest expedition (Antonio de Otermín, in Hackett and Shelby 1942: 292). The Spanish regarded such shrines as evidence of idolatry and routinely destroyed them along with *kivas* and ritual paraphernalia. The renewal of these shrines was one of the principal activities undertaken after the Revolt of 1680. According to informant accounts, Popé and Alonso Catiti, two of the leaders of the revolt, required all people to place in and near their villages "piles of stones on which they could offer ground corn and other cereals and tobacco, they saying that the stones were their God" (Testimony of Juan and Francisco Lorenzo, in Hackett and Shelby 1942: 251).

This brief overview of the conceptual terrain of the Northern Keres pueblos demonstrates the close interrelations of land, supernatural beings, and people in the Keres world view. Sacred mountains, hills, springs, and distinctive natural features defined the sense of "place" held by each community. These features were inhabited by an array of supernatural beings who held considerable power over the seasons, weather, crops, and animals. Ritual leaders periodically made pilgrimages to the houses of the supernatural deities on the sacred mountains and in these actions, they insured the continuance of the Keres world. Members of medicine societies typically went on summer retreats to caves and lakes, an act which was conceptualized as "going back to *shipap*," a renewal of vision and·purpose effected by communication with the supernatural founders of the societies. People of the pueblo prayed at artificial shrines built within the plazas and in the countryside immediately surrounding the village when they were in need. Two material systems of meaning were thus intertwined, with social meaning attached to natural features of landscape in combination with specifically constructed features placed within that landscape. Land and society thus reproduced each other.

These data provide a substantive baseline from which to interpret Ancestral Keres landscapes. Given the continuity, both historical and spatial, between the modern populations and their immediate predecessors, some correlation in the perception and manipulation of landscape over time is highly probable. This is not to say that change can be discounted, particularly since the intervening centuries have been marked by demographic collapse and other severe impacts brought about by the Spanish conquest. The perception of "place," however, is fundamental to the Keres world view, and the cardinal directions and four corners of the world appear to be basic structuring principles used in the maintenance of the ideological landscape. Within the parameters thus established, variation can be expected as a product of different historical circumstances and social interactions. The two archaeological examples discussed below permit the identification of some of this variability and allow for the exploration of the time depth of the structuring principles.

The Ideological Landscape of Los Aguajes

Our first case study is Los Aguajes (LA 5; figure 8.3), a probable Ancestral Keres community located near the southern end of the Caja del Río Plateau northeast of Cochiti Pueblo (see figure 8.1). At the center of the community is Pueblo los Aguajes, a double-plaza, H-shaped adobe "community house" with an estimated 160 rooms, located on the edge of a flat plain bounded by hills on three sides and

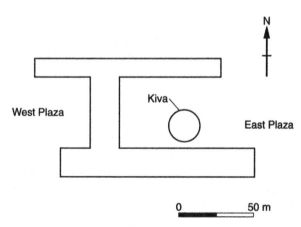

Figure 8.3 Pueblo los Aguajes (LA 5).

overlooking the Cochiti Basin to the southwest. Dendrochronological dates from excavations earlier in the twentieth century by Nels Nelson (Smiley et al. 1953; Vivian n.d.) along with associated ceramics indicate that Pueblo los Aguajes was occupied for a brief period in the fifteenth century AD, perhaps for no longer than a generation. Although it does not appear to be specifically mentioned in Keres oral history, architectural, ceramic, and locational data are consistent with the identification of Pueblo los Aguajes as an Ancestral Keres site. Survey of a 238-ha area centered on the pueblo in 1995 documented 52 sites associated with the community, including small structures, formal field features, trails, petroglyphs, artifact scatters, and shrines (Snead 1995).

Shrines at Los Aguajes fall into several formal categories. The first, and most recognizable, are circular and "C"-shaped features built of piled basalt and scoria cobbles. The most prominent of these, LA 10623, is located on a hilltop 800 meters due south of the community house, and is a circular mound 12 meters in diameter and a meter in height, composed of thousands of basalt cobbles (figure 8.4). This site is the most prominent architectural feature in the community, besides the pueblo itself. A similar, but less massive, circular shrine is located between this large shrine and the community house, while a C-shaped feature (LA 114032), open to the east, is present on a sloping ridge summit 800 meters north of the community house (figure 8.5).

Another evident shrine type consists of architectural features associated with petroglyphs. One of these, a small stone enclosure built against a basalt outcrop, overlooks a deep canyon, while another of similar plan sits against the cliff of a small mesa nearby. While idiosyncratic in design, sites consisting of this suite of features have been noted elsewhere in the region and have been suggested to be related to ritual activity (Chapman et al. 1977; Schaafsma 1990; Snead 1995).

The third category of shrines concerns natural features which have been marked or modified in ways which indicate that they were accorded particular significance. The principal water source at Los Aguajes is a catchment basin in the bottom of an adjacent arroyo; this is the largest of the *"aguajes"* for which the area was named. While small in size, it would have been the principal source of water for the entire community. The thousands of petroglyphs which mark the surrounding basalt indicate that its significance extended beyond the material realm and may have preceded the occupation of the community house by a considerable period. Shrines were also built on mountaintops in the immediate vicinity of Los Aguajes. The summits of both La Tetilla to the southeast and Cerro Colorado to the north feature constructed shrines.

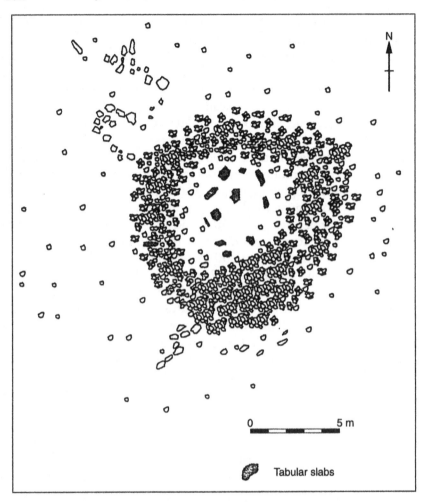

Figure 8.4   LA 10623, south directional shrine of Los Aguajes.

Interpreting the Los Aguajes shrines requires both comparative and spatial analysis. Circular and C-shaped shrines are common features of Ancestral Keres sites. There is a large circular shrine, similar to LA 10623, present on a ridge south of the site of Kuapa. A similar feature is found near the Caja del Rio North (LA 174) community house, 10 km to the north of Los Aguajes (Snead 1995). Herhahn (1995) illustrates a crescent-shaped field structure near La Bajada (LA 7) which is very similar to LA 114032. Hewett (1953) remarked that nearly every pueblo in the region had an associated shrine of one of these types.

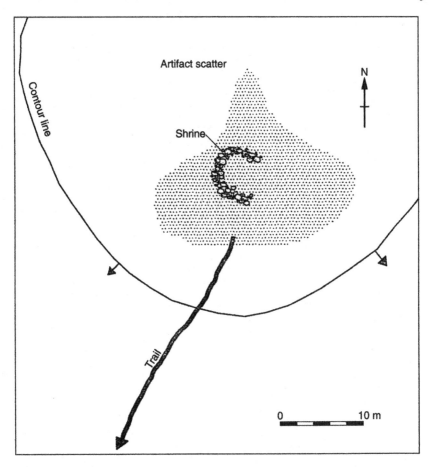

Figure 8.5 LA 114032, C-shaped shrine at Los Aguajes.

Spatially, the larger shrines of Los Aguajes are distributed along a north–south axis drawn through the community house. This layout is even more striking when a shrine on a low hilltop 2 km south of the community house is included (figure 8.6). Other ridgetops and summits within the survey area are devoid of shrine features. Survey has not been conducted in areas to the east and west of the community house to an extent sufficient to document the presence or absence of shrines in the other cardinal directions, but previous research and reconnaissance indicates that this is a strong possibility. Such a "system" of shrines closely resembles the directional shrines described for the Tewa by Ortiz (1969), which provide symbolic boundaries for community space. The area encompassed by the "north" and "south" shrines is roughly 3 km in diameter, which appears to define the core

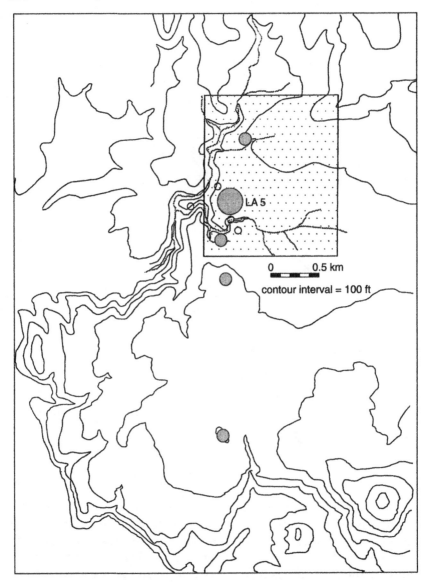

Figure 8.6 The Los Aguajes community, indicating the predominantly north–south alignment of shrines.

of the Los Aguajes community. The striking orientation of the Los Aguajes shrine system towards the cardinal directions indicates that order perceived in the natural realm was influential in its design.

The presence of shrines oriented towards prominent natural features, such as hilltops, viewpoints, and springs, also reveals a concern with domesticating the local topography. The visibility of springs and mountains and their cosmological role would have made them key landmarks, to which the addition of a constructed shrine may have symbolized the construction of a relationship between the builder and whatever the landmark symbolized. An analogy may have existed between local hills and the peaks which bounded the Keres world, which would have been strengthened by the construction of shrines atop them. Springs may have represented points of access to the underworld and by analogy *shipap*. White (1935: 167) records a number of these for Santo Domingo and notes that they typically include petroglyphs depicting supernatural deities. These shrines were visited by ritual practitioners during their summer retreats.

The scale of the shrines at Los Aguajes is also informative. The relatively high level of labor invested in LA 10623 suggests that its construction may have been coordinated at the community level. While other data suggest that communities of this period were weakly organized, collective involvement in the building of shrines would imply that acts of landscape definition were important community functions (Kolb and Snead 1997). This, in turn, demonstrates an interest in identity and legitimacy even in locations such as Los Aguajes, several kilometers distant from the nearest contemporary group.

Concern with naturalizing the Los Aguajes community within the landscape is also evident through the association of other shrines with prominent natural features. The large number and variable style of the petroglyphs surrounding the *aguaje* suggest that the location was important over a long period of time, possibly longer than the occupation of Los Aguajes itself. The identification of the community with the *aguaje*, and its possible associations with *shipap*, would also have linked the social group to an apparently long-standing tradition. This "invention of tradition" appears to have been an important community process, which would also have been sustained by ceremonies taking place in the *kivas* and on the dance grounds. The trail worn into the hillside leading to the shrine at LA 114032 is a tangible indication that ritual activity associated with such features was an ongoing part of community life.

The Ideological Landscape of Kotyiti

Our second case study is Kotyiti, also known as Old Cochiti and La Cieneguilla de Cochiti, the sixth of seven Ancestral Cochiti villages identified in Cochiti oral history (Benedict 1931; Lummis 1973).

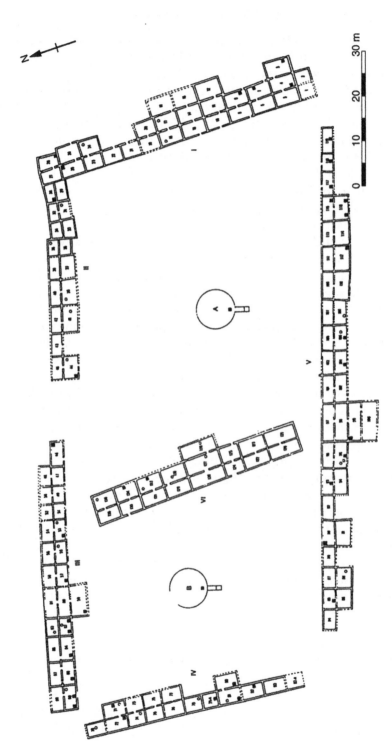

Figure 8.7 Main plaza pueblo of Kotyiti (LA 295).

Kotyiti is located on a prominent mesa northwest of Cochiti Pueblo (see figure 8.1). It is well known as one of the centers of resistance during the Pueblo Revolt and Reconquest Periods (1680–94) (Dougherty 1980; Preucel 1998). The main village (LA 295) of the community consists of six roomblocks enclosing two plazas, each of which contains a central *kiva* (figure 8.7). A secondary village (LA 84) consisting of an informal cluster of isolated rooms is located 150 meters to the east. The main village was excavated in its entirety by Nels Nelson in 1912 (Nelson n.d.). Dendrochronological samples taken in the 1930s suggest that there were two construction periods at the main pueblo, one dating between 1651 and 1666 (7 dates) and another between 1680 and 1691 (20 dates) (Robinson et al. 1978). These data imply that building activities took place concurrently with the Spanish missionizing activities and during the subsequent Revolt and Reconquest periods.

Kotyiti figures prominently in the seventeenth-century Spanish ethnohistorical accounts. The village and mesa of La Cieneguilla de Cochiti were the site of a pan-Pueblo meeting in 1681, at which representatives from all the Pueblos, except Hopi and Zuni, met to determine their response to Antonio de Otermín's reconquest expedition (Hackett and Shelby 1942: 236–7). Diego de Vargas, the Reconqueror of New Mexico, visited the community three times. On his first visit in 1692, he learned that the community was inhabited by people from Cochiti as well as San Marcos and San Felipe and unsuccessfully tried to bring them down off the mesa (Vargas, in Kessell and Hendricks 1992: 515–16). A year later he returned, with similar results (Vargas, in Kessell et al. 1995: 424–8). Finally, at the request of Zia, a Christianized pueblo which was threatened by the rebels, Vargas attacked the village on April 17, 1694, and seized 342 women and children as prisoners (Bandelier 1892: 173–7).

The main village of Kotyiti is a large multi-story dwelling with six separate roomblocks enclosing two plazas, each of which contains a single large *kiva*. There are 136 ground-floor rooms, all of which are constructed of shaped tuff blocks with mortar and irregular tuff chinking. The masonry work is quite good and, in some places, walls are still standing 3 meters high. Holes to receive roof beams (*vigas*) are present in upper areas of several walls and these provide direct evidence for roofs and perhaps second-story floors. Many of the rooms have features such as vents, doorways, and niches. Quite a few of the rooms have intact wall plaster. Several rooms yielded charred corn and fused tuff, and this is quite likely direct evidence for Vargas's burning of the pueblo on April 24, 1694.

The construction and layout of Kotyiti are directly associated with a revitalization movement which underwrote puebloan resistance against

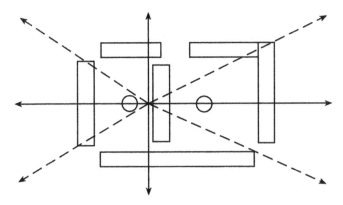

Figure 8.8 Schematic view of Kotyiti, indicating the convergence of the architecture and extramural shrines at the plaza shrine representing *shipap*.

the Spanish during the seventeenth century (Preucel 1997). This movement was grounded in a form of consciousness advocating a return to "the ways of the ancestors." The ethnohistoric evidence for this revival is quite strong. According to several informant accounts, prior to the famous Revolt of 1680 the Tewa leader Popé visited all the pueblos and instructed them to burn all images and temples, rosaries, and crosses, to discard their baptismal names and take new ones, to leave their wives wed in the church and remarry, to avoid mentioning the names of God, of the Virgin, or of the Saints, to stop speaking the Spanish language, and to burn the seeds of Spanish crops and plant only their native crops of maize and beans (Declaration of Juan, in Hackett and Shelby 1942: 235). People were then instructed to purify themselves by bathing in the rivers and streams.

At Kotyiti, this revival movement was encoded in architecture and expressed in the form and orientation of the main village (figure 8.8). Architectural data gathered by the Kotyiti Research Project indicates that the pueblo was very carefully planned as an open rectangle with gateways constructed between the two north roomblocks and in each of the four corners of the pueblo (Preucel 1997; 1998).[5] The northern gateway may provide metaphorical access to *shipap*. The northwest gateway may refer to the House of Thought Woman, the creator deity. The southwest gateway is possibly associated with the House of Spider Grandmother. The southeast entrance may have provided access to Turquoise House belonging to Butterfly and observations related to the winter solstice. The northeast entrance may have given symbolic access to the House of Mockingbird Youth and may have been important in lines of sight related to the summer solstice. Curiously, this entry-way was closed off, at some indeterminate time, by six rooms linking Roomblocks I and II (see figure 8.7).

The revival movement was also enacted by the construction of plaza and directional shrines. Within the west plaza and adjacent to Kiva B (probably the Pumpkin *kiva* by analogy to the modern pueblo of Cochiti) is a very large circular pile of tuff stones. This feature probably marks the ritual center of the village and is a physical representation of *shipap*.[6] This shrine both sanctified the village and protected it from danger and would be the place where ritual dances were initiated. Its presence in the west plaza and the absence of an obvious shrine in the east plaza may indicate that the west was the "main plaza" of the village. Possible directional shrines are located immediately outside the village in two of the cardinal directions. The east shrine consists of a discrete concentration of tuff stone containing a high proportion of broken grinding stones and hammerstones. Ortiz (1969: 10) interprets similar objects at Tewa shrines as offerings associated with souls and the sacred past, and a comparable use here seems quite plausible. The south shrine is a diffuse cluster of small tuff stones, three of which are standing upright. The poor condition of these shrines may be the result of intentional destruction by Vargas during the burning of the village.

These plaza and directional shrines were an integral part of the symbolic legitimation of the village. Their construction would have been a highly visible public act, important in the re-invention of tradition and particularly useful in the education of children.

> For their churches, they placed on the four sides and in the center of the plaza some small circular enclosures of stone where they went to offer flour, feathers and the seed of maguey, maize, and tobacco, and performed other superstitious rites, giving the children to understand that they must all do this in the future.
>
> (Declaration of Josephe, in Hackett and Shelby 1942: 240)

The organizational layout of the main village of Kotyiti and its associated shrines symbolically re-created the Keres world in a conscious attempt to embody traditional practices. This formal architecture would have reminded people of their connections to pre-Spanish cultural landscapes and their ancestral way of life. It is even possible that Kotyiti was originally conceived in the image of White House, the original Ancestral Keres village located in the north where the people and *katcinas* lived together in harmony.

Discussion and Conclusions

Our interpretation of the villages of Los Aguajes and Kotyiti reveals some striking similarities and a few differences in how the Keres world was constructed and reproduced over a period of half a millennium. We argue that these similarities and differences can be understood as the products of ongoing negotiations between political needs and ideological structures. One of our most striking findings is the continuity of a well-developed shrine system as a means of creating and maintaining a distinctive ideological landscape.

At Los Aguajes, this landscape appears to have been given structure and meaning through the construction of an extensive system of local shrines. It is probable that part of this network consisted of shrines located in the cardinal directions, which may have reflected cosmological beliefs. For lack of excavation data, we do not know if there were shrines within the plazas of Los Aguajes. It is clear, however, that the shrine system represents a considerable amount of labor investment. The creation of this system by a people newly colonizing an area was probably a social mechanism for the domestication of the landscape and the legitimation of the community establishing itself within it. It provided a means of attaching meaning to places in the countryside, thereby, to borrow a term from modern geopolitics, creating "facts on the ground." While similar to those documented ethnographically for Keres villages, the shrines at Los Aguajes also resemble another archaeological example, recorded at the Ancestral Tewa site of Poshuoinge by Jeançon (1923). This similarity may suggest the existence of aspects of a pan-puebloan ideology shared throughout the region prior to the historic period.

This ideological landscape was rooted in a natural world to which meaning was assigned as well. The construction of the community house adjacent to an important water source seems to have been significant on symbolic as well as pragmatic levels. Springs and water holes were associated with supernatural deities. The main *aguaje*, its sacred character reinforced by thousands of petroglyphs, may have been a central feature of community identity at Los Aguajes. The symbolic importance of the surrounding hills, likewise emphasized through shrine construction, may also have derived from analogy with the more distant mountains at the cardinal directions, such that the larger Keres world was re-created on the local level. The natural and built landscape at Los Aguajes thus reinforced both the particular identity of the local community and its integration with the broader Keres realm.

Kotyiti is sited principally with a view for defense. In its location, it is similar to the contemporaneous villages established on Black Mesa

(Harrington 1916: 294), Cerro Colorado (White 1962: 23), Astialakwa (Dougherty 1980), and Dowa Yalane (Ferguson 1996). Many of these villages were an amalgam of local resident groups and refugees. The short-lived nature of these communities attests to the difficulties of integrating different factions and ethnic groups during the period of the Spanish reconquest. Although formal surveys are still lacking (an exception being Dowa Yalane), most of these villages do not appear to have *kivas* (Dougherty 1980: 8). Kotyiti is thus remarkable in its clear evidence of ritual features – particularly its *kivas*, ceremonial rooms, and shrines. One possible explanation for this divergence is that Kotyiti may have been conceptualized from the very beginning as a permanent village and not a temporary or "refugee" settlement.

The main village of Kotyiti appears to embody the principles and values of the Cochiti people as they sought to re-invent the traditional ways of their ancestors. The placement and orientations of the different roomblocks probably invoked different deities by means of gateways and lines of sight. Similarly, small shrines located in the east and south defined the village's immediate boundaries. These shrines were probably used when people wanted to pray for rain or to ask for supernatural assistance. Integrating both the four corners and directional shrines is the plaza shrine located in the west plaza. This shrine would have served as the ritual center of the village, the middle place where offerings would have been made during ceremonial observances. This careful formal structure suggests that the village may have been conceptualized as an embodiment of White House, the primordial village occupied after emergence from the underworld. In this way, the natural may have been domesticated with reference to the social and the authority of the pueblo leaders legitimized.

Our ideological approach to settlement studies reveals some of the limitations of the standard ecosystem approach so prevalent in earlier processual studies. It draws out some of the principles that structured the relationships between the natural landscape and the built environment. In the Ancestral Keres examples discussed here, these general structuring principles, such as the world corners and cardinal directions, activated through the construction of different kinds of shrines, have remained remarkably stable. However, it is also evident that the specific expression of these principles has varied at different times and at different villages. Rather than simply reify ethnographic data, the consideration of ideological landscapes provides means to better understand both continuity and change in the settlement process and culture history. For the Ancestral Keres, as well as for their neighbors and relations across the Southwest, the landscape was more than a provider of nourishment; it was, in Keith Basso's (1984: 45) words, "a stern and benevolent keeper of tradition."

ACKNOWLEDGMENTS

We wish to acknowledge the assistance of J. Michael Bremer, Forest Archaeologist, Santa Fe National Forest, and Mike Walsh, Pajarito Archaeology Research Project Laboratory, UCLA. James Snead thanks the UCLA Institute of Archaeology for supporting field research at Los Aguajes, and his superb volunteer field crew. Bob Preucel thanks the Pueblo of Cochiti, the members of the Kotyiti Research Project, the American Philosophical Society, the University of Pennsylvania Museum, MASCA, the University Research Foundation, Ruth Scott, Annette Merle-Smith, and Douglas Walker. Finally, we wish to dedicate this paper to the memory of our professor and friend, James N. Hill.

NOTES

1   We consider "ideological landscapes" to refer to the social construction of space through reference to history, tradition, and mythology in order to legitimize a particular interest.

2   The Spanish distinguished the province of the "Quires" from that of the neighboring "Punames," whose chief village was Zia (Espejo, in Hammond and Rey 1966). This identification probably reflects a political rather than an ethnic or linguistic distinction since the name Puname is clearly a variant of "Buname" which means "people of the west" in Keres (Hodge 1910: 327).

3   Other important ethnographies include James and Matilda Cox Stevenson's (1894) study of Zia, and work at Cochiti by Father Noel Dumarest (1919), Ester Goldfrank (1927), Ruth Benedict (1931), Charles Lange (1959), and Robin Fox (1967).

4   Bandelier (1892: 161) states that local treasure hunters destroyed one of the lions.

5   This organization is also characteristic of the Tewa pueblos. Ortiz (1969: 16) writes that the Tewa "do not have a circular village structure but one of four parts in which the corners are always left open" and citing Villagrá, the chronicler of the Oñate expedition, he projects the ethnographic present back to 1598.

6   Similar shrines among the Tewa are called "Earth mother earth navel middle place" shrines (Ortiz 1969; Swentzell 1988).

REFERENCES

Anschuetz, K. F. 1995: Saving a rainy day: the integration of diverse agricultural technologies to harvest and conserve water in the Lower Rio Chama Valley, New Mexico. In H. W. Toll (ed.), *Soil, Water, Biology, and Belief in Prehistoric and Traditional Southwestern Agriculture*, Special Publications, 2, Albuquerque: New Mexico Archaeological Council, 25–39.

Anschuetz, K. F. 1996: Of pueblos, fields, and shrines: steps beyond archaeological landscapes in the northern Rio Grande. Paper presented at the 61st Annual Meeting, Society for American Archaeology, New Orleans.

Bandelier, A. F. 1892: *Final Report of Investigation among the Indians of the Southwestern United States, Carried on Mainly in the Years from 1880 to 1885.* Part II, Papers of the Archaeological Institute of America, American Series IV. Cambridge MA: Archaeological Institute of America.

Basso, K. H. 1984: "Stalking with stories": names, places, and moral narratives among the Western Apache. In E. M. Bruner (ed.), *Text, Play, and Story: The Construction and Reconstruction of Self and Society*, Washington, DC: American Ethnological Society, 19–55.

Basso, K. H. 1996: *Wisdom Sits in Places: Landscape and Language among the Western Apache.* Albuquerque: University of New Mexico Press.

Benedict, R. 1931: *Tales of the Cochiti Indians*, Bureau of American Ethnology, Bulletin 98. Washington, DC: Smithsonian Institution.

Bloch, M. 1995: People into places: Zafimaniry concepts of clarity. In E. Hirsch and M. O'Hanlon (eds), *The Anthropology of Landscape: Perspectives on Place and Space*, Oxford: Clarendon Press, 63–77.

Boas, F. 1928: *Keresan Texts*, Publication 8 (1, 2). New York: American Ethnological Society.

Boas, F. 1934: *Geographical Names of the Kwakiutl Indians*, Contributions in Anthropology, 20. New York: Columbia University.

Bonnemaison, J. 1994: *The Tree and the Canoe: History and Ethnogeography of Tanna.* Honolulu: University of Hawaii.

Bradley, R. 1997: *Rock Art and the Prehistory of Atlantic Europe: Signing the Land.* London: Routledge.

Bradley, R., Criado Boado, F., and Fabregas Valcarce, R. 1994: Rock art research as landscape archaeology: a pilot study in Galicia, North-West Spain. *World Archaeology*, 25, 374–90.

Chapman, R. C., Biella, J. V., Shutt, J. A., Enloe, J. G., Marchiando, P. J., Warren, A. H., and Stein, J. R. 1977: Description of twenty-seven sites in the permanent pool of Cochiti Reservoir. In R. C. Chapman and J. V. Biella with S. D. Bussey (eds), *Archaeological Investigations in Cochiti Reservoir, New Mexico*, vol. 2: *Excavation and Analysis, 1975 Season*, Albuquerque: University of New Mexico, Office of Contract Archaeology, 119–351.

Dillehay, T. D. 1990: Mapuche ceremonial landscape, social recruitment and resource rights. *World Archaeology*, 22, 223–41.

Dougherty, J. D. 1980: *Refugee Pueblos on the Santa Fe National Forest*, Cultural Resources Report 2. Santa Fe: Santa Fe National Forest.

Douglass, W. B. 1912: A world-quarter shrine of the Tewa Indians. *Records of the Past*, 11 (4), 159–72.

Douglass, W. B. 1917: Notes on the shrines of the Tewa and other Pueblo Indians of New Mexico, *Proceedings of the Nineteenth International Congress of Americanists*, Washington, DC: International Congress of Americanists, 344–78.

Dumarest, Father N. 1919: *Notes on Cochiti, New Mexico*, E. C. Parsons (transl.), Memoirs, 6 (3). Washington, DC: American Anthropological Association.

Farrington, I. S. 1992: Ritual geography, settlement patterns, and the characterization of the provinces of the Inka Empire. *World Archaeology*, 23, 368–85.

Ferguson, T. J. 1996: *Historic Zuni Architecture and Society: An Archaeological Application of Space Syntax*, Anthropological Papers, 60. Tucson: University of Arizona.

Fleming, A. 1988: *The Dartmoor Reaves*. London: B. T. Batsford.

Fox, R. 1967: *The Keresan Bridge: A Problem in Pueblo Ethnology*. New York: Humanities Press.

Goldfrank, E. S. 1927: *The Social and Ceremonial Organization of Cochiti*, Memoirs, 33. Washington, DC: American Anthropological Association.

Griaule, M., and Dieterlein, G. 1954: The Dogon. In D. Forde (ed.), *African Worlds: Studies in the Cosmological Ideas and Social Values of African Peoples*, London: Oxford University Press, 83–110.

Habichte-Mauche, J.A. 1993: *The Pottery from Arroyo Hondo Pueblo, New Mexico: Tribalization and Trade in the Northern Rio Grande*, Arroyo Hondo Archaeological Series, 8. Santa Fe: SAR Press.

Hackett, C. W., and Shelby, C. C. (eds and transl.) 1942: *Revolt of the Pueblo Indians of New Mexico, and Otermín's Attempted Reconquest, 1680–1682*, Coronado Cuarto Centennial Publications, 1540–1949, 2 vols. Albuquerque: University of New Mexico Press.

Hammond, G. P., and Rey, A. 1966: *The Rediscovery of New Mexico, 1580–1594: The Explorations of Chamuscado, Espejo, Castaño de Sosa, Morlete and Leyva de Bonilla and Humaña*. Coronado Cuarto Centennial Publications, 1540–1949, vol. 3. Albuquerque: University of New Mexico Press.

Harrington, J. P. 1916: *The Ethnogeography of the Tewa Indians*, Bureau of American Ethnology, Twenty-ninth Annual Report 1907–1908. Washington, DC: Smithsonian Institution.

Helms, M. W. 1988: *Ulysses' Sail: An Ethnographic Odyssey of Power, Knowledge, and Geographical Distance*. Princeton: Princeton University Press.

Herhahn, C. 1995: 14th-century dry farming features in the Northern Rio Grande Valley. In H. W. Toll (ed.), *Soil, Water, Biology, and Belief in Prehistoric and Traditional Southwestern Agriculture*, Special Publications, 2, Albuquerque: New Mexico Archaeological Council, 77–84.

Hewett, E. L. 1906: *Antiquities of the Jemez Plateau, New Mexico*, Bureau of American Ethnology, Bulletin 3. Washington, DC: Smithsonian Institution.

Hewett, E. L. 1953: *Pajarito Plateau and its Ancient People*, rev. by B. P. Dutton, School of American Research. Albuquerque: University of New Mexico Press.

Hobsbawm, E., and Ranger, T. (eds) 1983: *The Invention of Tradition*. Cambridge: Cambridge University Press.

Hodge, F. W. 1910: Punames. In *Handbook of American Indians North of Mexico*, Bureau of American Ethnology, Bulletin 30 (2), Washington, DC: Smithsonian Institution, 327.

Jeançon, J. A. 1923: *Excavations in the Chama Valley, New Mexico*, Bureau of American Ethnology, Bulletin 81. Washington, DC: Smithsonian Institution.

Kessell, J. L., and Hendricks, R. (eds) 1992: *By Force of Arms: The Journals of Don Diego de Vargas, New Mexico 1691–1693*. Albuquerque: University of New Mexico Press.

Kessell, J. L., Hendricks, R., and Dodge, M. (eds) 1995: *To the Royal Crown Restored: The Journals of Don Diego de Vargas, New Mexico 1692–1694*. Albuquerque: University of New Mexico Press.

Kolb, M., and Snead, J. E. 1997: It's a small world after all: comparative analysis of community organization in archaeology. *American Antiquity*, 62, 609–28.

Lange, C. H. 1959: *Cochiti, a New Mexico Pueblo: Past and Present*. Austin: University of Texas Press.

Lee, S. H. 1989: Siting and general organization of traditional Korean settlements. In J.-P. Bourdier and N. Alsayyad (eds), *Dwellings, Settlements, and Tradition: Cross-Cultural Perspectives*, Lanham, MD: University Press of America, 295–316.

Loud, L. 1918: *Ethnogeography and Archaeology of the Wiyot Territory*, Publications in American Archaeology and Ethnology, 14 (3). Berkeley: University of California.

Lummis, C. F. 1973: *The Land of Poco Tiempo*. New York: Scribners.

Munn, N. D. 1970: The transformation of subjects into objects in Walbiri and Pitjantjatjara myth. In R. M. Berndt (ed.), *Australian Aboriginal Anthropology: Modern Studies in the Social Anthropology of the Australian Aborigines*, Perth: University of Western Australia Press, 143–63.

Myers, F. R. 1986: *Pintupi Country, Pintupi Self: Sentiment, Place, and Politics among Western Desert Aborigines*. Washington, DC: Smithsonian Institution Press.

Nelson, N. C. 1914: *Pueblo Ruins of the Galisteo Basin, New Mexico*, Anthropological Papers, 15 (1). New York: American Museum of Natural History.

Nelson, N. C. n.d.: Excavations of Pueblo Kotyiti, New Mexico. New York: Archives of the American Museum of Natural History.

Ortiz, A. 1969: *The Tewa World: Space, Time, Being and Becoming in a Pueblo Society*. Chicago: University of Chicago Press.

Parsons, E. C. 1920: Notes on ceremonialism at Laguna. *Anthropological Papers of the American Museum of Natural History*, 19, 83–131.

Parsons, E. C. 1923: Notes on San Felipe and Santo Domingo. *American Anthropologist*, 25, 485–94.

Preucel, R. W. 1990: *Seasonal Circulation and Dual Residence in the Pueblo Southwest: A Prehistoric Example from the Pajarito Plateau, New Mexico*. New York: Garland Publishing.

Preucel, R. W. 1997: Making Pueblo Identities: Architectural Discourse at Kotyiti, New Mexico. Paper presented at the 62nd annual meeting, Society for American Archaeology, Nashville.

Preucel, R. W. 1998: *The Kotyiti Research Project: Report of the 1996 Fieldseason*. Report submitted to the Pueblo of Cochiti and the USDA Forest Service Southwestern District, Santa Fe.

Prince, L. B. 1903: *The Stone Lions of Cochiti*, Publications, 4. Santa Fe: Historical Society of New Mexico.

Prince, L. B. 1904: The Stone Lions of Cochiti. *Records of the Past*, 3, Washington, DC: Smithsonian Institution, 151–60.

Robinson, W. J., Hannah, J. W., and Harrill, B. G. 1978: *Tree-Ring Dated Sites from New Mexico: Central Rio Grande Area*. Tucson: Laboratory of Tree Ring Research, University of Arizona.

Schaafsma, P. 1990: The Pine Tree site: a Galisteo Basin Pueblo IV shrine. In M. S. Duran and D. T. Kirkpatrick (eds), *Clues to the Past: Papers in Honor of William M. Sundt*, Papers of the Archaeological Society of New Mexico, 16, Albuquerque: Archaeological Society of New Mexico, 239–57.

Smiley, T. L., Stubbs, S. A., and Bannister, B. 1953: *A Foundation for the Dating of Some Late Archaeological Sites in the Rio Grande Area, New Mexico: Based on Studies in Tree-ring Methods and Pottery Analyses*, University of Arizona Bulletin, 24 (3), Laboratory of Tree Ring Research Bulletin, 6. Tucson: University of Arizona.

Snead, J. E. 1995: Beyond pueblo walls: community and competition in the northern Rio Grande, AD 1300–1400. PhD dissertation, University of California, Los Angeles.

Steen, C. R. 1977: *Pajarito Plateau Archaeological Survey and Excavations*, vol. 1. Los Alamos: Los Alamos Scientific Laboratory.

Stein, J. R., and Lekson, S. H. 1992: Anasazi ritual landscapes. In D. E. Doyel (ed.), *Anasazi Regional Organization and the Chaco System*, Anthropological Papers, 5, Albuquerque: Maxwell Museum of Anthropology, 87–100.

Stevenson, M. C. 1894: *The Sia*, Bureau of American Ethnology, Eleventh Annual Report. Washington, DC: Smithsonian Institution.

Swentzell, R. 1988: Bupingeh: the Pueblo plaza. *El Palacio*, 94 (2), 14–19.

Thomas, J. H. 1991: *Rethinking the Neolithic*. Cambridge: Cambridge University Press.

Tilley, C. 1994: *A Phenomenology of Landscape: Places, Paths and Monuments*. Oxford: Berg.

Tonkinson, R. 1991: *The Marda Aborigines: Living the Dream in Australia's Western Desert*. New York: Holt, Rinehart, and Winston.

Toren, C. 1995: Seeing the ancestral sites: transformations in Fijian notions of the land. In E. Hirsch and M. O'Hanlon (eds), *The Anthropology of Landscape: Perspectives on Place and Space*, Oxford: Clarendon Press, 163–83.

Vivian, R. G. n.d.: Los Aguajes, LA 5, Manuscript. Santa Fe: Laboratory of Anthropology Library, Museum of New Mexico.

Wendorf, F. 1953: *Salvage Archaeology in the Chama Valley, New Mexico*, Monographs, 17. Santa Fe: School of American Research.

Wheatley, P. 1971: *The Pivot of the Four Quarters*. Chicago: Aldine.

White, L. A. 1932a: *The Acoma Indians*, Bureau of American Ethnology, Forty-seventh Annual Report. Washington, DC: Smithsonian Institution.

White, L. A. 1932b: *The Pueblo of San Felipe, New Mexico*, Memoirs, 38. Washington, DC: American Anthropological Association.

White, L. A. 1935: *The Pueblo of Santo Domingo, New Mexico*, Memoirs, 43. Washington, DC: American Anthropological Association.

White, L. A. 1942: *The Pueblo of Santa Ana, New Mexico*, Memoirs, 60. Washington, DC: American Anthropological Association.

White, L. A. 1960: The world of the Keresan Pueblo Indians. In S. Diamond (ed.), *Culture in History: Essays in Honor of Paul Radin*, New York: Columbia University Press, 53–64.

White, L. A. 1962: *The Pueblo of Sia, New Mexico*, Bureau of American Ethnology, Bulletin 184. Washington, DC: Smithsonian Institution.

Part III

Prehistoric Cases

9

Centering the Ancestors: Cemeteries, Mounds, and Sacred Landscapes of the Ancient North American Midcontinent

Jane E. Buikstra and Douglas K. Charles

What do people make of places? The question is as old as people and places themselves, as old as human attachments to portions of the earth. As old, perhaps, as the idea of home, of "our territory" as opposed to "their territory," of entire regions and local landscapes where groups of men and women have invested themselves (their thoughts, their values, their collective sensibilities) and to which they feel they belong. The question is as old as a strong sense of place – and the answer, if there is one, is every bit as complex.

(Basso 1996: xiii)

Introduction

With these words Keith Basso opens his discussion of places within the traditional Western Apache world. Yet his comments are equally cogent for studies of more ancient pasts. What were the attributes that characterized places chosen for hunting, for homes, for ceremonies? Where might the ancestors best be located, so that their insights could continue to guide the living?

These questions frame our current investigation of Midcontinental North Americans who inhabited the remarkably rich riverine landscape of West-central Illinois many millennia prior to recorded history (figure 9.1). The acme of their built environment comprised the earthworks erected by Middle Woodland peoples two thousand years ago. Mound groups dotted bluff crests, 100 meters or more above the floodplain (figure 9.2). Upon the floodplain were situated fewer, but larger and more structurally complex tumuli, immense and dominating the riparian environment (Buikstra et al. 1998; Struever 1960;

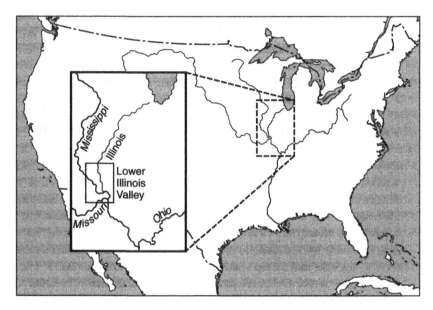

Figure 9.1 The location of the lower Illinois River valley within North America is illustrated.

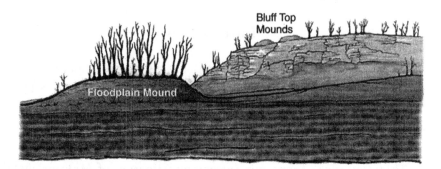

Figure 9.2 This reconstruction illustrates both the natural and built environment of ancient peoples from the North American Midcontinent. In the foreground, Middle Woodland Kamp Mound 8 rises prominently from the Illinois River floodplain, its monumentality a striking reflection of the much more ancient limestone bluffs that demarcate valley limits. Less prominent tumuli are located upon the bluff crest, above the floodplain.

1968a; 1968b; Struever and Houart 1972). Many, though not all floodplain sites were organized around open spaces where audiences once gathered for rites that positioned both the living and the dead within their worlds. These central places may have witnessed other collective rituals, including dances celebrating seasonal change and the fertility of plants and animals, both real and mythical. Political and social in nature, such events anchored their participants within a complex cosmos, vertically and horizontally differentiated.

Recovering Sacred[1] Landscapes

Features of the landscape identified as sacred may take many forms: a tree, a stream, a rocky outcrop, the direction from which the sun rises. For the archaeologist, recovering meaning from such natural phenomena may seem an insurmountable task. But not all that is sacred is of natural origin. People construct and remodel elements of the landscape, and these processes often leave archaeologically recoverable traces. Such residues facilitate our understanding of ancient societies, their politics and their ideologies.

In the riverine Midcontinent of North America, places where corpses and valued items had been buried were used for millennia to divide and mark the landscape in ways that carried social, political, and religious meaning. In an earlier explanation of Middle Archaic mortuary practices (Charles and Buikstra 1983), we relied heavily upon processual theories in developing an expanded application of Arthur Saxe's (1970) Hypothesis 8, as reworked by Lynne Goldstein (1976; 1980). In brief, the hypothesis links the development of specialized, permanent and bounded areas for exclusive disposal of the dead to ritual affirmation of corporate group control of crucial, restricted resources. Such processual approaches have undergone severe criticism, most commonly leveled by postprocessualists such as Hodder (1980; 1982) and Shanks and Tilley (1982). As Morris (1991) notes, the processual/postprocessual debate is no longer so prominent in studies of mortuary sites as it was during previous decades. This is especially true among British archaeologists, whose studies are overwhelmingly influenced by the postprocessualist critique (but see Chapman 1995).

On a world-wide basis, however, archaeological interpretations of mortuary sites continue to employ a range of theoretical perspectives. In North America, for example, some approaches are explicitly processual (e.g., Carr 1995), while others are most closely aligned with postprocessual paradigms (e.g., Hall 1997). Given such theoretical eclecticism, it is important that we position our interpretative stance within the processual/postprocessual continuum.

We agree with certain aspects of the postprocessual critique, especially its emphasis upon the way in which mortuary ritual can and often is manipulated to serve the needs of the living. We do, however, disagree quite emphatically with the postprocessualist dismissal of cross-cultural investigations, believing that such surveys can provide useful insights and *starting points* for interpretation, when coupled with appropriate sensitivity to specific cultural and archaeological contexts.

Recently, Ian Morris (1991: 163) has reviewed the status of the Saxe/Goldstein Hypothesis, and believes that "it is a rewarding idea, which, if used carefully and with due regard for human agency, can stimulate research into new areas of ancient society. Like any archaeological methodology, it is neither right nor wrong, only more or less helpful in specific empirical situations." We concur, and continue to believe that the Saxe/Goldstein Hypothesis is useful for our analyses of Midcontinental North American mortuary sites (see also Brown 1995).

One of the most valuable aspects of Morris's (1991) critique is his decoupling of mortuary ritual from ancestor cult, following Gluckman's (1937) definitions of "cult of the dead" and "ancestor cult." The former, renamed by Morris "mortuary ritual" to decrease intuitive ambiguity, describes the rite-of-passage ceremonies which separate the deceased from the living. "Ancestor cult" refers to those rituals which provide continued access to the deceased in the afterworld. The ancestors in this sense continue to be engaged in the affairs of their descendants, as participants in social, political, and economic relationships. As Fortes (1965) notes, death and mortuary rites do not in and of themselves confer "ancestorhood" (Morris 1991).

Morris (1991) emphasizes that the link between ancestor cults and descent or property transmission is relatively straightforward. The association between mortuary rituals and inter-generational transfer of property, power, and authority is much less direct. Yet ancestor cults and mortuary rituals affect one another, even though most archaeological residues reflect mortuary rituals rather than ancestor cults. We would argue, however, that there are times when the archaeological record provides evidence of both phenomena. One of these occasions is visible archaeologically within the lower Illinois valley, as the mound-building tradition began, approximately 7,000 years ago.

The overt separation between mortuary ritual and ancestor cults is analytically quite useful, as exemplified in Ahern's (1973) study of ancestor cults and inheritance in the Taiwanese village she called Ch'inan. Other Southeast Asian examples also reinforce the notion that ancestor cults emphasize "lineage unity and common property transmission," while mortuary rituals were arenas for competition. Morris (1991: 153) cites Watson (1988) in emphasizing that formal and stylized ancestral cult rituals define contemporary power arrangements, while "grave rites constitute one of the battlegrounds for disputing those arrangements. . . . Those aspects of the cult that focus on the ancestral grave are more concerned with political competition than with glorifying rigid status hierarchies or group unity." Working out the tensions inherent in such dualities serves to re-create society, perhaps in altered form. Rituals and their meaning may change, as may the statuses of the individuals performing sacred rites.

Although removed in time and space from our Illinois valley examples, Morris's observations and Watson's conclusions help inform our discourse on sacred landscapes. Interestingly, although Morris emphasizes the archaeological residues of grave rites, the ancestor cults described by Ahern and Watson, among others, would certainly provide monumental, archaeologically-recoverable evidence that the ancestors were being used to legitimize relationships among the living. In Ahern's example, she describes four agnatic lineages which each maintained an ancestral hall where tablets bearing the names of ancestors were displayed and worshipped. Archaeological remnants of such structures, bearing visible material residues of ancestor worship, could be recovered and interpreted.

In decoding the archaeological record of West-central Illinois we have, of course, no written records or ethnographic descriptions. We argue, however, that the distinction between ancestor cults and mortuary ritual is a useful construct, assisting in interpreting past sacred landscapes. In this case study, it is particularly helpful in exploring the social and political contexts that led to the development of the mound-building tradition.

A second, archaeologically useful distinction focuses upon levels of societal integration in the face of political and ideological competition. Evans-Pritchard (1948), Fortes (1945), and more recently, Turner (1974) have emphasized the differences between ritual landscapes of ancestral/political cults and of earth/fertility cults (see also Bell 1997). They contrast the placement of shrines associated with ancestral cults, which are commonly located within or adjacent to communities, and the peripheral position of earth shrines, which may become pilgrimage centers. For Turner (1974), ancestral shrines represent exclusivity and political divisions, associated with conflict. Common, overarching and unifying ideals and values (inclusivity) are reflected in earth and fertility cults. While developed within the context of African ethnographic study, this dichotomy, especially the exclusivity/inclusivity opposition, has proved useful to Crown (1994) in her investigation of ancient puebloan peoples of the North American Southwest. More recently, it has figured in Emerson's (1997a; 1997b) analysis of Mississippian power structures, principally at Cahokia and the American Bottom region of the Central Mississippi valley. We believe that the spatial, political, and ideological implications of the ancestral/political–earth/fertility cult distinction will also help inform our interpretative history of lower Illinois Valley landscape transformations.

The Sacred Landscapes of Archaic and Woodland Hunter–gatherer Gardeners

When Middle Woodland (Hopewellian) peoples entered the Illinois River valley c.2050 years ago, they encountered a natural landscape dominated by vertical relief. The Mississippian Era limestone escarpments rose 100 meters from a floodplain dissected by webs of outflow from nearby bluffs. Floodplain surface topography included relict terraces, slightly elevated sand ridges and natural levees, permanent and ephemeral backwater lakes, and the Illinois River, which flowed closest to the western bluffs. Horizontal distinctions developed from a water–land dichotomy where vegetational zones, including both floodplain and bluff crest, forest and prairies, aligned parallel to the river.

For 300 years Hopewellian peoples built monumental earthworks, evidence of mortuary ceremonialism. These special, still enigmatic places serve to capture archaeological imagination today because their monumentality begs interpretation. Yet we must recognize that the two places chosen for tumulus construction, the bluff crest and the floodplain, reflect deep traditions in less-than-monumental placement of the dead. In fact, both contexts had long been locations for human interments. Such time depth must reflect many distinctive ancient ideologies, economies, social and political structures, yet the fact that these two places were emphasized over millennia requires us to adopt a long-term view that embeds chronological change within the largest possible context for mortuary behavior. We argue that the mortuary monumentalism associated with Middle Woodland can be explained only by considering the lexicon of ritual choice inherited from the first people who buried their dead in these distinctive locations (Charles 1996). We therefore begin by considering Middle Archaic peoples.

By 7,000 years ago the Illinois River was entrenched near its present site, on the west side of the lower Illinois valley. East of the river, outflow from the bluffs had incised channels into ancient terraces, coursing southwestward, eventually to join the Illinois River. Some of these channels became deep lateral lakes, habitats attractive to aquatic animals and plants. Both the paleochannels and the lakes gradually infilled until major flooding approximately 3,000 years ago leading to the development of a yazoo-like system which reworked linear sand ridges, visible above the braided streams. Waters caught behind the natural levee of the Illinois River formed both permanent and seasonal backwater lakes, supporting a wide variety of aquatic resources. Through time, sedimentary infilling of the water courses rendered some sand ridges less distinct, thus leveling the landscape (Buikstra and Seddon n.d.; Hajic 1987; 1990; Styles 1985; Van Nest n.d.).

Between 8,000 and 4,500 years ago, Middle Archaic peoples occupied the Illinois valley. Some foraged opportunistically, moving their homes several times within the year, while others experimented with longer periods of residence. Brown and Vierra (1983: 190) describe alternative periods of logistic and residential mobility:

> prior to 7500 BP in the Early Archaic and Middle Archaic 1 phases, subsistence-settlement was based on the scheduled exploitation of various seasonally available resources through high residential mobility. After this date, occupation began to lengthen in duration at strategic locations in response to rising availability of prime foods in the floodplain. This began the trend that continued over the succeeding thousands of years toward greater reliance on these foods from this highly productive resource area while becoming increasingly more sedentary. In our view, the key factor in this development was the growth of the food-rich slack-water environment of the valley to the point where the valley pulled hunter–gatherer subsistence and settlement strategies predominantly toward this area to the exclusion of alternatives. With increasing floodplain productivity, this zone came to dominate, and with this came sedentism and economic intensification.

Middle Archaic mortuary sites also reflect the trend toward sedentism and economic intensification (Charles 1995). There were three distinctive patterns for the treatment of the Middle Archaic dead. Within residential sites, the infirm and many of the young were buried in middens, without grave goods or other elaboration. In complementary fashion, primarily middle-aged and young adults were interred in bluff crest knolls, prominences near their villages, with knives and other artifacts (Buikstra 1981; Charles, Leigh, and Buikstra 1988). The knolls became "mounds" as they grew accretionally, through sequential additions of bodies and enclosing sediments. Thus, these Middle Archaic structures lacked the formal organization of later Middle Woodland sites. Elsewhere, we have argued that such bluff top interments are strong statements of territorial ownership, where the ancestors validated privileged access to local resources (Charles and Buikstra 1983). These bluff crest interments generally conform to Morris's definition of an ancestor cult.

We have recently excavated a third, distinctly different, burial site (Buikstra and Seddon n.d.). Named for the centrally-located amateur excavations that brought the site to our attention, the Bullseye site was located on a linear sand ridge isolated by paleochannels from the nearby Keach School Terrace and from nearby slackwater lakes (figure 9.3). More than a hundred Middle Archaic interments and quantities of stone tools and debitage were recovered in the course of four field seasons conducted by the University of Chicago field school. In comparison with other Middle Archaic burial contexts, the Bullseye site is notable for a high density of artifacts overall, for a remarkable variety of projectile point types, for the presence of unassociated tools and debitage reflecting maintenance and extractive activities, for the predominance of reburials, which include two distinctive interments of several young adults with quantities of artifacts (Burials 25 and 66), and for a remarkable variety of bannerstones, or elongated spearthrower weights (figure 9.4) (Buikstra 1988; Buikstra and Seddon n.d.; Charles 1995; Charles and Buikstra 1995). Of 29 bannerstones, 24 are of banded slate whose source would have been northern Indiana or southern Wisconsin, and 5 are of locally available materials, similar in color to the banded slate (Hassen and Farnsworth 1987). While contexts for the bannerstones are uncertain due to their location in the central part of the site, some were said to occur in like-type pairs. The slate bannerstones were broken, perhaps intentionally, and they were frequently incomplete, while the local items were never finished.

We interpret the diversity of bannerstones and chipped stone artifact forms as evidence that the Bullseye sand ridge included a cemetery of Middle Archaic peoples during a period (or periods) of residential mobility. It was probably a seasonal camp where several communities of dispersed households gathered. They would have come together to discuss matters of mutual concern, to bury their dead, and to exchange mates, thus linking death and renewal, mortality and fertility. In such contexts, bannerstones may have served as symbols representing group membership. These symbols may have been ritually "killed" in competitive displays ostensibly dedicated to the ancestors but also deeply involved in negotiations for influence among the living. Competition stimulated ostentation, as individual and group status was based upon the ability to acquire and to dispose of portable wealth (Buikstra and Seddon n.d.; Charles and Buikstra 1995). Caches of artifacts not

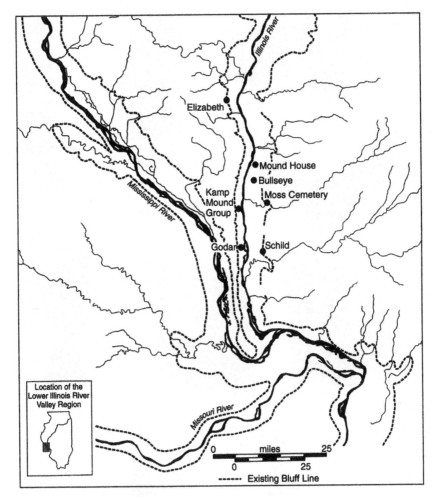

Figure 9.3 Map of the lower Illinois River valley, illustrating the location of sites mentioned in the text.

directly associated with burials bear witness to the fact that social rituals were not the exclusive provenance of mortuary behavior (Charles 1996; Charles, Goldstein, and Buikstra 1996). Both forms of disposal, the burial of valued items as caches and the graveside competitive displays, thus become contentions of the *status quo*. In this way they each served the social and political functions Morris (1991) ascribes to mortuary rituals.

We do not believe that ethnic differences alone are sufficient to explain the dissimilar bluff crest and the sand ridge burial programs.

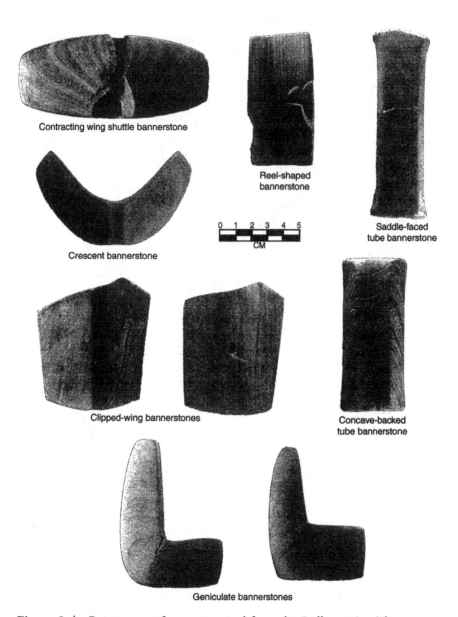

Contracting wing shuttle bannerstone

Reel-shaped
bannerstone

Saddle-faced
tube bannerstone

Crescent bannerstone

CM

Clipped-wing bannerstones

Concave-backed
tube bannerstone

Geniculate bannerstones

Figure 9.4 Bannerstone forms recovered from the Bullseye site. The clipped-wing and geniculate types are said to have been deposited in pairs.

Artifact assemblages at the two locations contain no mutually exclusive "badges" of group identity. The differences are quantitative, seen in artifact densities rather than the qualitative variation one might expect if contemporary corporate groups with distinctive origins and identities were choosing these contrastive locations (Charles 1995: table 1). The Bullseye assemblage is simply more diverse and dense, similar to other less completely reported Midcontinental Middle Archaic floodplain cemeteries such as the Godar site (see figure 9.3), also located within the lower Illinois River valley (Titterington 1950), and the Ferry site, which overlooks the Saline River near the Ohio River in eastern Illinois (Fowler 1957).

Nor do we think that the Bullseye cemetery simply represents those who happened to die during a seasonal occupation. The interments were primarily bundle reburials, curated for disposal in this context. On the southern periphery of the site, more than 200 pieces of red ochre were recovered with the commingled, disarticulated remains of three young adults (Burial 66) (Hoshower n.d.). This conspicuous burial may reflect ancestors brought by a single lineage to reaffirm territorial "ownership." We see similar display behavior in the spectacular Middle Archaic initiating event for Mound 1 at the Elizabeth site, a multiple interment of four males, three aged between 13 and 17 years, the other near 30 years of age at death. Each has two or three projectile points carefully arranged in the chest cavity, as well as belts or sashes beaded with anculosa shells around the waist (Charles and Buikstra 1983; Charles, Leigh, and Buikstra 1988).[2] While we cannot fully interpret the meaning behind such elaborations, we believe that this complexity effectively negates simple explanations that posit fortuitous disposal of those who happened to die at these locations during seasonal occupations.

While our preferred explanation characterizes the Bullseye burial program as part of a mobility phase of the Middle Archaic sedentarization process, we cannot control time sufficiently to be certain that our interments are not earlier than those at Middle Archaic bluff crest and base camp contexts. If this were the case, it would not fundamentally change our interpretation of the site as a multi-community cemetery, which formed in the context of a seasonal ritual cycle.

Though temporal relationships among Middle Archaic cemeteries remain ambiguous, it is clear that these contrastive mortuary behaviors are best understood in an analytical framework that emphasizes roles and statuses of the living, as well as those of the dead. Kin groups came to the floodplain Bullseye site to engage in the competitive behaviors that established their place among their contemporaries and to create alliances that would ensure the presence of future generations. Ostentatious mortuary rituals (*sensu* Morris 1991) were a significant aspect of these events. The real need to negotiate and to resolve the tensions inherent in the conflictive competitive displays while also engaging in alliance formation no doubt held the potential for altering both individual statuses and traditional structures over time. By contrast, the bluff crest Middle Archaic cemeteries comprised true monuments to the dead, evidence of Morris's "ancestor cult." Located above the community, in doubly liminal zones between the earth and sky, valley and uplands, these monuments were ideal platforms from which the ancestors might influence the world of the living. Thus began the mound-building tradition.

Late Archaic (*c*.4500–2850 BP) peoples interred their dead within bluff crest mounds, following a custom of their Middle Archaic predecessors, while Early Woodland (*c*.2550–2100 BP) folk favored floodplain locations (Charles, Buikstra, and Konigsberg 1986; Perino 1966; 1968). Although Middle Archaic cemeteries were confined to the main river valleys, Late Archaic mortuary sites were situated on elevated points of the landscape along tributaries, apparently reflecting an expansion of populations into upland regions (Charles and Buikstra 1983). The few modest Early Woodland main valley cemeteries may reflect depopulation and even eventual abandonment of the lower Illinois valley (Charles, Buikstra, and Konigsberg 1986; Farnsworth and Asch 1986).

Nearly invisible Early Woodland mortuary activity was followed by the most conspicuous built landscapes in the Midcontinent prior to Euro-American settlement. Middle Woodland, or Hopewellian, peoples again turned to the bluff crest, where formally organized community cemeteries led, over time, to the creation of mound clusters arranged in linear fashion. The earliest mounds tended to be positioned nearest the valley on the most prominent natural feature, with the more recent, frequently larger structures in less conspicuous locations (Charles 1985; 1992; Konigsberg 1990). In addition, Hopewellian peoples constructed a limited number of mound groups in the floodplain. Such mound clusters were frequently arranged around an open area or "plaza" and were dominated by one or more oval tumuli over 100 meters long and 6 meters in height. These larger, formally organized floodplain groups are thought to represent multi-community contexts, just as during the Middle Archaic.

Such Middle Woodland spatial diversity can be understood only by examining the larger lexicon of ritual alternatives common to ancient Midcontinental traditions. Within this larger framework, we must also appreciate local chronologies, especially the recolonization of the lower Illinois River region following Early Woodland times. At an even more specific level, an archaeological dissection of Middle Woodland earthworks provides significant evidence of cosmological import. Developed within this multi-layered analytical format, our interpretations are based in large part upon data from our recent excavations at the Elizabeth (Charles, Leigh, and Buikstra 1988) and the Mound House sites (Buikstra, Charles, and Rakita 1998). In these works we have thoroughly sampled Hopewellian cemeteries at their two most conspicuous locations, respectively the bluff crest and the floodplain.

Charles (1985; 1992; 1995) has argued convincingly for sequential Hopewellian recolonization of the lower Illinois River valley, beginning in the north, a position also supported by analyses of material culture and habitation site data (Farnsworth 1986; McGregor 1958). This development initiates near the Elizabeth site, at the mouth of Blue Creek, with the mortuary sequence at Elizabeth exemplifying our knowledge of emerging complexity during Middle Woodland times (figure 9.5).

Mounds 1 and 3 at the Elizabeth site are fairly uncomplicated Middle Woodland structures, generally organized as rings of interments. These represent early Hopewellian community cemeteries, with

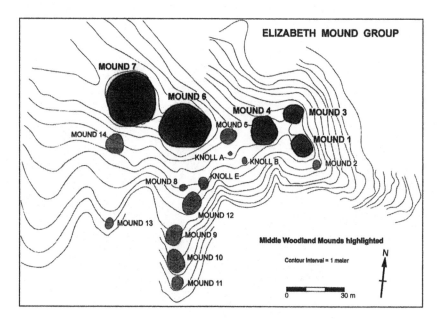

Figure 9.5 Map of the Elizabeth site.

Mound 1 composed simply of a burial ring while Mound 3 included both a central feature and encircling burials. Neither mound contained an elevated internal earthwork or ramp. We believe that such relatively simple structural formats were later embellished and expanded as communities attracted immigrants and inequalities emerged, a chronological sequence supported by a suite of radiocarbon dates (Buikstra, Charles, and Rakita 1998; Charles, Leigh, and Buikstra 1988; Kut and Buikstra 1998). For example, within the Elizabeth group, Mounds 6 and 7 are significantly larger than the earlier mounds, with considerable variation in treatment between the peripheral and central interments. Charles (1985; 1992) has argued elsewhere that this distinction may reflect the difference between a community's originating kin groups and those more recently recruited, which echoes earlier inferences by Brown (1981). Later mounds include "empty" tombs and are positioned near open spaces where audiences may have viewed the rituals staged from elevated ramps that encircled tomb structures (Charles 1992). These rituals served to anchor the Middle Woodland world, moving the dead across lofty platforms representing the upper world, through the flat disk of this world, into the dark, subsurface underworld (figure 9.6). A thin layer of light-colored sediments encircling the tomb at ground level is interpreted to represent this world (Buikstra, Charles, and Rakita 1998).

Elaborate rituals thus re-created the ternary Middle Woodland cosmos, just as they served to reify the political prominence of specific

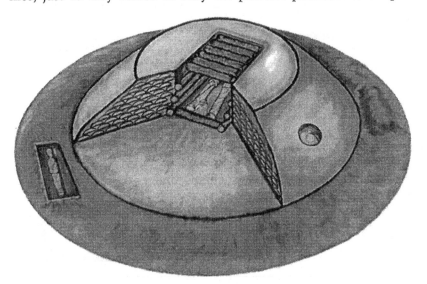

Figure 9.6   Rendering of "typical" Middle Wodland tumulus.

Hopewellian practitioners and their kin. We believe that the imposing floodplain cemeteries represent the intersection of ancient customs and Hopewellian belief systems. A long-standing tradition specified that multi-community political and social events be held in floodplain contexts, just as they had in Middle Archaic times. Rather than simply being contexts for competitive ostentation, however, the floodplain landscape now served the ever-larger audiences that met to celebrate the world order, as Hopewellian people knew it and re-created it through their rituals (Charles 1996; Charles and Buikstra 1995).

We have thus described locational continuity for corpse disposal areas over millennia within the lower Illinois River region. Bluff crest and sand ridge locations were sought 7,000 years ago, just as they were during Middle Woodland times. Previous explanatory models have tended to focus exclusively upon Hopewell mounds, and generally have a functionalist orientation. Bluff crest mounds were said to have been village cemeteries, located on the nearest economically-unimportant property, while the floodplain mounds were situated next to the river to facilitate access for multi-community groups who came to exchange exotic Hopewell items at selected intervals (Struever and Houart 1972). Confirming evidence for this economic model is said to be the fact that as the Illinois valley widens to the north, floodplain mounds are located adjacent to the river rather than the bluffs (Struever and Houart 1972). Contradicting this model, however, is the fact that the "transaction centers" were not utilized simultaneously. As previously noted, the lower Illinois valley received immigrants from the north, with ensuing north-to-south migration (Charles 1985; Farnsworth 1986; McGregor 1958). Furthermore, recent studies indicate that there is no special abundance of Hopewell items or evidence for their manufacture among floodplain earthworks (Buikstra, Charles, and Rakita 1998; Farnsworth 1990).

While transportation-based models may have intuitive appeal, they neglect to consider other possible explanations rooted in ancient ideologies. We suggest that there exist equally compelling alternative models, based in ethnographic and ethnohistoric accounts of eastern Woodlands Indians. For example, the riverine proximity for floodplain mounds may equally well reflect the importance of water, bathing and cleansing during world renewal rituals. Similarly, water may have been the symbolic entryway to the underworld, its proximity important to death rites. Water–air dichotomies pervade Hopewellian iconography, nowhere more compellingly than in the ceramic assemblage from Burial Feature 6, Mound 7, at the Elizabeth site. Twenty-one ceramic vessels were recovered with the remains of a young infant (Charles,

Leigh, and Buikstra 1988). Marine shell vessels were also present within the grave assemblage. Birds of the air and birds of the water are represented on the ceramics (figure 9.7), with vessels representing raptors always stacked below those of spoonbills, even though this placed smaller vessels below larger pots (Morgan 1988). Thus the natural order was reversed in a rite reflecting death, the ultimate disruptive event. These birds, and the many other animals such as frogs and beavers represented in Hopewellian imagery, can be perceived as liminal beings that move between landscape domains: air to land; land to water; water to air. Movement between these symbolic arenas is also represented within Middle Woodland mortuary structures, as noted above.

We therefore believe that Middle Woodland monuments re-created the cosmos, vertically and horizontally differentiated, just as they provided a forum for the negotiation of power relations among the living. Images from vessels and pipes suggest that both the living and the supernatural worlds were inhabited by naturalistic beings, with symbolic emphasis upon those who could move between two worlds. Complex sites such as Mound House and Elizabeth (Mounds 6 and 7) provide evidence for rituals that placed disposal of the dead within a larger context of world renewal. Thus, the rituals that created the Middle Woodland built environment were structured by kinship, were expressive of power relations, and were developed within a traditional, unifying cosmology.

Figure 9.7 Rollouts of ceramic vessels from Feature 6, Mound 7, Elizabeth site. These illustrate the contrastive raptorial (bird-of-the-sky) and water bird motifs.

Post-Hopewellian Reconfiguration of the Sacred Landscape

People who used early Late Woodland White Hall ceramics resided within the lower Illinois valley from 1150 to 700 BP and are thought to represent a cultural transformation of indigenous Woodland peoples (Studenmund 1998). Their chipped stone artifact assemblages included arrow points, unknown in earlier times. Ceramic vessels, while technically superior to those of earlier Woodland peoples (Braun 1991), lacked the overt iconography of their Hopewell forebears.

No White Hall cemeteries have been discovered, thus contrasting with Hopewell monumentalism. The remarkable absence of identifiable early Late Woodland items in burial contexts suggests a conscious denial of the elaborate rituals that served to negotiate the fragile power relations of the Middle Woodland social and political landscape. Elsewhere, Charles (1992; 1995; Charles, Goldstein, and Buikstra 1996) has argued that the Late Woodland period represents a time of political stability whereby local political and economic structures were negotiated and maintained via kin relations. As the lower Illinois valley became densely occupied, kinship networks assumed paramount importance in buffering the uncertainties inherent in local lifeways. Mortuary and ancestral aspects of the sacred landscape were de-emphasized, including the abandonment of floodplain sites, and replaced by a more archaeologically-ephemeral "landscape" of kin relations and understood ancestry.

Transformations of the natural landscape began again, however, among Late Woodland "Bluff" peoples (1300 to 750 BP) who were the first maize agriculturalists in the region. Biologically, these were indigenous groups (Buikstra 1976), whose material culture traditions differed markedly from those of their Hopewell ancestors. Absent from the monuments raised to these Late Woodland dead is the planned uniformity characteristic of Middle Woodland tumuli. While log and limestone-enclosed tombs occur in some Late Woodland sites, overall mound structure lacks the formality of an earlier era. Charnel structures were the final disposal location for numerous, sequentially placed Late Woodland corpses, suggesting that these tombs and perhaps the mounds themselves represent the disposal locus for a single kin group or lineage.

Other accretional mounds appear to follow a prescribed pattern, beginning with cremation, followed by a series of tombs that extend vertically, horizontally, and eccentrically. Chronologically recent within the Late Woodland sequence, these have been interpreted as evidence for the emergence of a ritual calendric that privileged annual cycles of change rather than the individual (Kerber 1986).

Few material remnants remain as clues to Late Woodland ideology. Nearly all ceramic vessels and pipes lack images of liminal animals. No exotic birds lie side-by-side with human corpses, as they did in Gibson Mound 3 (Perino n.d.a); few figurines represent human forms. Infrequently were items manufactured from foreign sources. Absent were the pigments and the crystals that linked Hopewellians with distant places and supernatural worlds. Most materials were utilitarian, made from locally available raw materials.

Yet these modest monuments do suggest a cosmology that included earth and fire as important symbolic referents, perhaps for the world renewal rituals rooted in fundamental Woodland beliefs. Similarly, the few animal images ceremonially displayed in mortuary contexts are naturalistic representations, as they were in earlier times. For example, the interment of an aged male with four sets of deer antlers (Yokem Mound 4, Burial 8), ordered by increasing age, led the excavator Gregory Perino (n.d.b) to speculate that the antlers had been used by a shaman who "may first have appeared wearing the antlers of the youngest buck, periodically disappearing and reappearing, wearing the antlers of successively older deer until he finally wore those of the oldest." While Perino's interpretation of deer ceremonialism is admittedly speculative, a naturalistic rather than supernatural referent is clear.

The few other naturalistic images include an effigy pipe representing a human figure holding an animal skin or pelt (Titterington 1935), and a pipe showing a human head surmounted by a bird which has variously been interpreted as a crow (Titterington 1935), a buzzard (Perino 1971), or a woodpecker (Farnsworth 1989). Bone hairpins from two Jersey Bluff mounds appear to be renderings of kingfishers (Farnsworth n.d.), and a "crude" bird effigy pipe was recovered by Perino (1973) from the Late Woodland component of the Pete Klunk mound group. These examples are remarkably few when compared with Hopewell images, and there is no evidence for unnatural beasts, which are characteristic of some Mississippian materials (Emerson 1997a; 1997b; Knight 1989).

In sum, the Late Woodland period is initially characterized by a studied absence of monumentalism, followed by the construction of varied tumuli that probably reflect local, kin-based disposal facilities. Evidence for a ceremonial calendric cycle can perhaps be found within some of the most recent Late Woodland mounds. Ritual use of fire and earth may have symbolized world renewal, just as it did for earlier Hopewellians. Another parallel with earlier traditions involves naturalist images which apparently inhabited both the real and mythic aspects of the Late Woodland cosmos.

One thousand years ago, a new cultural tradition appeared in the lower Illinois River region. Mississippian artifacts were distinctly different from those of earlier Woodland groups. Ceramics, tempered with shell, included the elaborately decorated ware of the Ramey tradition, whose sworls and chevrons have been interpreted as having cosmological referents (Emerson 1997a; 1997b; Pauketat and Emerson 1991). Ramey vessels are common grave inclusions and are linked to ceremonial events.

The Mississippian built landscape reached its apogee at the site of Cahokia where more than 100 mounds served variously as disposal arenas and as foundations for chiefly dwellings (Fowler 1969; 1989; 1991). The sacred landscape had thus undergone a transformation that placed the living elites at the pinnacle of the built environment, from which they exerted control over both the natural and the supernatural (Emerson 1997a). Burial mounds contained multiple tribute forms, including human sacrifices (Fowler 1991). Poles and henges helped monitor seasonal change within what must have been a complex calendric. Mississippian plastic art and engraved images included both the natural and the fantastic, sometimes intertwined. Within and near Cahokia are numerous examples of pipes and sculptures that symbolically referred to fertility, not unexpected among agrarian peoples (Emerson 1997a; 1997b).

The monumentality of the newly built Cahokia landscape contrasted with that of the contemporary lower Illinois River valley. Although a very few Illinois Valley Mississippian "residential" mounds have been identified (Farnsworth and Emerson 1989; Farnsworth, Emerson, and Glenn 1991; Perino 1971), the millennia-long tradition of mortuary monumentalism was obviously and radically altered. Bluff crest locations that had attracted ancestral remains for thousands of years no longer excited ritual attention. Though sometimes adjacent to earlier tumuli, Mississippian cemeteries and charnel structures were placed on south-facing hill-slopes, perhaps oriented to Cahokia. The row structure of smaller cemeteries, such as the Moss site (Goldstein 1980), may reflect kin groupings, in the same manner as Late Woodland charnel structures. Larger and more complex sites, such as the Schild cemetery, undoubtedly contained more interments than could have been generated locally (Farnsworth, Emerson, and Glenn 1991; Goldstein 1980). Schild, and even the Moss cemetery, are not located immediately adjacent to Mississippian residential areas.

Goldstein (1980), noting the presence of both charnel structures and burial rows, argues that there is little evidence of differential interment practices at the Schild site, certainly not of the scale seen at more complex mound centers. Even so, there were rare interment types where distinctive burial positions and unusual artifacts coincided, and may be considered minor evidence of unequal statuses.

Interesting, however, is the fact that relatively late Late Woodland (Jersey or Late Bluff) villages are found near Mississippian cemeteries within the lower Illinois valley. At the mouth of Dayton Hollow, near the Schild cemetery, is a large scatter of Jersey Bluff ceramics adjacent to the remnants of a rectangular mound upon which a structure had burned (Perino 1971; Farnsworth, personal communication, January 6, 1997). Given the documented presence of both diagnostic Jersey Bluff and Mississippian items within the lower Illinois valley between 1,000 and 800 years ago (Farnsworth 1989; Farnsworth, Emerson, and Glenn 1991; Studenmund 1998), it seems probable that more Mississippian concepts than people entered the lower Illinois River region during Cahokia's expansive Stirling Phase (Farnsworth 1989; Farnsworth, Emerson, and Glenn 1991). This inference is also supported by evidence of initial Late Woodland to Mississippian genetic continuity from the Schild site (Buikstra 1976). Overall the Schild Late Woodland and Mississippian peoples differed from each other genetically (Buikstra 1976; Droessler 1981); however, the main difference results from heterogeneity among males from the most recent portion of the Mississippian component (Buikstra 1976).

In his discussion of Cahokia, Emerson draws on Turner's (1974) models to contrast the unifying earth/fertility cults with the politically divisive ancestral cults. He characterizes fertility cults as ancient; ancestral cults as new. Considered from our nearby lower Illinois valley perspective, however, the situation is somewhat more complex. While some novel symbolic referents appear, and power inequalities are more firmly institutionalized during Mississippian times, tensions between cults of inclusion and exclusion (sensu Turner 1974) have a long mid-continental history. The built environment well symbolizes this duality.

As emphasized in this chapter, we can trace ancestral cults across millennia within the lower Illinois valley. Middle Archaic peoples placed their ancestors in bluff crest locations designed to facilitate ongoing intervention of the ancients in their descendants' daily lives. Archaic peoples attempted to become more powerful through grave-side ostentatious displays, though certainly not to the degree implied by Emerson in this discussion of the coercive, institutionalized power held by Mississippian elites. The monuments built by Hopewell people also reflect social and political aspirations of individuals, kin groups, and communities. These were all part of an architecture of power that reached its acme during Mississippian times.

The fertility ritualism described by Emerson (1997a, 1997b) is no doubt rooted in the much more ancient earth renewal ceremonialism symbolically reflected in the structure of Middle Woodland burial mounds. In fact, it appears that the later and larger Hopewellian tumuli reflected ritual elaboration that transcended disposal of the dead (Buikstra, Charles, and Rakita 1998). Thus was the partnership between death and fertility ceremonialism weakened, with the latter assuming symbolic dominance over the former.

During Middle Woodland times, ancestral cults and earth renewal rites were inextricably linked, as witnessed by internal mound structure. Human bodies were moved across elevations into the symbolic underworld, where death and fertility were united. Early Hopewell mound structure suggests that movement of the corpse was of paramount ritual significance, the living actors less so. Over time, however, as Middle Woodland communities grew in size, mortuary rituals increasingly served to re-create social and political inequalities among the living. The descendant actors upon the elevated Hopewell stage assumed enhanced significance; corpse disposal, less so. For Mississippians, the stage—or temple mound—was locationally distinct from burial structures, thus fully decoupling fertility/earth renewal from ancestral cults.

Why was the Mississippian "religion" accepted by Woodland peoples of the lower Illinois valley? Doubtless because it was both foreign and familiar. Influential local lineages who served the new religion were elevated to structures located on pyramidal mounds, an empowerment by both living and supernatural forces beyond immediate control. Older, more fragile tensions between kin groups were finally resolved, in favor of institutionalized inequalities. The trappings of this religion, ultimately based in earth renewal myths, now focused upon fertility. Familiar Woodland materials from distant lands, such as mica, quartz crystals, and hematite, were charged with new meanings mediated by rituals whose drink and smoke transported participants into other worlds.

The kin-based structuring of sacred space was thus an ancient Woodland concept, and it was scarcely surprising that newly Mississippianized local lords could both appropriate and transform monumentalism. They now lived upon high points within the sacred floodplain and denied their contemporaries the bluff crest locations that had long lodged the ancestors. At Cahokia, the elite interred their dead ostentatiously within mortuary monuments, thus appropriating and embellishing the ancient ancestral cult, belying its Archaic roots.

Conclusion

We have here described landform choice for mortuary sites that were maintained across millennia within ancient Midcontinental North America. The contrast between ancestor cults and mortuary ritual facilitates our understanding of the earliest regional cemeteries, dating to the Middle Archaic period approximately 7,000 years ago. More recent by 5,000 years, Hopewellian mounds enhanced the visibility of these natural landforms, reflecting complex rituals that positioned the living and dead within the natural and spiritual universe. Though meanings no doubt changed, explanatory rites were transformed and embellished, we believe that this remarkable consistency reflects a deeply-rooted ancient cosmology which lodged the ancestors in places where the ancient worlds conjoined.

Contrasting with Middle Woodland monumentality as a material reflection of political and social instability, the Late Woodland period is characterized by kin-based mortuary structures and an absence of the tensions that characterized earlier times. Ultimately, two deeply embedded midcontinental traditions, the ancestral cult, and the earth renewal/fertility cult, were expropriated and transformed by Mississippian peoples. Mortuary monumentality was reserved for the Cahokia elite, while the living lords were elevated to structures upon pyramidal mounds. Thus did the descendants assume the paramount elevations within the sacred landscape, seizing power previously shared with their contemporaries and with the ancestors.

NOTES

1 Our concept of "the sacred" in this context follows that of Carmichael et al. (1994), in their discussion of sacred places (Buikstra, Charles, and Rakita 1998).

> To say that a specific place is a sacred place is not simply to describe a piece of land, or just locate it in a certain position in the landscape. What is known as a sacred site carries with it a whole range of rules and regulations regarding people's behavior in relation to it, and implies a set of beliefs to do with the non-empirical world, often in relation to the spirits of the ancestors, as well as more remote or powerful gods or spirits.
>
> (Carmichael et al. 1994: 3)

We do not, however, wish to imply that there exists a clear dichotomy between sacred and profane, but would instead emphasize the pervasive nature of "the sacred" in preindustrial societies. In this sense, all sites of human–environmental interaction (*sensu* Crumley 1994) are to some degree sacred. Even so, as Carmichael et al. (1994) emphasize, there often exist within the broader landscape sacred *places* that center human behavior in relationship to the empirical and non-empirical world. This study focuses upon one such class of sacred places, the ancient tumuli that persisted across millennia in the North American Midcontinent.

Our scope is thus limited, not because we wish to neglect other features of ancient landscapes. We recognize that the fullest understanding of such places requires other archaeological evidence for economic, social, political, and religious activities. Nor do we believe that "sacred" sites are free of data that inform beyond ideational aspects of human existence, a perspective abundantly illustrated in this chapter.

A comprehensive understanding of change in ancient lifeways and landscapes must, of course, range across all forms of archaeologically recovered evidence. In this investigation of cultural transformations across millennia, we have chosen to investigate the most conspicuous, persistent elements of ancient Midcontinental built environments as a point of departure for subsequent study of the more ambiguous and incomplete elements of the archaeological record.

2   Interestingly, six skulls of young males recovered from an early feature in the Middle Woodland component of Mound 3 at the Elizabeth site (Feature 1) may represent a similar statement of ancestral rights by Hopewell peoples recolonizing the lower Illinois valley from the north (Charles and Buikstra 1983; Charles, Leigh, and Buikstra 1988).

REFERENCES

Ahern, E. 1973: *The Cult of the Dead in a Chinese Village*. Stanford: Stanford University Press.

Basso, K. H. 1996: *Wisdom Sits in Places: Landscape and Language among the Western Apache*. Albuquerque: University of New Mexico Press.

Bell, C. 1997: *Ritual: Perspectives and Dimensions*. New York: Oxford University Press.

Braun, D. P. 1991: Why decorate a pot? Midwestern household pottery, 200 BC–AD 600. *Journal of Anthropological Archaeology*, 10, 360–97.

Brown, J. A. 1981: The search for rank in prehistoric burials. In R. Chapman, I. Kinnes, and K. Randsborg (eds), *The Archaeology of Death*, Cambridge: Cambridge University Press, 25–37.

Brown, J. A. 1995: On mortuary analysis – with special reference to the Saxe–Binford research program. In L. A. Beck (ed.), *Regional Approaches to Mortuary Analysis*, New York: Plenum Press, 3–26.

Brown, J. A., and Vierra, R. K. 1983: What happened in the Middle Archaic? Introduction to an ecological approach to Koster site archaeology. In J. L. Phillips and J. A. Brown (eds), *Archaic Hunters and Gatherers in the American Midwest*, New York: Academic Press, 165–95.

Buikstra, J. E. 1976: *Hopewell in the Lower Illinois Valley: A Regional Approach to the Study of Biological Variability and Mortuary Activity*, Scientific Papers, no. 2. Evanston, IL: Northwestern University Archeological Program.

Buikstra, J. E. 1981: Mortuary practices, palaeodemography and palaeopathology: A case study from the Koster Site (Illinois). In R. Chapman, I. Kinnes, and K. Randsborg (eds), *The Archaeology of Death*, Cambridge: Cambridge University Press, 123–32.

Buikstra, J. E. 1988: *The Mound-Builders of Eastern North America: A Regional Perspective*. Amsterdam: Elbde Kroon-Voordracht Gehouden voor de Stichting Nederlands Museum voor Anthropologie en Praehistorie.

Buikstra, J. E., Charles, D. K., and Rakita, G. F. M. 1998: *Staging Ritual: Hopewell Ceremonies in the Lower Illinois Valley*, Kampsville Studies in Archeology and History, no. 1. Kampsville, IL: Center for American Archeology.

Buikstra, J. E., and Seddon, M. T. n.d.: *The Bullseye Site: A Middle Archaic Cemetery Complex in the Lower Illinois River Floodplain*, Kampsville Studies in Archeology and History, no. 3. Kampsville, IL: Center for American Archeology.

Carmichael, D. L., Hubert, J., Reeves, B., and Schanche, A. (eds) 1994: *Sacred Sites, Sacred Places*. London: Routledge.

Carr, C. 1995: Mortuary practices: their social, philosophical–religious, circumstantial, and physical determinants. *Journal of Archaeological Method and Theory*, 2, 105–200.

Chapman, R. 1995: Ten years after – megaliths, mortuary practices, and the territorial model. In L. A. Beck (ed.), *Regional Approaches to Mortuary Analysis*, New York: Plenum Press, 29–51.

Charles, D. K. 1985: Corporate symbols: an interpretive prehistory of Indian burial mounds in west-central Illinois. PhD dissertation, Northwestern University.

Charles, D. K. 1992: Woodland demographic and social dynamics in the American Midwest: analysis of a burial mound survey. *World Archaeology*, 24, 175–97.

Charles, D. K. 1995: Diachronic regional social dynamics: mortuary sites in the Illinois Valley/American Bottom region. In L. A. Beck (ed.), *Regional Approaches to Mortuary Analysis*, New York: Plenum Press, 77–99.

Charles, D. K. 1996: Death as a medium for social action. Paper presented at the 95th annual meeting, American Anthropological Association, San Francisco.

Charles, D. K., and Buikstra, J. E. 1983: Archaic mortuary sites in the Central Mississippi drainage: distribution, structure, and behavioral implications. In J. L. Phillips and J. A. Brown (eds), *Archaic Hunters and Gatherers in the American Midwest*, New York: Academic Press, 117–45.

Charles, D. K., and Buikstra, J. E. 1995: Structural evidence of ritual practice at the Hopewell Mound House site in west-central Illinois. Paper presented at the 60th annual meeting, Society for American Archaeology, Minneapolis.

Charles, D. K., Buikstra, J. E., and Konigsberg, L. W. 1986: Behavioral implications of terminal Archaic and Early Woodland mortuary practices in the lower Illinois valley. In K. B. Farnsworth and T. E. Emerson (eds), *Early Woodland Archaeology*, Kampsville Seminars in Archeology, vol. 2, Kampsville, IL: Center for American Archeology, 458–74.

Charles, D. K., Goldstein, L., and Buikstra, J. E. 1996: Sacred landscapes in the lower Illinois valley: trend and tradition, content and meaning. Paper presented at the 61st annual meeting, Society for American Archaeology, New Orleans.

Charles, D. K., Leigh, S. R., and Buikstra, J. E. (eds) 1988: *The Archaic and Woodland Cemeteries at the Elizabeth Site in the Lower Illinois River Valley*, Kampsville Archeological Center, Research Series, vol. 7. Kampsville, IL: Center for American Archeology.

Crown, P. L. 1994: *Ceramics and Ideology: Salado Polychrome Pottery*. Albuquerque: University of New Mexico Press.

Crumley, C. L. 1994: Cultural ecology: a multidimensional ecological orientation. In C. L. Crumley (ed.), *Historical Ecology: Cultural Knowledge and Changing Landscapes*, Santa Fe: SAR Press, 1–16.

Droessler, J. 1981: *Craniometry and Biological Distance: Biocultural Continuity and Change at the Late Woodland–Mississippian Interface*, Kampsville Archeological Center, Research Series, vol. 1. Evanston, IL: Center for American Archeology at Northwestern University.

Emerson, T. E. 1997a: *Cahokia and the Archaeology of Power*. Tuscaloosa: University of Alabama Press.

Emerson, T. E. 1997b: Cahokian elite ideology and the Mississippian cosmos. In T. R. Pauketat and T. E. Emerson (eds), *Cahokia: Domination and Ideology in the Mississippian World*, Lincoln: University of Nebraska Press, 190–228.

Evans-Pritchard, E. E. 1948: *The Divine Kingship of the Shilluk of the Nilotic Sudan*. Cambridge: Cambridge University Press.

Farnsworth, K. B. 1986: Black Sand culture origins and distribution. In K. B. Farnsworth and T. E. Emerson (eds), *Early Woodland Archeology*, Kampsville Seminars in Archeology, vol. 2, Kampsville, IL: Center for American Archeology, 634–41.

Farnsworth, K. B. 1989: Rediscovery of a lost Woodland site in the lower Illinois valley. *Illinois Archaeology*, 1 (1), 82–99.

Farnsworth, K. B. 1990: Evidence for specialized Middle Woodland camps in western Illinois. *Illinois Archaeology*, 2 (1,2), 109–32.

Farnsworth, K. B. n.d.: Late Woodland crested bird effigy bone hairpins from Jersey Bluff mounds in the lower Illinois valley. Manuscript.

Farnsworth, K. B., and Asch, D. L. 1986: Early Woodland chronology, artifact styles, and settlement distribution in the lower Illinois valley region. In K. B. Farnsworth and T. E. Emerson (eds), *Early Woodland Archeology*,

Kampsville Seminars in Archeology, vol. 2, Kampsville, IL: Center for American Archeology Press, 326–457.

Farnsworth, K. B., and Emerson, T. E. 1989: The Macoupin Creek figure pipe and its archaeological context: evidence for Late Woodland–Mississippian interaction beyond the northern border of Cahokian settlement. *Midcontinental Journal of Archaeology*, 14 (1), 18–37.

Farnsworth, K. B., Emerson, T. E., and Glenn, R. M. 1991: Patterns of Late Woodland/Mississippian interaction in the lower Illinois valley drainage: a view from Starr Village. In T. E. Emerson and R. B. Lewis (eds), *Cahokia and the Hinterlands: Middle Mississippian Cultures of the Midwest*, Urbana: University of Illinois Press, 83–118.

Fortes, M. 1945: *The Dynamics of Clanship among the Tallensi*. London: Oxford University Press.

Fortes, M. 1965: Some reflections on ancestor worship in West Africa. In M. Fortes and G. Dieterlin (eds), *African Systems of Thought*, Oxford: Oxford University Press, 122–4.

Fowler, M. L. 1957: *Ferry Site, Hardin County, Illinois*, Scientific Papers 8 (1). Springfield: Illinois State Museum.

Fowler, M. L. 1969: The Cahokia site. In M. L. Fowler (ed.), *Explorations into Cahokia Archaeology*, Illinois Archaeological Survey, Bulletin 7, Urbana: University of Illinois, 1–30.

Fowler, M. L. 1989: *The Cahokia Atlas: A Historical Atlas of Cahokia Archaeology*, Studies in Illinois Archaeology, no. 6. Springfield: Illinois Historic Preservation Agency.

Fowler, M. L. 1991: Mound 72 and Early Mississippian at Cahokia. In J. B. Stoltman (ed.), *New Perspectives on Cahokia: Views from the Periphery*, Madison, WI: Prehistory Press, 1–28.

Gluckman, M. 1937: Mortuary customs and the belief in survival after death among the south-eastern Bantu. *Bantu Studies*, 11, 117–36.

Goldstein, L. G. 1976: Spatial structure and social organization: regional manifestations of Mississippian society. PhD dissertation, Northwestern University.

Goldstein, L. G. 1980: *Mississippian Mortuary Practices: A Case Study of Two Cemeteries in the Lower Illinois Valley*, Scientific Papers, no. 4. Evanston, IL: Northwestern University Archeological Program.

Hajic, E. R. 1987: Geoenvironmental context for archeological sites in the lower Illinois River valley. Manuscript, St Louis: US Army Corps of Engineers.

Hajic, E. R. 1990: *Koster Site Archaeology*, vol. 1: *Stratigraphy and Landscape Evolution*, Kampsville Archeological Center, Research Series, vol. 8. Kampsville, IL: Center for American Archeology.

Hall, R. L. 1997: *An Archaeology of the Soul: North American Indian Belief and Ritual*. Urbana and Chicago: University of Illinois Press.

Hassen, H., and Farnsworth, K. B. 1987: *The Bullseye Site: A Floodplain Archaic Mortuary Site in the Lower Illinois River Valley*. Springfield: Illinois State Museum.

Hodder, I. 1980: Social structure and cemeteries: a critical appraisal. In P. Rahtz, T. Dickinson, and L. Watts (eds), *Anglo-Saxon Cemeteries*, BAR vol. 82, Oxford: British Archaeological Reports, 161–9.

Hodder, I. 1982: *Symbols in Action*. Cambridge: Cambridge University Press.

Hoshower, L. M. n.d.: The burials: skeletal analysis and mortuary behavior. In J. E. Buikstra and M. T. Seddon (eds), *The Bullseye Site: A Middle Archaic Cemetery Complex in the Lower Illinois River Floodplain*, Kampsville Studies in Archeology and History, no. 3, Kampsville, IL: Center for American Archeology.

Kerber, R. 1986: Political evolution in the lower Illinois valley. PhD dissertation, Northwestern University.

Knight, V. J. 1989: Some speculations on Mississippian monsters. In P. Galloway (ed.), *The Southeastern Ceremonial Complex: Artifacts and Analysis*, Lincoln: University of Nebraska Press, 205–10.

Konigsberg, L. W. 1990: Temporal aspects of biological distance: serial correlation and trend in a prehistoric skeletal lineage. *American Journal of Physical Anthropology*, 82, 42–52.

Kut, S. T., and Buikstra, J. E. 1998: Calibration of C-14 dates in the lower Illinois River valley. Paper presented at the 63rd annual meeting, Society for American Archaeology, Seattle.

McGregor, J. C. 1958: *The Pool and Irving Villages: A Study of Hopewell Occupation in the Illinois River Valley*. Urbana: University of Illinois.

Morgan, D. T. 1988: Ceramics at the Elizabeth site. In D. K. Charles, S. R. Leigh, and J. E. Buikstra (eds), *The Archaic and Woodland Cemeteries at the Elizabeth Site in the Lower Illinois Valley*, Kampsville Archeological Center, Research Series, vol. 7, Kampsville, IL: Center for American Archeology, 120–54.

Morris, I. 1991: The archaeology of ancestors: the Saxe/Goldstein hypothesis revisited. *Cambridge Archaeological Journal*, 1, 147–69.

Pauketat, T. R., and Emerson, T. E. 1991: The ideology of authority and the power of the pot. *American Anthropologist*, 93, 919–41.

Perino, G. 1966: A preliminary report on the Peisker site: part I – the Early Woodland occupation. *Central States Archaeological Journal*, 13, 47–51.

Perino, G. 1968: *The Pete Klunk Mound group, Calhoun County, Illinois: The Archaic and Hopewell Occupations (with an appendix on the Gibson Mound group)*. Bulletin 6, Urbana, IL: Illinois Archaeological Survey, 9–124.

Perino, G. 1971: The Mississippian components at the Schild site (no. 4), Greene County, Illinois. In J. A. Brown (ed.), *Mississippian Site Archaeology in Illinois*, Vol. I: *Site Reports from the St. Louis and Chicago Areas*, Bulletin 8, Urbana, IL: Illinois Archaeological Survey, 1–141.

Perino, G. 1973: The Late Woodland component at the Pete Klunk site, Calhoun County, Illinois. In *Late Woodland Site Archaeology in Illinois* I, Urbana, IL: Illinois Archaeological Survey, 58–89.

Perino, G. n.d.a: The Gibson Mounds Hopewell Project, Calhoun County, Illinois. Manuscript.

Perino, G. n.d.b: The Yokem Site Late Woodland Mounds, Pike County, Illinois. Manuscript.

Saxe, A. A. 1970: Social dimensions of mortuary practices. PhD dissertation, University of Michigan.

Shanks, M., and Tilley, C. 1982: Ideology, symbolic power and ritual communication: a reinterpretation of Neolithic mortuary practices. In I. Hodder (ed.), *Symbolic and Structural Archaeology*, Cambridge: Cambridge University Press, 129–54.

Struever, S. 1960: The Kamp Mound Group and a Hopewell mortuary complex in the lower Illinois valley. MA thesis, Northwestern University.

Struever, S. 1968a: A re-examination of Hopewell in eastern North America. PhD dissertation, University of Chicago.

Struever, S. 1968b: Woodland subsistence – settlement systems in the lower Illinois valley. In S. R. Binford and L. R. Binford (eds), *New Perspectives in Archeology*, Chicago: Aldine, 285–312.

Struever, S., and Houart, G. L. 1972: An analysis of the Hopewell Interaction Sphere. In E. N. Wilmsen (ed.), *Social Exchange and Interaction*, Anthropological Papers, vol. 46, Ann Arbor: Museum of Anthropology, University of Michigan, 47–79.

Studenmund, S. 1998: A reconsideration of the Late Woodland period in the lower Illinois River valley. Manuscript.

Styles, T. R. 1985: *Holocene and Late Pleistocene Geology of the Napoleon Hollow Site in the Lower Illinois Valley*. Kampsville, IL: Center for American Archeology.

Titterington, P. F. 1935: Certain bluff mounds of western Jersey County, Illinois. *American Antiquity*, 1, 6–46.

Titterington, P. F. 1950: Some non-pottery sites in the St. Louis area. *Illinois State Archaeological Society*, 1 (2), 1–13.

Turner, V. 1974: *Dramas, Fields, and Metaphors: Symbolic Action in Human Society*. Ithaca: Cornell University Press.

Van Nest, J. n.d.: Geoarchaeology at the Bullseye site. In J. E. Buikstra and M. T. Seddon (eds), *The Bullseye Site: A Middle Archaic Cemetery Complex in the Lower Illinois River Floodplain*, Kampsville Studies in Archeology and History, no. 3, Kampsville, IL: Center for American Archeology.

Watson, R. S. 1988: Remembering the dead: graves and politics in southeastern China. In J. L. Watson and E. Rawski (eds), *Death Ritual in Late Imperial and Modern China*, Berkeley: University of California Press, 203–27.

10

Ideational and Industrial Landscape on Prehistoric Cyprus

A. Bernard Knapp

What do these faces [of Mediterranean women] tell one except that
nothing Mediterranean can change for it is landscape-dominated; its
people are simply the landscape-wishes of the earth sharing their partic-
ularities with the wine and the food, the sunlight and the sea.
(Lawrence Durrell, *Réalités*, Paris, June 1961)

Introduction: Social and Cultural Landscapes

Over the past decade, and often with little regard for the poetic hyper-
bole of literary figures like Lawrence Durrell, Mediterranean archaeologists have canvassed several types of landscape: rural, urban,
ceremonial, civic. Granted that the study of landscapes is a "multidisciplinary project" (Johnston 1998), it is still possible to subsume all
variations of perceived landscapes under two general categories: the
cultural and the ideational (or cognitive). For Tilley (1994: 37), the
landscape is an "unstable" concept swinging between these polar
extremes. For Fowler (1995: 100–1), the meaning and understanding
of the "countryside" are relative, and result from human preconceptions or the expression of artistic and scientific viewpoints. For Bender
(1998: 8–9 and *passim*), landscapes are multiple, contested, embodied
and an integral part of everyday human activity. Such instability, relativity, and variability surely help to explain the appeal of exploring the
concept of landscape and the ways it impacts on different domains of
human action and experience. The concept of landscape, moreover, is
imbued with a pronounced socio-symbolic element; it is dynamic and
fully contextualized within the human experience.

The cultural landscape has been shaped by peoples' routines and
processes, by their morals and beliefs. The landscape record may be

modified, confused or destroyed by the dynamic interplay between natural and human factors. Such a realization has led UNESCO to categorize and define "outstanding" cultural or "natural" landscapes in the attempt to identify and preserve them. One main category defined by UNESCO – the *organically evolved landscape* – includes a "subspecies" (relict) "... associated with industries such as mining, quarrying and the production of metals, glass and textiles" (Cleere 1995: 66). Reference is made to classical Greek silver mines at Lavrion, and to nineteenth- and twentieth-century gold-rush regions of western North America and Australia. This category seems to be equivalent to what the US National Park Service defines as a "historic vernacular landscape;" the National Register lists specific criteria to help identify, define, and evaluate the historical significance and integrity of these typically rural landscapes (Feierabend 1990; Hardesty 1990).

The archaeological notion of a cultural landscape assumes that past patterns have somehow created or influenced the present through a predictable continuity (or "association"). This assumption, however, neutralizes many of the social factors that helped to construct the landscape and influenced various perceptions of it. Furthermore, this kind of "naturalistic" view portrays the landscape as a passive stage on which the human drama is acted out. Landscape, however, cannot be conceived of simply as a neutral, binary relationship between people and nature (Meinig 1979: 2). The "inherent" landscape – as defined by Robert Johnston (1998) – makes no distinction between "real" and "perceived" landscapes: in terms of a person's experience of "being-in-the-world" (Tuan 1977), the two concepts are indivisible. People perceive the three-dimensional landscape through their own cultural and cognitive filters, and single out certain locations as a result of differing intentions, naming, repeated use, or unusual qualities. In this alternative view, space becomes a medium for and the outcome of human activity: it does not exist apart from that activity (Tilley 1994: 10, 23).

Although some landscapes may become intensely marked and socialized as time passes, sites with remarkable "natural signifiers" are the ones often considered most powerful by various contemporary groups (e.g., Australian aborigines) (Taçon 1994: 126). In certain societies people consciously identify and modify their surroundings to demarcate these special, natural places. Both cultural and cognitive landscapes are conceptualized and constructed by people in order to perpetuate or change existing political, social, or economic configurations. The landscape therefore cannot be viewed as a natural, ready-made substrate on which a cultural design or mental template is imposed. There is a dynamic tension between the "natural" world and a socially constructed image of landscape (Richards 1996: 314). Landscape is neither "complete," nor is it "built" or "unbuilt": rather it is a "social expression," perpetually under construction (Head 1993: 486–9).

At this still-developing stage in the archaeological study of landscapes, we should try to transcend passive, impressionistic viewpoints, and instead consider how the landscape – as a source of the sacred and symbolic, or a place to enact them – also serves to establish social identity, power and authority, and to reinforce politico-economic or religious institutions. This chapter adopts an ideational approach, and seeks to reflect upon and treat recursively the archaeological record. If archaeologists are able to link landscape transformations to an understanding of diachronic social processes, they will gain insights into long-term social action unavailable to any other discipline (Gosden and Head 1994: 114–15).

Industrial and Ideational Landscapes

Landscape archaeology as conventionally understood frequently restricts itself to the study and analysis of "built" monuments. By so doing, it has omitted an entire class of material evidence which is critical, at certain times and in certain places, for the social construction of the inhabited landscape. The constitution and composition of the natural world – including mountains, rivers, trees, minerals, etc. – may be defined and interpreted through social practices and experience.

The ideational landscape of prehistoric Cyprus was intimately linked to industrial (specifically, mining) activities, and to the Bronze Age elites who exploited their perceived "supernatural" knowledge in exchange for control over the appropriation, distribution and consumption of labor, land and raw materials – especially copper. Whereas archaeologists have typically discussed the parameters of authority in the ancient Cypriot landscape by referring to the construction or elaboration of monumental architecture in urban centers, we should not ignore the strategic, symbolic value of ritually defined sacred space in rural settings, or any other aspect of the unbuilt landscape.

In this study, I look specifically at "rural sanctuaries," mining villages and agricultural sites, and prominent features within the striking industrial landscape of Cyprus's Troodos Mountain foothills. The massive slag heaps, abandoned mines, and regenerated forests that exist today impacted significantly, and throughout time, on the ideational landscape of Cyprus (figure 10.1).

Rural sanctuaries

One direct approach to conceptualizing past ideational landscapes is to consider the ceremonial activities that took place within them. Rural sanctuaries are crucial for assessing the symbolic aspects of such landscapes. On Cyprus during the Late Bronze Age (c.1600–1200 BC), it is widely agreed that there was an unprecedented scale of sociopolitical development (e.g., Keswani 1996; Peltenburg 1996: 27–37; Webb 1997), and a tripartite system of settlement and economy was proposed long ago (Catling 1962):

1   wealthy, coastal trading centers;
2   inland, rural, agriculturally based settlements; and
3   inland production sites associated with copper mining, chiefly found in the igneous zone of the Troodos foothills.

To this threefold division we might add at least a fourth category, the "rural sanctuary" (for detailed reconsideration of these categories, see Knapp 1997: 53–61). In addition to some sanctuaries situated within the new town centers (e.g., at Enkomi, Kition, Kouklia *Palaepaphos*, perhaps Maroni *Vournes* and Alassa *Paleotaverna*), there were several inland (not necessarily isolated) sites which are also thought to have been special-purpose (i.e., sanctuary or "ritual") sites, including Myrtou *Pigadhes*, Ayios Iakovos *Dhima*, Korovia *Palaeoskoutella*, perhaps Eylenja *Leondari Vouno* and Athienou *Bamboulari tis Koukounninas*. Although Catling (1975: 193) first suggested that these "rustic sanctuaries" may have functioned as intermediary points in an internal trade that brought copper and surplus international goods to the town centers, he did not distinguish them in his scheme from any other inland, agricultural settlement. Webb (1988) identified eighteen possible Late Cypriot "cult units," most of which she regards as public or ceremonial sites (on *Dhima*, *Palaeoskoutella*, and *Leondari Vouno* as funerary cult sites, see Webb 1992: 92–6).

Wright (1992: 274–6) adopts a diachronic perspective and on that basis characterizes the location of "rural sanctuaries" as follows:

1   proximity to agricultural settlements but distance from urban centers;
2   concentration in the area delimited by Athienou, Idalion, and Tamassos (Archaic period);
3   absence of sanctuaries from the mountain districts;

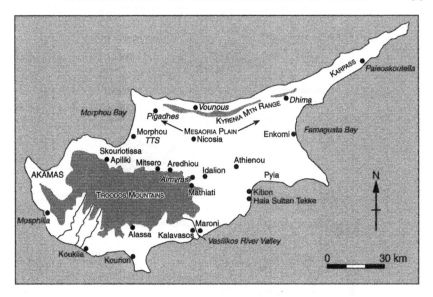

Figure 10.1(a)   Map showing the approximate location of sites mentioned in the text.

4   the boundedness of the sacred with the "state of nature," repre-
    sented by a tree or grove of trees;
5   the altar as the focal point of a cult;
6   the "servient" rather than dominant nature of all buildings within a
    sacred precinct.

Reconstructed notions about ideology and authority within Chalcolithic–Early/Middle Bronze Age Cyprus (Prehistoric Bronze Age: *c*.2400–1700 BC) are based on the study and analysis of building models (Peltenburg 1994) and figurines (Knapp and Meskell 1997), which offer interesting supplementary information on the concept of the rural sacred landscape. By the Late Bronze Age (Protohistoric Bronze Age: *c*.1700–1000 BC), the spatial patterning of settlement, cemetery and sanctuary had changed, and there is indisputable evidence for ceremonial structures in both urban and rural centers, the latter characterized by their relative isolation in the landscape and by placement on some topographic prominence.

Three of the best known "rural sanctuaries" in Late Bronze Age Cyprus are Ayios Iakovos *Dhima*, Athienou, and Myrtou *Pigadhes*. The layout of the Late Bronze (=Late Cypriot) II "rural sanctuary" at Ayios Iakovos *Dhima* (Wright 1992: 269–70, and fig. 1) is not spatially dissimilar to that represented in the earlier (Chalcolithic–Early/Middle

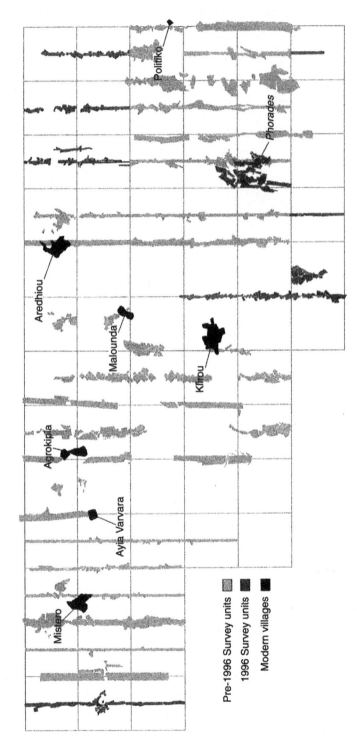

Figure 10.1(b) Map showing the area of the Sydney Cyprus Survey Project, including local village sites mentioned in the text, as well as Politiko *Phorades*.

Bronze Age) terracotta models from *Mosphilia*, *Vounous*, or Kotchati. The site of *Dhima* appears to be representative of the rural sanctuary as it existed over the course of 2,500 years (*c.*1500 BC–AD 1000): it is small, isolated and elevated. At Athienou *Bamboulari tis Koukounninas*, excavations produced thousands of miniature "votive" juglets in association with an array of items suggestive of metallurgical activity. It is likely that the primary smelting of copper took place at the nearby mines, with further processing being undertaken at Athienou (Maddin et al. 1983: 136–8; but cf. Muhly 1985: 33nn., 91–2). However, the production and storage of up to 11,000 liters of olive oil at Athienou may also have played a major economic role and served the needs of those who managed the "sanctuary" (Keswani 1993: 78), perhaps those of the local miners and metalworkers as well. At Myrtou *Pigadhes*, the sanctuary had a single room which revealed clear, albeit limited evidence for metallurgical activity (Du Plat Taylor 1957: 20, fig. 12). Amongst the finds from Myrtou *Pigadhes* were a small bronze bull figurine, terracotta bull figurines, a hoard of bronze tripods and ring stands, "horns of consecration," and similar paraphernalia (Du Plat Taylor 1957: 103–12; al-Radi 1983: 81–2; Ionas 1985). These unique installations and artifacts suggest that the main structure at *Pigadhes* served some ceremonial function.

In the Archaic period, there are several rural sanctuaries centering on the city-kingdom of Tamassos (Given 1991: 52; fig. 14), an example being Kalokhorio *Zithkionas* (Gunnis 1936: 244; *ARDAC* 1953: 17). The only rural sanctuary associated specifically with slag or copper working in the north central Troodos region is at Mathiati, where terracottas were found in direct association with a slag heap (*BCH* 1984: 964–5). In the village of Tamassos itself, there are copper workshops immediately adjacent to the principal Archaic sanctuary (Buchholz 1985: 240–2), whilst a considerable amount of slag is spread throughout the neighboring buildings and in the courtyard of the sanctuary itself. As well as copper slag, other products of the countryside are present in the city sanctuary at Tamassos, including the bones of wild and domestic animals, olive pits, grain, and, judging from the vessels, oil and wine. Copper was clearly just one of the products brought in from the surrounding countryside to the center and dedicated or processed in a ceremonial setting (Given 1991: 54–5).

The basic conclusion to be drawn from this brief overview is that a noticeable proportion of Late Cypriot and Archaic town or village sites have ceremonial precincts or sanctuaries (see also Knapp 1997: 54–5, table 2). Of these, the three briefly discussed above may be regarded as rural sanctuaries, and two of the three are firmly associated with

metalworking activity of some sort. Is there any more substantive connection between prehistoric rural sanctuaries and archaeometallurgical
sites? Before attempting to answer that question, it is necessary first to
consider the industrial landscape of prehistoric Cyprus; in so doing, I
draw mainly upon recent field work – survey and excavations – carried
out by the Sydney Cyprus Survey Project (SCSP) (Donnelly et al.
1998; Knapp and Given 1996; Given et al. n.d.; Knapp et al. 1994).

The mining landscape

The materiality of the mining experience is a major factor in the social
construction of a mining community, and by extension of the mining
landscape (see various studies in Knapp et al. 1998). Consider, for
example, the huge (modern-day) spoil heap of the *Kokkinopezoula* mine
overlooking the village of Mitsero in the foothills of Cyprus's north
central Troodos Mountains (figure 10.2). The mines gave villagers not
only employment but also a sense of their own economic and social
identity: this remarkable human modification of the landscape altered
the traditional agricultural character of Mitsero and served to recon-
struct it as a village with a mixed agricultural and industrial economy.
This spoil heap dwarfs the local built environment and in a very real

Figure 10.2 Modern spoil heap from mid-twentieth-century mining
operations at Mitsero *Kokkinopezoula*, with modern village in foreground.

sense imitates the encompassing topography. The dominant spoil heaps and slag heaps in this region reflect the daily grind of mining; in time they assumed social significance as part of the industrial landscape that configured everyday life.

Similarly, a bright gossan in an outcrop of rock may have a special significance for someone involved in the mining and production of copper, be they prospector, miner, or farmer producing food for a mining community (Constantinou 1992). In the eyes of the mining community, certain aspects come to the fore in the appropriation of a local landscape: natural resources; agricultural land; places for working and spaces for dwelling; communications; and, in some cases, the ideology of mining practice. But gossans and ores are by no means the only components of a mining landscape, ancient or modern. Fluxes (notably manganese oxide and silica) are needed to lower the melting point and viscosity of the gangue when smelting, thus facilitating its separation from the metal. In Cyprus's Pillow Lavas, manganese oxide occurs mainly in the form of umber and manganese concretions, which usually appear at the interface between the Lower Pillow Lavas and the sedimentary zone. The characteristic deep brown layers of the umber and black nodules of the manganese concretions take on special significance in a mining landscape (see also Given and Knapp n.d.).

Because mining galleries usually need pit-props, and smelting needs fuel, inevitably the production of metal needs forests. The most common timber preserved in ancient mining galleries (e.g., as pit props at Skouriotissa or at Mitsero *Kokkinoyia*) was pine (*Pinus brutia* and *Pinus halepensus*), a species particularly suited to the Pillow Lavas. Even allowing for extensive deforestation since antiquity, *Pinus brutia* remains quite common in the Pillow Lava zones, and regenerates naturally on the spoil heaps of modern mines. Dwarf oak (*Quercus alnifolia*), hawthorn and olive would have been the commonest hardwoods; they produce long, hot burns and can easily be coppiced; accordingly they would have been ideal as a source of fuel for roasting and charcoal for smelting. The denuded landscape of certain areas on modern-day Cyprus, not far distant from the Pillow Lavas of the Troodos Mountains, must have resulted at least in part from 4,000 years of copper mining and production.

The relationship between mining, settlement, and landscape varies according to the scale and organizational level of production (Raber 1987: 301–2). For example, the intermittent small-scale, localized production of the Medieval period on Cyprus contrasts markedly with the larger-scale industries and major labor forces typical of the Imperial Roman period. Moreover, it is often assumed that, once the Roman

Empire collapsed, the mining of copper sulfides for metal would have ceased. Recent work carried out by the SCSP in the northern Troodos suggests that we must reassess this presumption (Clough, in Knapp and Given 1996: 308–16). When copper was produced and exported on a large scale, as it was during the Bronze Age and the Roman era, a fully functional and simple system of communications was essential. Whenever copper production exceeded the local or regional scale, mining communities were perforce linked into interregional, national, or global networks of communication and exchange. Invariably this development would have impacted on the mining landscape in the form of imports, migrant labor, and possibly even new settlement plans in the face of other socio-structural change.

How can these Classical to contemporary industrial images further our understanding of earlier, prehistoric landscapes? In attempting to answer that question, I rely largely on field work conducted by the SCSP over the past five seasons (1992–7).

During the 1995 field season, an archaeometallurgical team made sections at two major ancient slag heaps (Mitsero *Kouloupakhis* and Mitsero *Sykamies*), and at the major, modern spoil heap at Agrokipia *Kriadis*. At *Kouloupakhis*, we uncovered clear, stratified evidence of a major structure embedded within the slag heap (figure 10.3). This building may pre-date the slag heap, it may be contemporary with it, or both. Although the association of structures with slag heaps should

Figure 10.3 Classical(?) period structure within the slag heap at Mitsero *Kouloupakhis*.

be of major interest to anyone interested in copper mining and the mining community, scant attention has been paid to this issue. Structures were likewise embedded in slag heaps at Skouriotissa (also in the northern Troodos) and at Kalavasos *Petra* (southern Troodos). Koucky (in Wallace 1982: 243) reports that the foundations of "medieval buildings" (fifteenth to sixteenth centuries) were built on top of the slag heaps near the *Kokkinoyia* mine at Mitsero: Koucky must be referring to the rubble remains associated with the abandoned village settlement at *Mavrovounos* (Knapp and Given 1996: 324–5), directly adjacent to the slag heap at Mitsero *Sykamies*. This area has been investigated in a preliminary manner, and was examined in much greater detail during SCSP's 1998 study season.

In attempting to define the relationship between industrial processes and structures at *Kouloupakhis*, we must also consider the chronological position of that site. Analysis of the sections leads to the following observations (see also Clough, in Knapp and Given 1996: 315–16, figs 12–15):

1   amongst the building remains, some have walls at least 15 meters long with sections standing to a height of 3 meters; these walls were constructed of mortared limestone with some finely cut blocks.

2   The stratigraphy of one construction section reveals substantial building activity prior to the beginnings of copper production at *Kouloupakhis*. No slag was found in the buried walls, or on the floors and layers with building waste and pottery. One building seems to have been abandoned prior to the smelting operations; pottery from the relevant level suggests that this structure may have been built in the Classical period.

3   Slag covers and is in direct contact with some of the standing walls, which suggests that the walls lay in ruins at least during the later stages of the copper-producing industry.

4   Roman tiles, pottery and mortars within the "workshop" walls indicate that they may have been refurbished during the lifespan of the copper industry.

5   The wall exposed at the lower face (Lower Terrace, west section) suggests that although it had been constructed prior to the development of copper production, it was used for some part of the industrial process prior to being turned into a dump. This particular wall was constructed of cut limestone blocks and mud mortar, with thick white plaster (1–2 cm) remaining in parts.

6   The relationship between the workshop floors and the walls also indicates that the structures were used in industrial activities.

7   Most pottery collected from the surface in the fields surrounding
     the slag heaps can be dated to pre-Roman periods (Classical–
     Hellenistic), whilst the pottery from the upper levels of the slag
     heap is definitely mid–late Roman.

Some tentative conclusions follow: prior to the industrial activity
which produced the slag heaps, there existed substantial, apparently
Classical/Hellenistic structures that spread beyond the bounds of the
later production site. Some of these buildings were substantial, and
may have been associated with administrative, military, industrial, or
religious activities. At some point the buildings were integrated with a
major copper smelting industry and there are indicators of refurbish-
ments during the Roman period. The ultimate impression gained is
that the *Kouloupakhis* slag heaps and the surrounding area represent a
lengthy human occupation and investment in the copper industry,
spanning several hundred years. The architecture is impressive, and
may represent more than small-scale occupation. However, the full
significance of Mitsero *Kouloupakhis* can only be realized through more
intensive investigation and excavation.

The slag heaps at *Kouloupakhis* show several parallels with the slag
heap at Mitsero *Sykamies*, to the west and on the opposite side of the
village from *Kouloupakhis*. Both sites are similar in scale and have similar finds: large slag cakes, fragments of furnace lining, significant
amounts of slagged stones used in the construction of the furnace, and
pottery. The main difference is that, at *Kouloupakhis*, large built structures were found in association with the slag, along with well-defined
floors connected to metallurgical activities. While the *Sykamies* slag
heap clearly can be associated with the mine at Kokkinoyia, we
cannot be sure of the origin of the ores smelted at *Kouloupakhis*
(perhaps Agrokipia *Kriadhis*). The mines associated with *Kouloupakhis*
may well have been buried or even removed during twentieth-century
gold-extracting operations, carried out just to the north of the slag
heaps.

The variety of slags found elsewhere on the island is mirrored closely
by the variation seen in the slag heaps at Mitsero *Kouloupakhis* and
Mitsero *Sykamies*. Whereas it has proved more difficult to identify pre-
Classical industrial (roasting, smelting) sites, there is indisputable and
widespread evidence for ancient ore extraction and copper production
throughout the survey area. Before the 1996 field season, however,
none could be associated strictly with the Bronze Age. With the discovery of Politiko *Phorades*, however, we recorded what seems to be the
earliest smelting site yet known on Cyprus, and at least 1,500 years

Figure 10.4 Overview of the excavations at Politiko *Phorades* (from west).

earlier than the most intensive period of activity indicated by the Mitsero sites.

Politiko Phorades   This site is situated about 3 kilometers southwest of Politiko village, and about 500 meters east of the nearest gossan and mineral deposit (*Kokkinorotsos*). *Phorades* consists of a buried creek bed and a copper smelting site exposed in the current creek bed section (see figure 10.4). The contemporary creek runs more than 4 meters below the old creek bed preserved in section, which indicates that the creek has changed its course since the metallurgical activity occurred. The smelting remains are buried beneath erosional material and topsoil deposited since the site was abandoned. Slag and furnace material were evident on the horizontal surface above the creek bed. The quantity of slag involved at *Phorades* is no more than a few tons, as opposed to several hundred thousand tons at Mitsero *Sykamies*. Such a smelting operation is much smaller than most others known on Cyprus, and in this regard the closest parallel is the Cypro-Archaic–Hellenistic smelting site at Ayia Vavara *Almyras* (Fasnacht and Kassianidou 1992; Fasnacht et al. 1996).

Several different types of evidence make it possible to propose a tentative date for ancient metallurgical activity at *Phorades*.

1 A 3,000–5,000-year-old soil profile that developed on deposits overlying the materials from the smelting area makes a Bronze Age or early Iron Age date for the smelting workshop plausible.

2 AMS dating at the University of Oxford's Radiocarbon Accelerator Unit of a single sample of charcoal taken from furnace material gave a calibrated date in the twelfth-to-tenth century BC (Donnelly et al. 1998).

3 Stratigraphic layers containing archaeometallurgical material have revealed Black Slip II, Base Ring, Proto-White Slip and White Slip I, and Coarse Ware sherds, all of which suggest a date at the very end of the Middle Bronze or beginning of the Late Bronze (sixteenth century BC); further charcoal samples have now been submitted to the Oxford Lab for AMS dating.

We are confident that *Politiko Phorades* is the earliest primary smelting site yet discovered on Cyprus, by nearly 1,000 years, and that its excavation is critical for our understanding of early industrial societies, not just on Cyprus but in the Mediterranean world generally.

Excavations at Politiko *Phorades* during both 1997 and 1998 confirmed that the site consisted of a remnant slag heap within and partly alongside an ancient river channel. The slags from *Phorades* are unique on Cyprus. At Apliki, for example, most slag came in the form of large, tapped slag cakes (Muhly 1989: 306), whilst at Kition some of the slags were crucible shaped, that is, plano-convex (Tylecote 1982: 89). At *Phorades*, plano-concave cakes indicate that the slag may have cooled on top of an ingot of copper. The slag was of a very low viscosity which allowed the full separation of the metal and slag phases. In order to produce such a slag the smelters had to be fully cognizant of applying the appropriate type and amount of flux required for the particular ore type and smelting conditions.

Forty-five complete or nearly complete *tuyères* (clay tubes through which air travels to the reaction zone within a smelting furnace) have been recovered during the two excavation seasons (figure 10.5). This represents a collection that more than doubles in size and quality all the *tuyères* from Enkomi and Apliki (Dikaios 1971; Du Plat Taylor 1952: 152 and 161). The *tuyère* fragments are of four kinds: (1) cylindrical *tuyères* with slagged tips; (2) unslagged cylindrical *tuyères*;

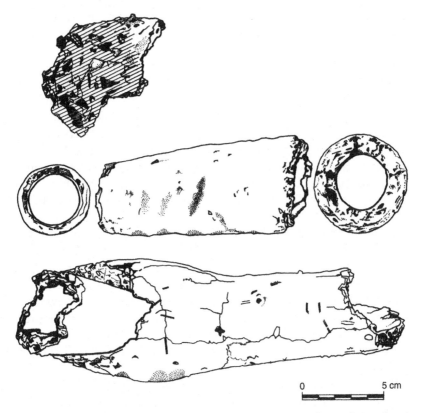

0   5 cm

Figure 10.5 Some *tuyères* from Politiko *Phorades*: (top) slagged tip of *tuyère* which has been overheated and started to melt; (center) unslagged *tuyère* tip broken on both ends (slagged tip may be missing, or else it may be part of a double *tuyère*); (bottom) one of the several double *tuyères*.

(3) double *tuyères* (where one is encased within another); and (4) a *tuyère* with fine tip but unslagged.

Despite this recovery of a magnificent collection of *tuyères*, hundreds of fragments of furnace lining, an unprecedented type of slag, and other associated debris, the highly disturbed nature of the site still prevents us from demonstrating that features or installations are *in situ*. A small stone-lined feature discovered at the end of the 1997 season (near which were recovered a number of almost complete *tuyères* – some slagged) is hypothesized to represent some kind of installation related to pyrotechnological activity within the old creek channel. There appears to be a complete *tuyère* extending from the inside of this feature through the stones to the outside. Three smaller features have also been located cutting into this same anthropogenic bank. A final season of excavations will be required to clarify the integrity of these features.

Politiko *Phorades* reveals unprecedented technological developments on an island that has been a center for Mediterranean copper production over the past 4,000 years. The extensive material remains of mining activity, as revealed both by our survey work in the northern Troodos area and by other archaeological activity island-wide, represent increasingly specialized production and distribution. At this stage, we have enough archaeometallurgical finds from a primary smelting workshop to help us address several complex questions that surround concepts of Late Bronze smelting technology on Cyprus (Donnelly et al. 1998).

To return to the concept of the mining landscape: small industrial sites like *Phorades* may have been much more common throughout the Pillow Lavas that encircle the Troodos Mountains, before the advent of twentieth-century mining. For example, our field work at Agrokipia *Kriadis* (Knapp and Given 1996: 316–21) has shown that evidence for ancient beneficiation (ore crushing and sorting) and other ore preparation is buried within modern spoil heaps. Moreover, modern-day mining operations in the Skouriotissa region have obliterated the Bronze Age site of Apliki.

In order to understand better the mining landscape of prehistoric Cyprus, we need to consider first, why *Phorades* was located where it was, and secondly, what were the technological and functional differences between *Phorades* and *Kouloupakhis*. In deciding where to establish a smelting workshop in antiquity, some key factors would have been the location of ore deposits and the appropriate fluxes, as well as the availability of fuel, water, and refractory clay (for the manufacture of the furnace lining and the *tuyères*). The clay had to be able to withstand high temperatures and be resistant to the corrosive nature of the slag. The distance (some 800 m) of the workshop at Politiko *Phorades* from the nearest copper ore deposit may be explained at least in part by its location on a creek, which would have provided the necessary raw materials for constructing the furnaces. Moreover, there may have been adequate fuel in the same area. No ground stone tools for crushing or grinding the ore have yet been identified at *Phorades*, nor were there any ore roasting layers or roasting conglomerates: we presume that these steps were carried out nearer the mine. Amongst the finds from 1997 was a piece of metallic matte, a rare intermediate product of the smelting process. During the 1998 season, one long piece and two shorter pieces of metal were also found amongst the remains of anthropogenic material associated with the slag heap. This "functional" interpretation of various features at *Phorades* should not be seen as precluding other, social factors in site/settlement choice and landscape conception.

Based on two seasons of excavations at *Phorades* and on the results of a highly intensive, regional survey carried out between 1992 and 1997, it is possible to offer the following reconstruction of the Bronze Age industrial landscape. The ores smelted at *Phorades* would have derived from mines on the gossan ridge above the smelting site, whilst ore preparation and roasting took place at an intermediate point, farther down the hill. Smelting would have been carried out at *Phorades* itself, some 500–800 meters distant, along the river bank. Geobotanical indices as well as geomorphological parameters indicate a markedly different landscape around the smelting site: this tends to substantiate the notion of a multi-phase process with specialized production units represented by the various "sites" and installations in this micro-region of the Troodos. In these same micro-regional terms, I have elsewhere proposed a localized settlement pattern within a wider settlement hierarchy (Knapp 1997). Taking material from *Phorades* into consideration alongside other, already known Late Cypriot data (Keswani 1993; 1996; Knapp 1986; 1994; Muhly 1986; 1989), we can postulate more securely a self-contained metallurgical site with essential raw materials, a distinct social organization, and a viable communication network, all of which would have fueled an archaeometallurgical and pyrotechnological revolution.

Some obvious, and certainly not unexpected changes occurred in the mining landscape of Cyprus between the Bronze Age, the Iron Age, and the Classical–Medieval periods. Whereas it is clear that all the SCSP sites discussed in this study – *Phorades*, *Kouloupakhis* and *Sykamies* – as well as Ayia Varvara *Almyras*, were involved in the smelting of sulfide ores, the diverse types of evidence available from all these sites indicates very different kinds of pyrotechnological and organizational activity. Although there is abundant furnace lining from *Phorades*, we cannot yet distinguish between roasting and smelting furnaces as has been possible at *Almyras* (Fasnacht and Kassianidou 1992: 81–3); moreover, the slag heaps at *Kouloupakhis* and *Sykamies* have not revealed any furnace lining. In terms of the social relations of production at these different sites and in different time periods, we have proposed for Phorades a small-scale, micro-regional, specialized production unit that was probably linked into an overall settlement hierarchy, one which became increasingly centralized during the course of the Late Bronze Age. By the Archaic period, at Ayia Varvara

Almyras, it seems clear that production was centralized and probably controlled from Idalion, even if conflict developed during the Classical–Hellenistic periods (Fasnacht and Kassianidou 1992: 84–8). SCSP evidence for the Classical period at *Kouloupakhis* is patchy, but there is no doubt that some sort of Classical–Hellenistic settlement was located in the immediate vicinity, and that the structures situated in the slag heap had their origins at this time. Ongoing analyses of the pottery suggest that this industry flourished mainly in mid/late Roman times, although it is equally possible that the structures could be associated with earlier extractive metallurgy. Only excavation can expand our understanding of this preliminary work.

Overview and Conclusion

Our understanding of the industrial landscape of both prehistoric and historic Cyprus has been enhanced by the interdisciplinary survey, excavation, exploration, and metallurgical analyses currently being undertaken by the Sydney Cyprus Survey Project. Places such as Politiko *Phorades*, Mitsero *Kouloupakhis* and (twentieth-century) Mitsero *Kokkinoyia* are often imbued with immense ideological and economic significance: here the landscape impacts on both personal and cultural identities. It is important to relate archaeologically-visible mining "settlements" such as *Phorades* to the abstract concept of mining "communities" (Knapp et al. 1998). Situated of necessity in close proximity to ore bodies, such communities also required water, timber, agricultural land, and a viable transport system. Although primary production took place in close proximity to the mines, other factors may have affected the various sequences of social production, political expediency, and economic demand: these might include access to the ores; micro-environments for effective smelting, beneficiation, and the like; the organization of the labor force (free, forced, or servile?); and the role of rural sanctuaries in the system overall.

The notion of a settlement *system* as part of the social landscape offers archaeologists a useful conceptual and empirical framework. Elsewhere, in light of information on economic organization and social structure, I have suggested the existence of a four-tiered site hierarchy, which would have been in place at least by the fourteenth century BC (Figure 10.6) (Knapp 1997: 53–61):

1 primary coastal centers;
2 secondary inland towns;

Figure 10.6 Late Cypriot Settlement Hierarchy.

3 tertiary inland sites (rural sanctuaries); and
4 agricultural support villages, mining sites, and pottery-producing
villages.

The inland rural sanctuaries, which served primarily ceremonial
functions, were also involved in the production and transport of
raw materials, and the limited storage of agricultural products such as
olive oil. Various material markers typify these sites (Alcock 1993:
172–214): distinctive architecture and installations; repositories for
storing cultic items; and precious or unique artifacts, such as figurines
and bucrania. Frequently, as indicated earlier, some structures at these
rural sanctuaries contain workshops or production units associated
with metalworking.

Agricultural support villages (such as Aredhiou *Vouppes* in the survey
area – see Knapp et al. 1994: 337–8, or Analiondas *Paleoklichia* nearby
– see Webb and Frankel 1994) would have produced surplus agricultural goods and redistributed them either to mining villages or "up the
line" to secondary or primary centers. Production sites like Politiko
Phorades – and industrial sites like Mitsero *Kouloupakhis* and *Sykamies*
during the Iron Age – fulfilled the basic production needs of the economy, in terms of both raw materials and finished goods. Local elites
who controlled production, storage, and distribution within
the Bronze Age agricultural villages were perhaps allied with more
powerful elites in the secondary and primary town centers. The secondary and tertiary centers (administrative and/or ceremonial centers)
controlled the production or flow of copper and exchanged goods,
and served as transhipment points where local merchants and officials
articulated with regional and interregional systems.

Some of these sites, installations and settlements clearly formed
part of the ideational landscape. The location of many secondary

(administrative towns) or tertiary (rural sanctuaries) sites on routes between the copper mines and the coastal ports indicates that elite ideology (expressed through local cults?) helped to bring together the production-oriented periphery (inland) and the consumption- or distribution-oriented core (coastal). The placement of rural "sanctuaries," then, may have served in part to demarcate a "ritually defined social space" (Alcock 1993: 202). In other words, these locations were not haphazard, but instead were linked closely to human settlement and social needs in the landscape.

How then can we envision the "sacred" landscape of prehistoric Cyprus? First, I would define the landscape as ideational rather than sacred, and would argue that people collectively develop and maintain certain places, or even regions, in ritual, symbolic or ceremonial terms. These places, in turn, create and express social identity. Within the landscape, people enact the "sacred" and symbolic, which in turn helps to establish their social identity and ideological authority, and to reinforce socio-economic or religious institutions. Landscape features, monuments, "sanctuaries" and shrines serve as social spaces where public or ceremonial activities are carried out and where local history is generated and maintained. The ideational landscape helps to create specific social, cultural, and politico-economic configurations. Archaeologists interested in "sacred" space need to understand how such elements in the landscape impact upon human relations, and how processes of legitimization and empowerment are played out in spatial and temporal terms.

The ideational landscape cannot be separated from social reality. Not all members of a society will share the dominant ideology, and they may have differing perspectives on spatial as well as social relationships. Within most prehistoric societies, it is difficult to determine how a particular ideology was generated and perpetuated, even if its principal aim was to mask appropriation by a dominant group. On prehistoric Cyprus, the situation is perhaps more straightforward, inasmuch as a great deal of the symbolism involves depiction of copper oxhide ingots or ingot-bearers — on seals, bronze stands, and pottery alike (Knapp 1986). All of this material, from seals and miniature ingots to archaeometallurgical installations and rural "sanctuaries," forms part of the ideational landscape. And within that landscape individuals — as members of groups — negotiated differing interests and manipulated their socio-spatial world: it is the closest link we can make between mind, meaning, and symbolism in the prehistoric context.

ACKNOWLEDGMENTS

I have drawn upon ideas and suggestions shared by Vasiliki Kassianidou, Michael Donnelly, and Sven van Lokeren, as well as on various papers produced in our work together on the excavations at Politiko *Phorades* and on the survey project that first identified this site. I wish to thank Michael Given, field director of that same Sydney Cyprus Survey Project, for reading and commenting on the manuscript. I am very grateful to Wendy Ashmore for her comments on an earlier draft of this study, and for all her energy and effort in pushing the idea of this volume, which has appealed greatly to both of us for some time. Research on this project began when I held an Australian Postdoctoral Fellowship in the School of History, Philosophy, and Politics at Macquarie University, Sydney; it was completed in the Department of Archaeology, University of Glasgow. I thank both institutions for all the support provided.

REFERENCES

Alcock, S. E. 1993: *Graecia Capta: The Landscapes of Roman Greece*. Cambridge: Cambridge University Press.

al-Radi, S. M. S. 1983: *Phlamoudhi-Vounari: A Sanctuary Site in Cyprus*, Studies in Mediterranean Archaeology, 65. Göteborg: P. Åström's Förlag.

ARDAC (Annual Report of the Department of Antiquities, Cyprus) 1953. Nicosia: Government of Cyprus.

BCH (Bulletin de Correspondance Hellénique) 1984.

Bender, B. 1998: *Stonehenge: Making Space*. Oxford: Berg.

Buchholz, H-G. 1985: Der Beitrag der Ausgrabungen von Tamassos zur antiken Baugeschichte Zyperns. In V. Karageorghis (ed.), *Archaeology in Cyprus, 1960–1985*, Nicosia: Leventis, 238–55.

Catling, H. W. 1962: Patterns of settlement in Bronze Age Cyprus. *Opuscula Atheniensia*, 4, 129–69.

Catling, H. W. 1975: Cyprus in the Late Bronze Age. In I. E. S. Edwards, C. J. Gadd, N. G. L. Hammond, and E. Sollberger (eds), *Cambridge Ancient History*, volume 2 (2), Cambridge: Cambridge University Press, 188–216.

Cleere, H. 1995: Cultural landscapes as world heritage. *Conservation and Management of Archaeological Sites*, 1, 63–8.

Constantinou, G. 1992: Ancient copper mining in Cyprus. In A. Marangou and K. Psillides (eds), *Cyprus, Copper and the Sea*, Nicosia: Government of Cyprus, 43–74.

Dikaios, P. 1969–71: *Enkomi. Excavations 1948–1958*. Mainz-am-Rhein: Philip von Zabern.

Donnelly, M., Kassianidou, V., and Knapp, A. B. 1998: Excavations at Politiko *Phorades* 1997. *Report of the Department of Antiquities, Cyprus*, 247–68.

Du Plat Taylor, J. 1952: A Late Bronze Age settlement at Apliki, Cyprus. *Antiquaries Journal*, 32, 133–67.

Du Plat Taylor, J. 1957: *Myrtou-Pighades: A Late Bronze Age Sanctuary in Cyprus*. Oxford: Ashmolean Museum.

Fasnacht, W., and Kassianidou, V. 1992: Copper at Almyras: a mining and smelting site on Cyprus. In A. Marangou and K. Psillides (eds), *Cyprus, Copper and the Sea*, Nicosia: Government of Cyprus, 77–90.

Fasnacht, W. (with V. Kassianidou, A. Connoly, C. Deslex, J. Kunz, T. Maradi, K. Zubler, and P. Roll) 1996: Excavations at Ayia Vavara *Almyras*: fifth preliminary report. *Report of the Department of Antiquities, Cyprus*, 95–125.

Feierabend, C. 1990: Historic mine lands as cultural landscapes. In L. R. Barker and A. E. Houston (eds), *Death Valley to Deathwood: Kennecott to Cripple Creek*, San Francisco: National Registers Program, 24–7.

Fowler, P. J. 1995: Writing on the countryside. In I. Hodder, M. Shanks, A. Alexandri, V. Buchli, J. Carman, J. Last, and G. Lucas (eds), *Interpretive Archaeology: Finding Meaning in the Past*, London and New York: Routledge, 100–9.

Given, M. J. M. 1991: Symbols, power, and the construction of identity in the city kingdoms of ancient Cyprus, *c*.750–312 BC. PhD thesis, Cambridge University.

Given, M., and Knapp, A. B. n.d.: The Sydney Cyprus Survey Project and the archaeology of mining. In G. C. Ioannides (ed.), *Proceedings of the Third International Conference on Cypriot Archaeology* (April 16–20, 1996), Nicosia: Society of Cypriot Studies.

Given, M., Knapp, A. B., and Meyer, N. (with T. E. Gregory, V. Kassianidou, J. Noller and L. Wells, N. Urwin, and H. Wright) n.d.: The Sydney Cyprus Survey Project: an interdisciplinary investigation of long-term change in the North Central Troodos, Cyprus. Submitted to *Journal of Field Archaeology*.

Gosden, C., and Head, L. 1994: Landscape – a usefully ambiguous concept. *Archaeology in Oceania*, 29, 113–16.

Gunnis, R. 1936: *Historic Cyprus: A Guide to its Towns and Villages*. London.

Hardesty, D. L. 1990: Mining property types: inventory and significance evaluation. In L. R. Barker and A. E. Houston (eds), *Death Valley to Deathwood: Kennecott to Cripple Creek*, San Francisco: National Registers Program, 39–43.

Head, L. 1993: Unearthing prehistoric cultural landscapes: a view from Australia. *Transactions of the Institute of British Geographers*, n.s. 18, 481–99.

Ionas, I. 1985: The altar at Myrtou-*Pigadhes*: a re-examination of its reconstruction. *Report of the Department of Antiquities, Cyprus*, 137–42.

Johnston, R. 1998: Approaches to the perception of landscape: philosophy, theory, methodology. *Archaeological Dialogues*, 5, 54–68.

Keswani, P. S. 1993: Models of local exchange in Late Bronze Age Cyprus. *Bulletin of the American Schools of Oriental Research*, 292, 73–83.

Keswani, P. S. 1996: Hierarchies, heterarchies, and urbanization processes: the view from Bronze Age Cyprus. *Journal of Mediterranean Archaeology*, 9, 211–49.

Knapp, A. B. 1986: *Copper Production and Divine Protection: Archaeology, Ideology and Social Complexity on Bronze Age Cyprus*, Studies in Mediterranean Archaeology, Pocketbook 42. Göteborg: P. Åström's Förlag.

Knapp, A. B. 1994: Problems and prospects in Cypriot prehistory. *Journal of World Prehistory*, 8, 377–453.

Knapp, A. B. 1997: *The Archaeology of Late Bronze Age Cypriot Society: The Study of Settlement, Survey and Landscape*, Department of Archaeology, Occasional Paper 4. Glasgow: University of Glasgow, Department of Archaeology.

Knapp, A. B., and Given, M. 1996: A report on the Sydney-Cyprus Survey Project (SCSP) – third season (1995). *Report of the Department of Antiquities, Cyprus*, 295–366.

Knapp, A. B., Held, S. O., Johnson, I., and Keswani, P. S. 1994: The Sydney-Cyprus Survey Project – second preliminary season (1993). *Report of the Department of Antiquities, Cyprus*, 329–43.

Knapp, A. B., and Meskell, L. M. 1997: Bodies of evidence on prehistoric Cyprus. *Cambridge Archaeological Journal*, 7, 183–204.

Knapp, A. B., Pigott, V., and Herbert, E. (eds) 1998: *Social Approaches to an Industrial Past: The Archaeology and Anthropology of Mining*. London: Routledge.

Maddin, R., Muhly, J. D., and Stech Wheeler, T. 1983: Metal working. In T. Dothan and A. Ben-Tor, *Excavations at Athienou, Cyprus, 1971–1972*, Qedem 16, Jerusalem: Institute of Archaeology, Hebrew University, 132–8.

Meinig, D. W. 1979: Introduction. In D. W. Meinig (ed.), *The Interpretation of Ordinary Landscape*, Oxford: Oxford University Press, 1–7.

Muhly, J. D. 1985: The Late Bronze Age in Cyprus: a 25 year retrospect. In V. Karageorghis (ed.), *Archaeology in Cyprus 1960–1985*, Nicosia: Leventis Foundation, 20–46.

Muhly, J. D. 1986: The role of Cyprus in the economy of the eastern Mediterranean during the second millennium BC. In V. Karageorghis (ed.), *Acts of the International Archaeological Symposium: Cyprus between the Orient and the Occident*, Nicosia: Cyprus Department of Antiquities, 45–60.

Muhly, J. D. 1989: The organisation of the copper industry in Late Bronze Age Cyprus. In E. J. Peltenburg (ed.), *Early Society in Cyprus*, Edinburgh: Edinburgh University Press, 298–314.

Peltenburg, E. J. 1994: Constructing authority: the Vounous enclosure model. *Opuscula Atheniensia*, 20, 157–62.

Peltenburg, E. J. 1996: From isolation to state formation in Cyprus, *c*.500–1500 BC. In V. Karageorghis and D. Michaelides (eds), *The*

Development of the Cypriot Economy: From the Prehistoric Period to the Present Day, Nicosia: Bank of Cyprus, University of Cyprus, 17–44.

Raber, P. A. 1987: Early copper production in the Polis region, western Cyprus. *Journal of Field Archaeology*, 14, 297–312.

Richards, C. 1996: Henges and water: towards an elemental understanding of monumentality and landscape in Late Neolithic Britain. *Journal of Material Culture*, 1, 313–36.

Taçon, P. S. C. 1994: Socialising landscapes: the long-term implications of signs, symbols and marks on the land. *Archaeology in Oceania*, 29, 117–29.

Tilley, C. 1994: *A Phenomenology of Landscape: Places, Paths and Monuments*. Oxford: Berg.

Tuan, Y. F. 1977: *Space and Place: The Perspective of Experience*. London: Edward Arnold.

Tylecote, R. F. 1982: The Late Bronze Age: copper and bronze metallurgy at Enkomi and Kition. In J. D. Muhly, R. Maddin, and V. Karageorghis (eds), *Early Metallurgy of Cyprus, 4000–500 BC*, Nicosia: Pierides Foundation, 81–100.

Wallace, P. W. 1982: Survey of the Akhera area. *Report of the Department of Antiquities, Cyprus*, 237–43.

Webb, J. M. 1988: The archaeological and iconographic evidence for the religion of Late Bronze Age Cyprus. PhD dissertation, University of Melbourne.

Webb, J. M. 1992: Cypriot Bronze Age glyptic: style, function and social context. In R. Laffineur and J. L. Crowley (eds), *EIKON. Aegean Bronze Age Iconography: Shaping a Methodology*, Aegaeum 8, Liège: Université de Liège, 113–21.

Webb, J. M. 1997: Device, image and coercion: the role of glyptic in the political economy of Late Bronze Age Cyprus. Paper presented at the 20th annual meeting of the Archaeological Institute of America, Chicago.

Webb, J. M., and Frankel, D. 1994: Making an impression: storage and staple finance at Analiondas *Paleoklichia*. *Journal of Mediterranean Archaeology*, 7, 5–26.

Wright, G. R. H. 1992: The Cypriot rural sanctuary: an illuminating document in comparative religion. In G. C. Ioannides (ed.), *Studies in Honour of Vassos Karageorghis*, Nicosia: Society of Cypriot Studies, 269–83.

11

The Mythical Landscapes of the British Iron Age

John C. Barrett

Landscapes Transformed

A significant change appears to occur in the organization of the landscape over many parts of Britain during the later prehistoric period. Later prehistoric is taken here to mean the periods of the Neolithic, Bronze, and Iron Ages. These run from the fifth through the end of the first millennia BC. The change began mid-way through the Bronze Age at the end of the second millennium. Up to this point the monumental constructions of the Neolithic and earlier Bronze Age had been dominated by the formation of highly ritualized foci and by the raising of ancestral tombs and burial mounds. Many of these monuments clearly went through a number of phases of development as well as a lengthy history of use. Settlement activity in the period on the other hand, although it extended across these landscapes, did not focus upon specific sites which were either enclosed, long-lived, or had any monumental characteristics. There are also few indicators of enclosed agricultural landscapes at this time; in other words, there is no indication of intensive agricultural systems employing a short-fallow cycle of regeneration (cf. Barrett 1994). All the indicators are that the Neolithic and earlier Bronze Age landscapes were structured around a dominant constellation of references to a spiritual or ancestral presence. The living communities mapped their own histories upon these sacred references through the temporal cycles of communal celebration and routine production. These activities brought the larger ritual community together at particular locations in the landscape and it was these locations which were embellished by monumental constructions.

During the earlier Bronze Age, the living community established a further linkage to that ever-present spiritual world via their burial rites. Many of these burials were located near, but not within, the large communal monuments and, after considerable elaboration were finally covered by substantial earthwork mounds. The whole of the fifth to second millennia therefore witnessed the lengthy if intermittent elaboration of a series of complex sacred landscapes. By the end of the second millennium the construction and maintenance of monuments associated with the sacred landscape ended and no further elaboration took place. At the same time, distinctive settlement foci emerged, with the building of enclosed settlements containing houses and ancillary structures with activities characteristic of a lengthy and continuous history of settlement. Alongside this seemingly more permanent settlement record comes evidence for land enclosure and the more intensive exploitation of arable through cycles of short fallow cultivation (Barrett 1994). By the fifth century BC the contrast appears complete; the landscape was structured around enclosed settlements and land-divisions and, occupying foci around which parts of the productive cycle were integrated, the hillforts emerged. The latter typify the nature of the change. Monumental in scale, they are occupied by clusters of round-houses and storage facilities. The evidence indicates that some of these hillforts stored grain produced and transported from a number of locations in the surrounding landscape (Jones 1984). Productive activities, including the working of metal, glass, shale and bone, also occurred at a number of other, different locations across the landscape.

Where ritual activity can be located in the later period, it appears to have occupied a quite restricted place. Votive deposits were made away from settlements, focusing in particular upon rivers (Bradley 1990), whilst, in the settlements themselves, it has been proposed that deposits of human and animal bones, artifacts and food debris represent the highly formalized treatment of materials associated with agricultural reproduction and feasting (Barrett 1989; Hill 1995). The contrast with the earlier period may be characterized almost as an inversion, for where previously settlement activities were contained within the settings of a sacred landscape the sacred was, by the Iron Age, either marginal to or subsumed within the structure of a settled agricultural landscape.

It is important to recognize that the distinction outlined above does not arise simply as a consequence of taphonomic processes. In other words what we are seeing is a change in the structural arrangements by which the landscape was inhabited, and not merely a change in the relative survival of different categories of archaeological material.

Interpreting the Landscape

The sequence of monuments which has been described in the highly generalized outline above, and which admittedly draws heavily upon the evidence from southern and eastern Britain, indicates that the principles around which the landscape was organized changed during the second millennium BC. In purely descriptive terms the sequence is one of changing form and function; sequences of monument types characterize the passing of time and each of these types fulfilled different functions. Thus not only did the landscape look different as a consequence of its redesign, but particular activities were associated with a changing configuration of places and structures through time. What were undoubtedly common if conflicting requirements among all communities – to secure or question their political institutions by reference to certain ideologically grounded truths, to accommodate the death of their members, to construct shelter and produce, prepare and consume food – appear over time to have taken place in different material settings and at different places. For example, many burial rites initiated the construction of elaborate covering mounds at the end of the third and beginning of the second millennia BC, and yet by the middle of the first millennium such rites appear to have required less prominent marking, or to have been relocated around areas of settlement, or indeed to have become almost invisible archaeologically (Whimster 1981).

I want now to consider the ways we might interpret a sequence like this to facilitate an adequate consideration of the wider landscape context of monuments. In particular I want to effect a shift away from accounts which give primacy to the acts of building as a way of characterizing a particular period – in other words where the mere corpus of monument types created over a given period is used to define the archaeology of that period (cf. Bradley 1993: 4) – towards a recognition that the construction of monuments is always an interpretation of a pre-existing world. There are three crucially important points in the argument I hope to develop. The first is that the world as it already existed will always have been imbued with meanings and have been used as a background of reference against which contemporary acts, including monument building, were played out. Indeed those acts may often have sought to make explicit the meanings which were soaked into the landscape, or to find ways to focus them more directly upon contemporary concerns. This brings me to my second point, which is that monument building may have involved strategies of appropriation by which values previously immanent to the world as a whole came to be revealed or enunciated by certain actions and in such a way that those very acts and their participants became the essential media for the transmission of that which had previously been given. This was a process of political appropriation by which the timeless values which seemingly governed order in the world were increasingly mediated and therefore controlled by the actions of a restricted group. Monuments thus acted as a focus or a "lens" through which the wider world of experience was to be viewed, enabling certain groups to act on behalf of the wider community to reveal that sacred order (cf. Tilley 1994). Finally, although we can distinguish between the material form of the world as it was given and the instigation of new projects of construction undertaken in the creation of new political realities, this is not the same as a distinction between the "natural" features of the topography and the "cultural" features of the transformed landscape. In the ways a pre-existing landscape offered an environment of potential experiences and signification no distinction need have been drawn between its "natural" and its earlier but now relic "cultural" components. Both equally had the potential to reveal the truths of a mythical past. The transformation of the landscape lay not so much in its physical modification as in its interpretation.

To establish this framework for our interpretation it will be necessary for us to diverge from more traditional archaeological approaches towards the analysis of landscape organization. Such analyses have tended to begin from the point already noted, namely to characterize a particular period by reference to the range of monuments and other material residues which were created in that same period. Having so characterized the material record of a period, that record is then taken to represent the way human life was organized in that same period according to social structural, political, or economic arrangements. Such reasoning means that it is incumbent upon the archaeologist to establish adequately the material correlates of particular types of social formation, be they chiefdoms, early states, or whatever. Consequent upon such analysis is the emergence of a history in which the passing of each period traces out a sequence of social formations. The material remains merely confirm the existence of these formations and illustrate their internal logic by exposing the ways in which the system functioned. The problem such histories pose is to understand the transformation from one type of social formation to another, a problem which can only be resolved in the relatively abstract terms of social and economic theory. By treating monuments as representative of a certain type of social formation those monuments are effectively disengaged from the actual reproduction and transformation of social life. Rather than being seen as part of the medium by which social practices gained their vitality, monuments are simply treated as a record of those practices. At the same time the wider "natural" environment appears to have operated as a set of relatively passive constraints upon which various social practices were enacted.

The divergence which I seek from this traditional thinking requires that we perceive monument building as a transformative process. Such programs drew upon previous understandings of the world and, by acts of building, certain signifiers were appropriated to create a new set of material conditions which life was then faced with having to accommodate. Monuments did not represent certain social conditions, rather it was through their construction that those conditions were gradually transformed. And in this context there existed the background landscape of places, forms, and experiences whose understandings informed the strategies of appropriation which the various monumental programs attempted to synthesize.

The shift in perception required to rethink the later prehistoric sequence of monuments allows us to see them not as the signifiers of particular social formations but as the signifiers of the cultural values appropriated in certain dominant strategies of social reproduction. These strategies were historically and materially situated, and while they expressed certain desires and aims by those who executed them, their consequences – the effects of monument building and the ways they were accommodated in future patterns of life – may have escaped the original intentions of the builders.

The archaeological recovery of certain material conditions demands that we consider how those material conditions could be occupied to enable the continuation of certain forms of life. This is an archaeology of inhabitation in which the material no longer simply represents the consequence of processes which we need to discover but becomes instead the historically constituted and necessary conditions of a world inhabited, interpreted, and acted upon. Whereas previously, archaeological remains were regarded as a trail of debris generated by the passing of the processes of history, where each epoch left its own distinctive signature upon the record, now each generation can be regarded as having to confront its own archaeology as the material remains of its past piled up before it.

Consider the material so far presented. Traditionally it is taken to represent a sequence: the distribution of settlements and fortified sites replaces the earlier distribution of ceremonial centers and burial monuments. This sequence is traditionally explained as indicative of a sequence of social transformations in which one particular type of social formation had been replaced with another by the end of the second millennium. The alternative, presented here, situates the material quite differently by placing it in the context of past human understanding. Now humans are seen to have confronted the cumulative material conditions which they inhabited. The earlier remains were no longer absent from the later period for the simple reason that the Iron Age was actually an inhabitation of Bronze Age residues. Indeed we might go further and recognize that the Iron Age could only have arisen in the way that it did as an interpretation or as a reading of the physical manifestation of its own landscape heritage.

We can now review the processes at work in a little more detail. My central question is to inquire as to the means by which places in the landscape, once the focus for intensive ritual activity and, through that, of recurring physical modification, became transformed into places which saw no further votive or ritual modification.

The burial mounds which were constructed and embellished during the earlier part of the second millennium BC in Britain (i.e., in the early Bronze Age) were built to contain a variety of burial deposits during that period. But they also endured to become Iron Age monuments. The difference was that during the Iron Age they received no further physical modification, but they did continue as a significant element in the Iron Age landscape and as such were presumably recognized and drawn into an understanding of that landscape. As such, the monuments were not modified by physical intervention but by the changing landscape context from whence they were viewed. The history of these mounds can therefore be described in terms of the distinction which is being considered by this volume. In their foundation and physical development these are the practically modified places where funeral rituals terminated with the burial of a corpse, or the deposition of the cremated remains of the dead. By the Iron Age they became an unmodified element of the cultural landscape. Traditionally archaeologists studying the Iron Age in southern Britain have operated as if these mounds were simply lost at this point; they do not for example appear on the distribution maps which we so often produce of Iron Age monuments. However, it is my case that these monuments remained a crucial and integrated component of the Iron Age landscape, and that their lack of further modification holds a key to understanding how the inhabitation of that landscape accommodated them.

Inhabiting the Landscape

Inhabiting the world establishes a recognition or an understanding for the inhabitants as parts of the world are "brought into view" by them (Hirsch 1995: 3). Such knowledge is geographical in as much as it has a perspective, a place from whence it is developed (cf. Thrift 1985). That place is the point at which the inhabitants have arrived in their own lives with their accumulation of biographical experiences, it is a place understood and described according to certain traditions and conventions to which the inhabitants have some access and to which they contribute through their own practices, and it is also a place at which the inhabitants themselves may be located and defined according to the desires and decrees of others. Thus the inhabitants not only find ways to situate themselves within, and thus to act effectively upon, the world, but in such actions they also submit to the desires of others, either willingly or through various forms of coercion. This geography of being is therefore a geography in which the inhabitants are able to find a place for themselves by reference to their own biography but in which that place is also fixed, and is recognized as being so fixed, according to a larger social order. The act of inhabiting a place is meaningful to the inhabitants according to their own experiences and desires, but it becomes socially meaningful when their actions are objectively recognized by others and thus set into a widely accepted frame of reference, which is often expressed in terms of the "social" or the "cosmological" orders which appear to arrange the world.

The issue which I have tried to describe in outline here is that inhabitation becomes meaningful when it is situated between different frames of reference. In the simple terms which I have employed, the inhabited place is known with reference to past experiences and by actions at that place which are played off against a wider "reality" of social continuity and order (Bell 1992). These frames of reference and the actions which link them are constructed out of the actions of inhabitation and they empower different groups in different ways. There are, for example, observers who are able to explain the actions of others according to certain social norms – they expose why people may behave the way they do, not so much by reference to individual motivations and desires as by reference to sets of ideal and socially recognized values. There are also those who may mediate between these frames of reference, or reveal by their actions – for example as ritual specialists–the sacred frame against which the routine practicalities of life are played out. And there are those who claim that their actions embodied the norms of social cohesion and upon that basis claim the political obligations to which they are due.

By thinking about inhabitation in this way it is possible to begin to recognize how the pragmatic and strategic decisions of a person's life, which draw personal understandings into play in the institutional activities of day-to-day experiences, are set within a wider frame of social traditions and norms. At the same time we must emphasize that these social traditions are themselves not simply given but constructed within the inhabited world; they too may be rethought and reworked through the "discovery" of some "deeper" or "wider" truth against which their own veracity may be assessed (Connerton 1989). Movement between these frames of reference may be considered as a movement between temporalities, between the time of an individual's own biography and that of the social rhythms of institutional activity and the timeless continuities of cultural order, or as I have attempted here, spatially between the near and foregrounded experiences of everyday life and the distant background or horizon of order, law, and stability (Helms 1988). Thus while the landscape may map spatial relationships it also contains different temporalities. Smith expresses this well when he draws a distinction between an engagement with the immediate practicalities of life and the "pleasure of detachment" in the moment of reverie as the eyes are lifted to the horizon, the sunset, and an appreciation of the apparent timelessness of the world inhabited (Smith 1993: 79).

Inhabitation is not about occupying a place. A landscape archaeology which simply maps places according to the role they may have played in the operation of some larger, and entirely abstract, social and economic system misses the point. Inhabitation is a process of understanding the relevance of actions executed at some place by reference to other times and to other places. In the simplified terms with which I have attempted to develop the argument here, the references which may be made are those which draw on the biographical experiences gathered in the journey to that place, and the projection of those actions against an apparently unchanging horizon of social and cultural order. Inhabitation also empowers: the actions which take place and the lives of which they are a part find their legitimacy and their security in terms of such references; people can cope with the world and work their desires upon it. But it also empowers in another way: as people find themselves framed and objectified by others who claim that their own lives and actions sustain some part of the larger social order, they stand between those framed and the common horizon and from such a position act upon those people's lives, upon their bodies. They mediate in ritual, extract dues, pass judgment, enslave and kill.

Redefining the Horizon

We can now review the contrast with which we began, between landscapes in which ritual, ceremonial, and burial monuments were raised, and those in which the monumental focus became the settlement itself. This contrast need no longer be regarded simply as one in which the different functional requirements of the social and economic system were located at different places or in different material contexts within the landscape. This did indeed occur, but that transformation was achieved more fundamentally by practices which redefined the references by which those places were known. In other words new places were made through new biographical experiences, by the definition of new horizons of social order, and by the realization of new networks of power.

During the Neolithic the construction and use of the ceremonial monumentality was part of the routine of social action which worked upon and transformed the landscape. It was as if these actions reinscribed upon the landscape its inherently sacred form. Although the descriptive term "ritual landscape" is misleading, it does have the virtue of evoking the idea that routine life was mapped upon the essential and timeless landscape. In this way, to inhabit the landscape was to evoke or revitalize the ever-present ancestral and spiritual order embedded in that same landscape. The actions of construction, and the inhabitation of these places, thus overlay the sacred structure of the landscape in such a way that the past and present effectively existed alongside each other. What the monuments achieved was an appropriation of that other timeless order as enclosures, and the architecture of the tombs, increasingly facilitated the arrangement of the participants and heightened the identity of ritual specialists.

This tradition of inhabitation, which effectively extended back to the Mesolithic, changed when a distinction began to be drawn more clearly between a past as the origin of cultural and sacred order and a present of inhabitation. This distinction was facilitated by the construction of a linear representation of time which projected back to a time of origins. This construction, I would contend, was partly achieved through the development of the burial rites which emerged during the early Bronze Age of the second millennium. Here, for the first time, funeral rites used earth-dug graves, thus not only leaving deposits in the ground and fixing the place of burial geographically, but also setting up the possibility of building sequentially upon the initial deposit through the addition of succeeding burials. It is notable that the early graves were indeed redug, and often on more than one occasion. And as the burial mounds were developed and enlarged over succeeding generations, so these monuments became complex depositories for lineages of the dead. A lineal sequence, recognized through the succeeding burial rites, literally created a human past distinct from the present. That past acted as a container for an origin, perhaps the founding of a lineage or dynasty, and the burial ground offered the physical manifestation of a sequence linking that past, and thus that origin, to the present.

During the second millennium, the place of the symbolic orders which had been mapped through many of the routine practices of social life became displaced into a past world which was no longer immediately present, and thus was not available to be reworked, in those routines themselves. But that past was still represented in the newly conceived history of the landscape itself. And it was still an essential component of that landscape, acting as an horizon to which the acts of inhabitation could refer. The institutionalized practices of social life now maintained a new order which created the enclosed and long-lived foci of settlement as well as the enclosed and intensively cultivated field systems of the period. The legitimacy of all such practices was presumably expressed partly in the new historical terms of an inherited legitimacy – rights which linked the present to a past through a direct, recognizable, and accepted line. That past, necessarily absent, must none the less have been represented by the relics of the earlier period, perhaps most evocatively by the burial mounds themselves. Burials no longer took place in or even around these mounds, but this very lack of intervention best expresses the role the mounds now played. The mythical past stood apart from the present. In its form the landscape contained the relics of those times occupying, almost literally, the horizon beyond the routines of daily life. Those routines reproduced the political relations of the time whose validity would have lain in the references made to their mythical origins. Such origins could not be drawn back into the contemporary world, the mounds may have stood as mute testimony to their previous existence, whilst the contemporary presence of the past lived on in the lives of its political inheritors.

Conclusion

What I have attempted to review in this chapter are the paths traced by a number of transformations. First is the transformation traditionally characterized by archaeology, where the form and function of the landscape changes and in which the nature of monuments and their associated deposits are taken to represent the organization of an ancient society. That transformation has then been reconsidered by references to the ways of inhabiting the landscape; from this perspective, places gain their significance because of their inhabitants' abilities to establish references to other times and other places, to remember their own histories and to lift their eyes to the more distant horizons. The transformation of the inhabited landscape therefore hinges not so much upon functional change as upon the reworking of these referents and the politics of their control.

The various elements of these landscapes, and the distinction between those elements of the cognitive landscape which were modified (i.e., cultural products) and those which remained unmodified but were assigned sacred significance (including natural features) are best understood in terms of the reference through which inhabitants must have recognized their own identities as manifest in the physical form and cultural values represented by the built and modified environment. This was achieved as personal biographies traced out the path of an individual's life across landscapes where the coincidence of biographical experiences and a larger symbolic order occurred at certain moments and places. Thus, what we perceive today as an essentially abstract landscape made up of the distribution of certain monument categories was lived as a personal landscape of experience as the spatial order of places was linked in a temporal sequence of movement. Individuals literally rediscovered or reworked the order of their own world through the practices of their own lives.

In the earlier of the cases examined here (that of the Neolithic), social practices reworked, literally excavated and revealed, the presence of a general order which was one of creation and origins but remained vital and ever present. Here certain political authorities may have acted to effect that revelation, they divined its potency and allowed their own actions to bring it into being. In the later case (that of the Iron Age) the past was displaced, it lay on a distant horizon linked to the present by a trajectory of legitimate inheritance. Political authority was both the true inheritor and the representative of that past; it spoke with the authority of the past now absent, and bequeathed its inheritance to future generations.

The transformation between these two kinds of landscapes and these two histories may have been achieved largely through the material construction of burial lineages. As the grave sequences were dug and the covering mounds enlarged, so the points of origin became increasingly hidden and distant. Eventually those remains stood simply as a mute testimony to an unchangeable order, observed perhaps, as Jonathan Smith has recently described, in moments of reverie in the same way as we might observe the landscape or a sunset (Smith 1993). But without that concept of the past, it seems unlikely that the political structures of control, which laid claim to the land and its resources, would have been possible to justify. The political structures of the Iron Age inherited their rights over land and people from that past and bequeathed those rights to the future. The Iron Age was indeed the product of the Bronze Age, but not in the way in which archaeologists usually mean: in other words, not as the product of a process of social evolution. Instead the Bronze Age created the Iron Age because it made available the conditions by which the Iron Age communities were themselves able to read of and to recognize the mythical histories by which they made themselves.

ACKNOWLEDGMENTS

I am grateful to both Wendy Ashmore and Bernard Knapp for their invitation to contribute to these proceedings and for their comments, along with those of Jane Downes, on earlier versions of this chapter.

REFERENCES

Barrett, J. C. 1989: Food, gender and metal: questions of social reproduction. In M. L. S. Sorensen and R. Thomas (eds), *The Bronze Age–Iron Age Transition in Europe: Aspects of Continuity and Change in European Societies, c.1200 to 500 BC*, Oxford: British Archaeological Reports, International Series 483, 304–20.

Barrett, J. C. 1994: *Fragments from Antiquity: An Archaeology of Social Life in Britain, 2900–1200 BC*. Oxford: Blackwell.

Bell, C. 1992: *Ritual Theory, Ritual Practice*. Oxford: Oxford University Press.

Bradley, R. 1990: *The Passage of Arms: An Archaeological Analysis of Prehistoric Hoards and Votive Deposits*. Cambridge: Cambridge University Press.

Bradley, R. 1993: *Altering the Earth: The Origins of Monuments in Britain and Continental Europe*, Monograph Series, 8. Edinburgh: Society of Antiquaries of Scotland.

Connerton, P. 1989: *How Societies Remember*. Cambridge: Cambridge University Press.

Helms, M. W. 1988: *Ulysses' Sail: An Ethnographic Odyssey of Power, Knowledge, and Geographical Distance*. Princeton: Princeton University Press.

Hill, J. D. 1995: *Ritual and Rubbish in the Iron Age of Wessex*, BAR, British Series 242. Oxford: British Archaeological Reports.

Hirsch, E. 1995: Landscape: between place and space. In E. Hirsch and M. O'Hanlon (eds), *The Anthropology of Landscape: Perspectives on Place and Space*, Oxford: Clarendon Press, 1–30.

Jones, M. 1984: The plant remains. In B. W. Cunliffe (ed.), *Danebury: An Iron Age Hillfort in Hampshire*, volume 2. London: Council for British Archaeology, Research Report 52, 483–95.

Smith, J. 1993: The lie that binds: destabilizing the text of landscape. In J. Duncan and D. Ley (eds), *Place/Culture/Representation*, London: Routledge, 39–56.

Thrift, N. 1985: Flies and germs: a geography of knowledge. In D. Gregory and J. Urry (eds), *Social Relations and Spatial Structures*, London: Macmillan, 366–403.

Tilley, C. 1994: *A Phenomenology of Landscape: Places, Paths and Monuments*. London: Berg.

Whimster, R. 1981: *Burial Practices in Iron Age Britain: A Discussion and Gazetteer of the Evidence, c. 700 BC–AD 43, BAR, British Series 90*. Oxford: British Archaeological Reports.

Part IV

Commentaries

12

Sacred Landscapes: Constructed and Conceptualized

Carole L. Crumley

> To infer ... religious institutions and spiritual life may seem superficially
> [easier than that of economic or sociopolitical organization], and for the
> first few steps it may sometimes be so. Paleolithic art clearly has much
> to do with institutions of hunting-magic and, in the case of the so-
> called "Venuses," with expressions of desire for human fertility. Grave
> goods ... indicate a belief that the dead need material supplies or equip-
> ment, as though still alive. But how much further can one go than
> that? Besides the animal and human portrayals in Stone Age art, are
> there not very many abstract signs whose meaning most often is just
> unknowable? What part were the dead, furnished with grave goods,
> supposed to play in the life of the community still living? You can use
> ethnological data obtained from modern primitives to stimulate your
> imagination by suggesting the sort of religious institutions and spiritual
> life your prehistoric people may or could have had, but you cannot this
> way demonstrate what they did have, and you know you cannot even
> hope to unless you can show some real connection between this modern
> and that prehistoric. I have heard the thing attempted ... from the side
> of the modern South African Bushmen and the significance of their
> paintings, back to prehistoric African, and then maybe European, Stone
> Age paintings and their significance. But it is a very long shot, and
> even the possibility of it ... is very rare. In general ... [textual and
> ethnographic] inference from material remains to spiritual life is the
> hardest inference of all.

So writes Christopher Hawkes (1954: 162), admonishing archaeologists that they should not expect to retrieve what today might be
called "mind." Undeterred by his gloomy forecast, archaeologists
began the search for the individual (Binford 1973; Hill and Gunn
1977), and for evidence of all forms of collective intentionality (e.g.,
economic, social, political, and spiritual organization). This volume

reflects the intellectual gains made in the past half century as archaeology has investigated cognition, and marks the centrality of this endeavor to archaeological theory.

Hawkes was correct, inasmuch as neither the dualistic model of human–environment relations ("man" and "Nature") then in fashion, nor the rising tide of postwar processualist/scientistic thought could be made to reveal belief, perception, or intent. Now, a half-century later, archaeological theory is dominated by the debate over not *if*, but *how* mind is recoverable. It is now recognized that humans both affect and are affected by the material world; furthermore, mental activity can be recorded in material remains, and material structures and conditions affect perception.

This dialectical understanding allows important modifications of the classic dimensions of space, time, and form identified by Spaulding, who defines dimensions as "an aspect or property of the subject matter which requires its own special measuring device" (1960: 438). Now both mental and material sources of change may be investigated by contrasting dimensions of space, time, and mind (e.g., Marquardt 1992; Marquardt and Crumley 1987). Contemporary archaeological theorists, by introducing the broad category of cognition, have expanded on an older framework based on the form and function of materials. This opens the door to new measurement devices, such as landscape analysis, that employ other scales and dimensions. Thus the choice of form, only one aspect of the way mind alters materials, is subsumed but not eliminated, while retaining the fundamental importance of formal analysis to archaeology.

As in the analysis of form, the site remains an enduring unit of archaeological analysis. Now, however, it is understood that sites are neither the best nor the only objects of study if the goal is recovery of past beliefs and understandings (Bender 1993; Dunnell 1992; Tilley 1994). People identify not only with the places where they live and work and bury their dead, but also with notable features of their surroundings. Springs, caves, mountains, and other ostensibly "natural" elements connect the individual with the cosmic frame that gives life meaning (Feld and Basso 1996). These features, although outwardly unchanged, are artifacts, inasmuch as they are factors in thought and action. The next logical step in the cultural elaboration of landscapes is that these features are duplicated in stone, wood, or other material (Brady and Ashmore, this volume).

Landscape, a term familiar in several disciplines, offers both specific means of study and broad interpretive latitude (Crumley 1994; Crumley and Marquardt 1990). Transitory and enduring elements, related to one another in complex ways, comprise landscapes. In some (but obviously not all) circumstances, perceptions and beliefs (cognition) may be inferred by noting physical continuity and change across time and space. While this is another primary assumption in archaeology, the implications of repeated site choice by different cultural groups is only beginning to be explored (Buikstra and Charles, this volume; Green et al. 1987; Schmidt 1996; 1997).

Manipulation of the physical circumstances of specific landscapes, whether intentional or unintentional, leaves evidence that illuminates how humans conceptualize their surroundings. Of course not everyone, in even the most harmonious groups, shares identical understandings. An enduring theme in archaeology is the reading of social power from modified landscapes. Although it is more difficult to know what those whose actions were constrained by the power of others might have thought or believed, sometimes they too have left a material record that archaeologists may read. Contradiction is the raw material of change, and as Knapp notes, landscapes are perpetually under construction.

In the study of sacred landscapes, the importance of memory and culture cannot be overstated. Culture acts like a "carrier wave," transmitting information across time and space. Even when the connection between memory and meaning is severed (as when a ritual is retained but its meaning lost), information can still be delivered to future generations. The most effective carriers of social memory are landscape elements that have both practical utility and cosmic meaning, such as caves, springs, or gardens. Such elements offer a personalized mnemonic that is "good to think." The greater the range of thoughts and behaviors and the richer the meanings that such concepts evoke, the greater likelihood that diverse information bundled around that concept will be transmitted.

A wide variety of landscape elements is addressed by chapters in this volume: springs, lakes, managed water systems, rivers and river systems, floodplains, and oceans; deserts; boulders, "spirit" stones, mountains, bluff crests, hillforts, and other high points; holes, caves, tunnels, and passages; paths and passes; gardens; mounds and pyramids; mines, slag heaps, clay beds, and other sources of materials.

Barnes documents a form of Buddhist rock art, the distribution of *buddha* and *bodhisattva* images on non-architectural features of the landscape. In early Buddhism, these sculptures were near cave temples in Afghanistan and northern China; later, and farther east, the importance of mountains in Chinese cosmology altered their location. This is an excellent example of how indigenous meanings attributed to

landscape features can influence religious practice imported from elsewhere. The fractal-like repetition of Buddhist cosmology at many
scales is interesting, as well as the reduction of three-dimensional
sculpture associated with asceticism to two-dimensional representations associated with salvation of the masses.

Barrett questions long-standing archaeological assumptions that
lock physical and cognitive changes together in the same period.
Instead he explores how landscape elements erected or modified by
previous inhabitants affect the perceptions of those who subsequently
inhabit the area. Early Bronze Age landscapes of experience were personal, inclusive, and their sacrality was diffuse; by the late Bronze Age
the meaning of those same landscape elements had become more specialized in function and more political. The past had come to stand
apart from, rather than being inclusive of, the present. In essence,
Barrett argues that monuments lead and society follows: while they
may be differently interpreted, the elements of previous landscapes
always modify current thinking.

Brady and Ashmore address a central theme in the volume, the
(seemingly universal) belief that caves and mountains are entry points
into the supernatural world. They make this point with Maya examples, including architectural mimics of caves and mountains built to
better manipulate power. The ritual purity of water is also explored,
the surface of which can mirror the spirit world. As demonstrated in
Barrett's chapter, the ability to control distance across time, space, and
states of existence is an enduring definition of political power. As in
Barnes's chapter, the fractal replications of elements at multiple scales
anchor the created landscape to those of mythic worlds and other
times.

Buikstra and Charles focus on an ancient regional tradition, that of
using two areas – bluff crest and floodplain – as locations for interment of the dead. They propose that bluffs are associated with the
practice of sedentism, group homogeneity, and ancestor cults that continue access to the dead; floodplains are associated with group mobility, diversity, and mortuary ritual (following Gluckman). In the
Mississippian period, ancient Midcontinental ceremonial traditions of
ancestor worship and rituals of world renewal are combined; as in
Barnes's chapter, new traditions draw on old templates.

Several papers raise issues that require a distinction between spiritual landscapes and the more comprehensive idea of symbolic landscapes. While spiritual landscapes are undeniably symbolic, not all
symbolic landscapes are spiritual; an example of the latter would be a
development that centers around golf: there would be a manicured

course and swank clubhouse, surrounded by an expensive residential neighborhood. This elaborate complex underscores the prestige of golf, relative to, for example, hockey.

Although Hawkes was almost as skeptical of reconstructions of society as of belief, from today's vantage point we can invoke widely accepted theory that guides the rediscovery of intangible social relations through the study of space, time, and materials. As with landscapes that encode belief, so too can social, political, ethnic, and other distinctions be embedded in the landscape.

Kealhofer explores the construction of social identity in a landscape new to its creators, English colonists in Tidewater Virginia. Tracing the ongoing evolution of identity requires varied scales and attributes; over time, the changing social system reinscribes its mark on the landscape at every scale, from personal house and garden plot to collective regional practice. Disparate individual activities are naturalized and collectively recognized, transforming the social and economic landscape into one with sacred properties tied to patriarchal and biblical myths.

Knapp evokes the power of the rural Bronze Age Cypriot landscape, also one in which economic, social, and religious aspects are inextricably intertwined. Primary materials extraction and transport sites are linked to stratified and densely populated coastal areas through elite ideology, which is practiced both in rural sanctuaries and in coastal temples. The prevalence of ingots and other symbolism related to ore extraction makes explicit the mutuality of economic success, ritual observance, and the maintenance of elite power.

Richards addresses the issue of "inhabitation" (Barrett, this volume), arguing for the inextricability of landscape, history, and ritual in the maintenance of both the cosmological and the social order. She offers a powerful example of what happens when the heretic Pharaoh Akhenaten violates the formula. As also seen in the chapters by Barnes and by Brady and Ashmore, natural features are necessary but not sufficient for imbuing landscape with meaning.

Snead and Preucel explore the implications of current research into prehistoric Southwestern US landscapes, one branch of which considers the constraining and enabling aspects of architecture, while the other considers the agricultural landscape as an integral part of the built environment. They take a dialectical approach to the ways prehistoric Keres peoples related their knowledge and perceptions of the landscape to structure community and society. As do Barnes, and Brady and Ashmore, they underscore the universal sacrality of mountains, caves, and springs and the fractal, multi-scalar quality of the positioning of shrines. Of particular interest is the way construction of the site of Kotyiti has written in spatial terms the puebloan revitalization movement, which was a response to Spanish depredations.

Taçon argues persuasively that communication, tool use, and art traditionally make us human, but the concept of landscape integrates all other markers. It is fortunate that networks of Australian rock art sites, the oldest evidence for perceived landscapes in the world, are accessible by means of both archaeology and ethnography. Taçon clearly identifies a pattern echoed throughout this volume: sacred precincts everywhere are modeled on a core set of natural places (mountains, caves, rock outcrops, springs, etc.) and embellished with culturally distinct symbols. These places are considered liminal, tucked between the mundane and the spirit world; they are entry points into another consciousness. The human past and the history the landscape holds are always woven together, defining both past and present human relationships.

Van de Guchte engages the search for mind by focusing on alterity, defined as irregularity or difference. He contrasts two pre-Hispanic Andean societies, Huari and Inca, that inhabited the same region but marked the landscape in contrasting ways. He employs ethnohistory, which "complements, contrasts, complicates, and occasionally contradicts the empirical record." Focusing on the evocation of liminal states, everywhere associated with religious experience (Campbell 1988; Turner 1995), van de Guchte's point is an important one; anomalies in the landscape are used as mnemonic devices to remind the beholder of the sacred in all things (Feld and Basso 1996).

Hawkes concludes (1954:167) that "the culture of all mankind rests in the last resort on things common to all men as a species, inherent in their culture-capacity from the start." Undeniably, the phenomenological experience of caves, mountains, springs, and other remarkable landscape features is common to humankind, and individual and social identities are formed by their mental and material embellishment. History and culture are formed from the raw materials of individual and collective memory, but it is still wise to remember that the past and the present always have real effects on one another.

While landscapes may take on or shed functions and meanings independent of other aspects of society, a holistic view that emphasizes linkages appears to be widespread in time and space. Through ritual, societies link economic success, belief, and elite power. Elites employ the strong tugs of individual and group experience and identity to demonstrate their mastery of time, space, and mind.

While landscapes make it difficult to decouple identity from the sacred, we are put on notice that it is not impossible to banish the sacred from everyday life. The destruction or homogenization of distinctive landscape elements, along with the substitution of trivial collective symbols devoid of personal meaning, threaten us today from all quarters. Individual identity must be reconnected with the sacred, through the mnemonic of landscape, at all scales of time and space: from the short human breath to the respiration of the Earth. May this volume be a plea to defend our very humanity from the bulldozer and its spore.

REFERENCES

Bender, B. (ed.) 1993: *Landscape: Politics and Perspectives*. Oxford: Berg.

Binford, L. R. 1973: Interassemblage variability – the Mousterian and the "functional" argument. In C. Renfrew (ed.), *The Explanation of Cultural Change*, Pittsburgh: University of Pittsburgh Press, 227–54.

Campbell, J. 1988: *Renewal Myths*. Dallas: Spring Publications.

Crumley, C. L. 1994: Historical ecology: a multidimensional ecological orientation. In C. L. Crumley (ed.), *Historical Ecology: Cultural Knowledge and Changing Landscapes*, Santa Fe: SAR Press, 1–16.

Crumley, C. L., and Marquardt, W. H. 1990: Landscape: a unifying concept in regional analysis. In K. M. S. Allen, S. W. Green, and E. B. W. Zubrow (eds), *Interpreting Space: GIS and Archaeology*, London: Taylor and Francis, 73–9.

Dunnell, R. C. 1992: The notion site. In J. Rossignol and L. Wandsnider (eds), *Space, Time, and Archaeological Landscapes*, New York: Plenum Press, 21–41.

Feld, S., and Basso, K. H. (eds) 1996: *Senses of Place*. Santa Fe: SAR Press.

Green, P. R., Berry, W. E., and Tippitt, V. A. 1987: Archaeological investigations at Mont Dardon. In C. L. Crumley and W. H. Marquardt (eds), *Regional Dynamics: Burgundian Landscapes in Historical Perspective*, San Diego: Academic Press, 41–119.

Hawkes, C. 1954: Archaeological theory and method: some suggestions from the Old World. *American Anthropologist*, 56, 155–68.

Hill, J. N., and Gunn, J. D. (eds) 1977: *The Individual in Prehistory*. New York: Academic Press.

Marquardt, W. H. 1992: Dialectical archaeology. In M. B. Schiffer (ed.), *Archaeological Method and Theory*, 4, Tucson: University of Arizona Press, 101–40.

Marquardt, W. H., and Crumley, C. L. 1987: Theoretical issues in the analysis of spatial patterning. In C. L. Crumley and W. H. Marquardt (eds), *Regional Dynamics: Burgundian Landscapes in Historical Perspective*, San Diego: Academic Press, 1–18.

Schmidt, P. R. 1996: Rhythmed time and its archaeological implications. In G. Pwiti and R. Soper (eds), *Aspects of African Prehistory: Papers from the 10th*

Congress of the PanAfrican Association of Prehistory and Other Related Studies, Harare: University of Zimbabwe Press, 655–62.

Schmidt, P. R. 1997: *Iron Technology in East Africa: Symbolism, Science, and Archaeology*. Bloomington: Indiana University Press.

Spaulding, A. C. 1960: The dimensions of archaeology. In G. E. Dole and R. Carneiro (eds), *Essays in the Science of Culture*. New York: Crowell, 437–56.

Tilley, C. 1994: *A Phenomenology of Landscape: Places, Paths and Monuments*. Oxford: Berg.

Turner, V. 1995: *The Ritual Process: Structure and Anti-structure*. New York: Aldine de Gruyter.

13

Exploring Everyday Places and Cosmologies

Peter van Dommelen

Dealing with Landscapes

Landscape is a remarkable object of study which has fascinated archaeologists since the early days of the discipline and which continues to do so today, regardless of the region or period involved. The wide geographical and chronological range of the contributions to the present volume testifies clearly to the versatility of landscape as a research theme. All the chapters, moreover, demonstrate how landscape studies are as much a part of processual and postprocessual approaches as they once were of culture-historical perspectives, a point also made by Knapp and Ashmore (this volume) in their rapid survey of landscape studies (see also Johnston 1998).

The prominence of landscape studies in archaeology and related disciplines such as geography must be related to the ubiquitous materiality of landscape – it is simply everywhere and people live in it on a daily basis. As a consequence, definitions of landscape have long tended to focus one-sidedly on the material aspects of landscape and, as a corollary, have drawn a sharp distinction between the natural and the human or social dimensions of landscape. Carl Sauer's claim that "the cultural landscape is fashioned out of a natural landscape" (1925: 343) is a typical example of this so-called "explicit" perspective on landscape (Johnston 1998: 57–60). In recent years, however, this dichotomy has gradually been blurred by an increasing awareness that the materiality of landscape is not as straightforward as it may seem: as Knapp and Ashmore note in their introduction to this volume, landscape is now increasingly viewed as "an entity that exists by virtue of its being perceived, experienced, and contextualized by people." As opposed to the "explicit" approach, this view has been termed "inherent," because the people inhabiting and experiencing the landscape no longer stand out-side it, exploiting it more or less efficiently; on the contrary, they are just as much part of the landscape they live in as are the so-called "natural" features (Johnston 1998: 61–4). Following the line of Johnston's arguments, the novelty of some recent landscape studies stems not so much from an emphasis on the social and symbolic dimensions of landscape but rather from a radical reconceptualization of landscape in and of itself.

As demonstrated by ethnographic accounts, landscape cannot easily be separated from society because it often plays an integral part in the reproduction of the existing social order. A fine example has been doc-umented on Malaita in the Solomon Islands, where the intriguing statement "land owns people" unmistakably signals the difference between the Malaitans' attitude to land and Western views about land tenure. To the 'Are'are, the landscape relates them to their ancestors in a very immediate and tangible way, because it was the ancestors who created the land and it is the present inhabitants who live from it. The Malaitan landscape is thus inextricably bound up in a complex set of relationships between people and their ancestors which in the end define 'Are'are society (cf. Barraud et al. 1984). To the people of Malaita, the landscape is therefore not just an environment of "named land tracts and settlement sites;" rather they experience it as pro-foundly "structured by history" (Keesing 1982: 76). As a consequence, the conclusion inevitably must be that "land is clearly not simply soil, but rather an entity always fused with the ancestors, under whose joint authority the living are placed" (de Coppet 1985: 81).

The Malaitan example nevertheless makes it clear that an inherent conception of landscape is just as much grounded in the materiality of the landscape as are the various explicit approaches, even if the "inher-ent" understanding of landscape is ultimately very different. In effect, in evident contrast to those other views, an inherent approach refuses to think of landscape as a mere background of human action. Instead, landscape is regarded as the outcome of particular processes of engage-ment between people and the world in which they live (cf. Hirsch 1995). Any landscape, therefore, represents a product of specific his-torical and local conditions that is continuously open to reinterpreta-tion and subject to reproduction. In this perspective, the *unity* of natural and cultural features is emphasized and attention is focused on the ways in which a particular landscape has taken shape, which ele-ments are significant in it, and which meanings and implications it contains for its inhabitants (cf. Coones 1992). Since it is the materiality of landscape in which the meanings and readings of the landscape are grounded, landscape can effectively be understood as "the most solid appearance in which a history can declare itself" (Inglis 1977: 489) – not unlike landscape as experienced by the 'Are'are and Kwaio of Malaita.

Studying "Sacred Landscapes"

Despite the unanimous concentration on the social and symbolic dimensions of landscape by the contributors to the present volume, which in itself is hardly innovative (noted by the editors in passing), the actual approaches adopted in the various chapters differ considerably. As is perhaps best demonstrated by the recurrent attempts of several authors to define landscape, most studies in the present volume assume a material landscape reality which stands apart from its social or symbolic perception. Particularly telling in this respect is, for instance, the claim that "landscape cannot be understood without reference to a world view which integrates place and space in the production of meaning" (Snead and Preucel, this volume). This view falls under the heading of Johnston's "explicit approach," since it regards landscape as a neutral "resource" which is "domesticated" and "placed in a cultural frame of reference" by its inhabitants (Snead and Preucel, this volume). In a similar vein, Barnes (this volume) argues that "some landscape features may be intentionally and explicitly 'marked' as to what their intended meaning is in specific systems of thought." The implication of such a view is, of course, that meaning is not embedded in the landscape itself but rather that "knowledge [is] created in the mind as guided by the anthropogenic landscape" (Barnes, this volume). In practice, both chapters share a strong focus on historically and ethnographically documented cosmologies which are almost literally "pinpointed" in the landscape by specific natural or cultural features. At the same time, little or no attention is paid to the landscape as a whole: we do not learn, for instance, how *buddhas* and *bodhisattvas* were integrated in the wider landscape and how they were part of people's daily lives, despite assertions that they were.

A closely related approach can be discerned in the study of the prehistoric lower Illinois valley by Buikstra and Charles, who distinguish a "sacred landscape" made up of burial mounds and ritual sites. They assert that these represent focal points in the landscape, which, as in the Rio Grande or East Asia, can be regarded as the material manifestations of a transcendent world view, "a deeply-rooted ancient cosmology which lodged the ancestors in places where the ancient worlds conjoined." In the absence of written records or ethnographic accounts about this prehistoric world view, however, ancient perceptions of the "sacred places" cannot be grasped more precisely. The detailed analysis of the locational characteristics does nevertheless reveal interesting shifts in the ways the inhabitants of the Illinois valley dealt with their landscape. I would argue – from an inherent perspective – that the sites examined should not just be seen in terms of a separate "sacred landscape" but that they should rather be viewed as part of everyday life *and* death in the Illinois valley, as the authors acknowledge. It is precisely this notion of transcendent meanings which is criticized by the inherent perspective on landscape and which has been argued to represent a specifically modern Western concept (Lemaire 1970: 59–86; 1997: 6–11). For China in particular, the immanence of meanings in the landscape has been emphasized in evident contrast to Western notions (Berque 1997).

The chapters by Taçon and Richards on, respectively, Australian rock art and two Egyptian ritual sites similarly focus on a "sacred landscape" and draw on a well documented cosmology. Both chapters moreover emphasize the relationships between the sites concerned and the surrounding physical environment. Taçon sets out from the observation that rock art sites "were organized very particularly in relation to natural signs and features of rock surfaces" and links these directly to contemporary Aboriginal art and sacred sites. While concluding that in the end it is all "about coming to terms with changing landscapes," he fails to elaborate the connections between rock art and landscape, merely claiming that "places were socialized through rock art and ritual, including cupule marking." These links need not have been direct, however, as contemporary Aboriginal perceptions of the physical landscape are embedded in ancestral and mythical representations, which actually "distance the present world" (Morphy 1995: 192–6). The contemporary *political* situation, for instance, has been argued to constitute a far more influential factor in the perception and shaping of Aboriginal landscapes (Morphy 1993; 1995: 187–9). While the Australian rock art sites consequently remain somewhat isolated from their social context, Richards' discussion of Egyptian Abydos and Amarna successfully brings out the complex interweaving of cosmology, landscape, architecture, and society. She shows in particular how a similar use of comparably impressive physical conditions resulted in rather distinct landscapes, because of the different social and political contexts. In the case of Abydos, she makes it particularly evident that the site is not just a "sacred site" but at the same time also the place where social inequalities were reproduced and re-defined. It is this embedding of the "sacred sites" in their wider social context and the awareness that the landscape is not just sacred but also political which denote the inherent approach to landscape of this chapter and which set it apart from the previous ones.

The very notion of an exclusively "sacred" landscape as found in the foregoing contributions is questionable in itself – at least from an inherent perspective – because it detracts from the unity of landscape. By focusing on a single issue, alternative or even competing perceptions and uses of the same landscape are ignored. In central Italy, for example, Etruscan burials lined the roads outside the settlement areas and were therefore at the same time as much part of the daily landscape of the living as they constituted a sacred and ancestral landscape: while it is in fact the daily context which allows these places to be perceived as different in the first place, their liminal associations were also reinforced by their location. Abandoning the term "sacred" altogether in favor of labels such as "ideational" or "conceptual," as discussed by the editors, does not seem very helpful, however, because their claim that all pre-industrial landscapes are somehow "sacred" could be extended to *all* landscapes, including (post-)modern ones, which may equally be regarded as "ideational" or "conceptual" (Augé 1992; Lemaire 1997; Schama 1995).

Monuments and Everyday Life

A conception of landscape which goes well beyond a narrow focus on "sacred landscapes" underlies the remainder of the contributions to the present volume. Unlike the previous chapters, however, the latter ones consistently relate ritual sites or places to, and integrate them in, the wider landscape of everyday life. The significance of this broader view is not only that it goes beyond an exclusive approach to landscape but also that it matches the archaeological attempts to understand landscape as a "seamless totality" (Coones 1992: 31) which is more than a collection of discrete sites (cf. Knapp and Ashmore, this volume). The "sacred sites" and more mundane features such as houses together make up "an ensemble which is under continuous creation and alteration as much or more from the unconscious processes of daily living as from calculated landscape design" (Meinig 1979: 6). It is the conjunction with the "ordinary" context of everyday life, which creates the conditions in which certain landscape features can be perceived as sacred, since "mythical orderings of landscape are not given facts, but are constantly produced by social practices" (Fontijn 1996: 85). In the

Etruscan case, for instance, the location of burials alongside roads was not coincidental, since cemeteries evidently echoed domestic architecture and were, in a later phase, even laid out as settlements. Life and death were clearly not separated in the Etruscan view – as in so many non-Western views – and their burials and ancestors must have been perceived as very much part of the same landscape as that inhabited by the living. If the "cultural biography" of the burial mounds was not just written at a limited number of ritual occasions but also largely shaped by people's routine activities in the landscape, the integration of these burials in the landscape must have been profound.

The contributions by Brady and Ashmore on the role of caves and water in Maya landscapes and by Knapp on Bronze Age mining in Cyprus represent this approach most explicitly. Brady and Ashmore in particular show that both the ritual caves and the royal palace at Dos Pilas were part of one and the same landscape, in which cosmology and physical environment were closely interwoven. The recurrence of the associations with rock and water in even the simplest of houses shows that, not unlike at Egyptian Abydos, the landscape at the same time brought together the different layers of Maya society and constituted the arena in which social differences were reproduced and asserted. While the term "ideational" landscape might imply an explicit separation between cosmology and the "real" landscape, Brady and Ashmore rightly stress, in an inherent fashion, the pervasiveness of the associations and the mixing up of built and unbuilt environment which underscore the unity of the Maya landscape. While Knapp's focus on mining and smelting sites turns our attention to a rather lowly landscape, he draws a much stricter divide between this "industrial" landscape and a "sacred landscape" of rural sanctuaries in a way reminiscent of the explicit approach to landscape. As a consequence, he is unable to examine the two elements as integral parts of one and the same late Bronze Age landscape, although he does note that several places not only served ceremonial functions but were also involved in productive functions. Since this effectively undermines Knapp's classification, I can only agree with his final assertion that "the ideational landscape cannot be separated from social reality."

The remaining papers by Barrett, Kealhofer, and van de Guchte share a strong focus on what Meinig has called "ordinary landscapes," because all three explore how landscapes of everyday life were perceived and (re-)shaped by those experiences. In his chapter on British Iron Age landscapes, Barrett insists that pre-existing Bronze Age monuments "endured to become Iron Age monuments," arguing that their role in the Iron Age landscape consequently needs to be understood in the "frame of reference" of the latter period. Yet by focusing more on the monuments themselves than on the Iron Age landscape as a whole, he fails to elaborate on their role in the settled agricultural landscapes of the Iron Age.

It is, however, the two meticulously documented case studies by Kealhofer and van de Guchte which particularly stand out in the present volume and which present fine examples of the ways in which an inherent perspective can contribute to a profound understanding of landscape. In his chapter on Inca textiles, urban layout, and landscape, van de Guchte demonstrates how the differences between these categories of material culture are more apparent than real, suggesting that "alterity" can be identified as a key feature in Inca perception. As underlined by his conclusion that "the Incas conceived of an animate landscape, parallel and similar to their own social fabric," van de Guchte's inherent approach to landscape not only underscores the unity of natural and cultural landscape features – ranging from textiles to settlement plans – but also emphasizes its materiality. Kealhofer's discussion of two gardens in seventeenth-century colonial Virginia equally foregrounds the materiality of landscape, as she demonstrates how the gardens were used and perceived in early colonial America as a means almost literally to ground identities in the colonized soil. Landscape and meaning thus were evidently "very much part of an ongoing process of individual social and political negotiation" (Kealhofer, this volume).

Conclusion: The Many Dimensions of Landscape

The chapters by van de Guchte and Kealhofer demonstrate that landscape is an extraordinarily encompassing notion which resists classifications into subsets defined as sacred, industrial, conceptual, or whatever. A common feature of landscape which has recurrently surfaced in the chapters discussed is in fact what I would term the "multiplicity" of landscape: the constitutive elements of landscape are profoundly contextual and always comprise something different and unexpected in every case considered. Van de Guchte's inclusion of textiles in his discussion of Inca landscapes is a good case in point. The label also refers to the observation that many landscape features can be grouped under a range of headings, as shown for instance by the Malaitan landscape in the Solomon Islands, which is ancestral and belongs to the living at the same time. It is this multiplicity, and its often apparent lack of consistency, which are captured by Hirsch's characterization of landscape as "a series of related, if contradictory, moments – perspectives – which cohere in what can be recognized as a singular form: landscape as a cultural process" (1995: 23).

The simple fact that landscape always retains its materiality and omnipresence, no matter how embedded or interwoven it is in other domains, not only accounts for its pervasiveness but also holds a key to its understanding, for it can be understood as material culture. This point is indirectly made by both Kealhofer and van de Guchte, who significantly do not attempt to identify or define landscape in any way but demonstrate how landscape was used by people as a *means* in their social and political strategies. This does not imply that landscape can be reduced to a political tool manipulated by elites, but rather amounts to, as Kealhofer explicitly argues, "an active role [of land- scapes] in shaping economic and political systems." As I pointed out above, the idea of landscape as a political or social arena can also be found in the chapters by Richards and by Brady and Ashmore.

To summarize, then, I would like to foreground not so much the wide geographical or chronological range covered by the contributors but rather the various approaches that I have discussed. While there clearly are widely diverging ideas about landscape and how it can or should be studied archaeologically, there is also broad agreement that landscape is much more than an environment to be exploited. As sev- eral of the chapters forcefully demonstrate, however, the social and symbolic dimensions of landscapes are not restricted to "sacred" sites, and pervade the entire landscape in all its known and unexpected dimensions. It is this shift away from monuments, and the growing attention for vernacular and non-monumental landscapes, which seem to me the principal developments signaled by the present volume, because they realize the potential of landscape studies in archaeology by blurring conventional archaeological categories such as "settlements" and "burials." Landscape thus presents a meaningful context for a joint consideration of different classes of evidence and offers a way to put into practice the observation that it is "inconceivable to work the land without imagining the landscape at the same time" (Bradley 1997: 48).

ACKNOWLEDGMENTS

I wish to thank Bernard Knapp and Wendy Ashmore for inviting me to contribute to this volume. I am indebted to Ayla Çevik for discussing with me some of the issues raised in this comment, while the frequent discussions with Jan Kolen have been a great source of inspiration.

REFERENCES

Augé, M. 1992: *Non-lieux: Introduction à une Anthropologie de la Surmodernité*. (La Librairie du XXe siècle). Paris: Seuil.

Barraud, C., de Coppet, D., Iteanu, A., and Jamous, R. 1984: Des relations et des morts. Quatre sociétés vues sous l'angle des échanges. In J-C. Galey (ed.), *Différences Valeurs Hiérarchie. Textes Offerts à Louis Dumont*, Paris: Éditions de l'École des Hautes Études en Sciences Sociales, 421–520.

Berque, A. 1997: There is only Mount Jingting. *Archaeological Dialogues*, 4, 22–3.

Bradley, R. 1997: Working the land: imagining the landscape. *Archaeological Dialogues*, 4, 39–52.

Coones, P. 1992: The unity of landscape. In L. MacInnes and C. Wickham-Jones (eds), *All Natural Things: Archaeology and the Green Debate*, Oxbow Monographs, 21, Oxford: Oxbow Books, 22–40.

de Coppet, D. 1985: Land owns people. In R. Barnes, D. de Coppet and R. Parkin (eds), *Contexts and Levels: Anthropological Essays in Hierarchy*, JASO Occasional Papers, 4, Oxford: JASO, 78–90.

Fontijn, D. 1996: Socializing landscape: second thoughts about the cultural biography of urnfields. *Archaeological Dialogues*, 3, 77–87.

Hirsch, E. 1995: Landscape: between place and space. In E. Hirsch and M. O'Hanlon (eds), *The Anthropology of Landscape: Perspectives on Place and Space*, Oxford: Clarendon Press, 1–30.

Inglis, F. 1977: Nation and community: a landscape and its morality. *The Sociological Review*, 25, 489–514.

Johnston, R. 1998: Approaches to the perception of landscape: philosophy, theory, methodology. *Archaeological Dialogues*, 5, 54–68.

Keesing, R. 1982: *Kwaio Religion: The Living and the Dead in a Solomon Island Society*. New York: Columbia University Press.

Lemaire, T. 1970: *Filosofie van het landschap*. Baarn: Ambo.

Lemaire, T. 1997: Archaeology between the invention and destruction of the landscape. *Archaeological Dialogues*, 4, 5–21.

Meinig, D. 1979: Introduction. In D. Meinig (ed.), *The Interpretation of Ordinary Landscapes: Geographical Essays*, Oxford and New York: Oxford University Press, 1–7.

Morphy, H. 1993: Colonialism, history and the construction of place: the politics of landscape in northern Australia. In B. Bender (ed.), *Landscape: Politics and Perspectives*, Oxford: Berg, 205–43.

Morphy, H. 1995: Landscape and the reproduction of the ancestral past. In E. Hirsch and M. O'Hanlon (eds), *The Anthropology of Landscape. Perspectives on Place and Space*, Oxford: Clarendon Press, 184-209.

Sauer, C. 1925: The morphology of landscape. In *Land and Life: A Selection from the Writings of Carl Ortwin Sauer*, Berkeley: University of California Press, 315-50.

Schama, S. 1995: *Landscape and Memory*. London: HarperCollins.

Index